With **Andy Stanley, Francis Chan, Bill Hybels, Thom Rainer, Craig Groeschel**

CHURCHLEADERS.COM

TOP 100

THE BEST LEADERSHIP ARTICLES, PRACTICAL HOW-TOS, AND FEATURES OF THE YEAR

2012 Edition

With **Andy Stanley, Francis Chan, Bill Hybels, Thom Rainer, Craig Groeschel,** and many others

CHURCHLEADERS.COM

TOP 100

THE BEST LEADERSHIP ARTICLES, PRACTICAL HOW-TOS, AND FEATURES OF THE YEAR

2012 Edition

ChurchLeaders.com Top 100

ISBN: 978-1-9355-4150-9

Editor: Brian Orme
Assistant Editor: Toni Ridgaway
Cover and Interior Design: Tim Downs and Alexia Garaventa
Contributing Editors: Terrace Crawford, Alan Danielson, Ray Hollenbach, Melissa Riddle-Chalos, Scott Williams

Printed in the United States of America

Contents

PART 4

CHURCH GROWTH

PART 5

WORSHIP & CREATIVE

Contents *continued*

Editor's Note:

At ChurchLeaders.com, we're dedicated to resourcing, equipping, and connecting a community of church leaders for greater impact worldwide. Since our launch in August 2010, ChurchLeaders.com has received 1.8 million visits from more than 750,000 readers. Our contributors include more than 500 authors from the church leader community, offering more than 10,000 articles, videos, and other free resources daily.

This book is an extension of our online ministry to help leaders in all areas of the church lead better every day. The *ChurchLeaders.com Top 100* covers a diverse range of leadership and ministry topics—from listening to God's voice, serving your staff, and guarding your vision to church growth secrets, leading a successful small group, and equipping teens to share their faith.

In many ways this Top 100 list was chosen by you, the ChurchLeaders.com reader. Your engagement on the site—through clicks, comments, Facebook shares, Tweets, and emails—helped us identify the top articles, most relevant features, and freshest voices for your leadership and ministry growth.

Our prayer is that this book will serve as an effective tool to launch you and your ministry into a new season of high-impact leadership. Thank you for your commitment to the church, your passion for serving God and others, and for joining us in the mission through ChurchLeaders.com.

I now present to you—the *ChurchLeaders.com Top 100*.

Best,

Brian Orme
General Editor
ChurchLeaders.com

1

PERSONAL GROWTH
& LEADERSHIP

Our greatest fear
should not be of failure
but of succeeding at things in life
that don't really matter.
—*Francis Chan*

The State of Heart Leadership

Andy Stanley

In Matthew 15:19, Jesus warned that *"…out of the heart come evil thoughts, murder, adultery, sexual immorality, theft, false testimony, slander."*

Can you think of anyone who derailed his or her organization or career because of anything on that list? I'll bet you can. In fact, I know far more stories of failure rooted in these issues than those resulting from a lack of competence or skill.

The simple truth is that leaders who fail to monitor their hearts jeopardize their organizations. If we neglect the arduous work of monitoring what's going on inside of us, our organizations will suffer.

Look at Jesus' words again. Everything we say and do springs from our hearts. The implications of this verse are huge for those who manage people. What's in our hearts eventually affects our ability to lead effectively. Consequently, learning to guard our hearts is critical to our success as leaders. There are three things in particular that if ignored have the potential to create chaos in the heart of a leader and, consequently, in his or her sphere of organizational influence.

The first is guilt. Leaders that carry unresolved guilt are forced to hide a part of themselves from those closest to them. They have secrets. They expend time and energy ensuring that no one finds them out because they know *they* are not completely trustworthy. And because they are suspect, they begin to suspect others. Their inability to trust others makes it almost impossible for them to build cohesive teams.

The second enemy of the heart is anger. Angry people live as if the world owes them something—something they can never quite identify. Angry leaders are impossible to please. They attract employees that are more concerned with making their bosses happy than doing what's best for the organization. This leads to poor decisions, eventually putting them at odds with their angry bosses, and the cycle of dysfunction continues.

The third heart issue that can derail a leader is jealousy. Professional jealousy is understandable, maybe even unavoidable to some extent. But when it is unrecognized and ignored, it has the potential to destroy the synergy of a team. Jealous leaders measure their success by the failure of others. An organization cannot sustain momentum when its leadership is focused on how well others are *not* doing rather than looking for ways to move forward. Maybe most crippling of all, leaders who carry jealousy in their hearts rarely surround themselves with competent and talented people. They feel threatened. And their insecurity stifles the growth all organizations need.

If you can identify with the ailments cited above, welcome to the human race. We all wrestle with guilt, anger, and jealousy at some level. That's why we need a Savior. The good news is that through Christ we can bring these enemies of the heart under control. They might never be eliminated, but they certainly don't have to control our lives or contaminate our organizations.

If you have a secret, tell somebody. Confess. Confession eradicates guilt. Chances are you've confessed to God. Now go confess to the person you've wronged. Angry? Forgive. Forgiveness is simply a decision to cancel a debt. Take time to decipher what you think the people who've hurt you owe you and cancel those debts. Otherwise, you will make the people closest to you pay. Jealous? Look for ways to celebrate the successes of people who've pulled ahead of you. Write 'em a letter. Praise their accomplishments in public. Refuse to allow jealousy to take up residence in your heart.

The writer of Proverbs 4:23 summarized it this way: *"Above all else, guard your heart, for it is the wellspring of life."* You live from the heart. You love from the heart. And yes, you lead from your heart. So pay attention to your heart. It impacts everything you do.

Adapted from Enemies of the Heart *(Multnomah Books: 2011) by Andy Stanley.*

Are You an Aquarium-Keeping Leader?

Steven Furtick

People ask me all the time how we've been able to see so many people come to Christ in five years.

Outside of the favor of God, I could give you a lot of specifics and tell you a lot of things that we've done. But none of it will help you until you make a decision we made in the early days of our church.

And that was the decision to be more focused on the people we're trying to reach than on the people we're trying to keep. As others have said, to be fishers of men, not just keepers of the aquarium.

We're not going to cater to the personal preferences of the few in our pursuit of the salvation of the many. And that includes if the few is 10 people when we're pursuing 100. Or 5,000 when we're pursuing 10,000. Or 10,000 when we're pursuing 20,000.

Most people and churches aren't willing to do that. They're keepers of the aquarium. They say they want to reach people, but in reality, they're more focused on preservation than expansion—on keeping people rather than reaching them.

They let saved people dictate style. Saved people dictate focus. Saved people dictate vision. The result is a room full of saved people, not people getting saved. Why? Because the people you're trying to reach aren't interested in the church that has been created by the people you're trying to keep. If they were, they'd be coming. But they're not.

For some reason, right here is where people usually play the discipleship card. They're trying to *disciple* the people they're trying to keep. They accuse you of pitting evangelism against discipleship.

But that isn't the case. I just believe true disciples should care more about making disciples than freeze-framing the church the way it was when they became one. Or wanting 26 programs customized to their liking. If the mark of Christian maturity is a bunch of people who want to create a museum glorifying and preserving their personal preferences and then sanctify it by calling it a church, count me out.

Some people say, "Why can't we have both?" You can. Focus on the people you want to reach, and you'll keep the people you want to keep. Let the rest walk. They'll find a church elsewhere to graze. The way I see it is they're just occupying the space of a person who needs to hear the gospel. You'll fill their seat.

And it will be with the person who needs it the most.

There are 750 Halls of Fame in America and 450 Who's Who Publications, but you won't find many real servants in those places. Notoriety means nothing to real servants because they know the difference between prominence and significance.

—*Rick Warren*

Why We Need to Throw Out the Term "Good Christian"

Francis Chan

I think it's time we stop asking ourselves the question: "Am I a good Christian?" We live in a time when the term "Christian" has been so diluted that millions of immoral but nice people genuinely consider themselves "good Christians." We have reduced the idea of a good Christian to someone who believes in Jesus, loves his or her family, and attends church regularly. Others will label you a good Christian even though your life has no semblance to the way Christ spent His days on Earth. Perhaps we should start asking the question, "Am I a good *Christ*?" In other words, do I look anything like Jesus? This question never even entered my mind until a friend of mine made a passing comment to me one day.

Dan is a longtime friend of mine. In fact, he's the pastor who performed my wedding. He was talking to me about a pastor named Von. Von has been working with youth in the San Diego area for decades. Many of his students have gone on to become amazing missionaries and powerful servants of God. Dan described a trip to Tijuana, Mexico with Pastor Von. (Von has been ministering to the poor in the dumps of Tijuana for years.) Dan didn't speak of the awful living conditions of those who made their homes amidst the rubbish. What impacted Dan the most was the relationship he saw between Von and the people of this community. He spoke of the compassion, sacrifice, and love that he witnessed in Von's words and actions as he held these malnourished and unbathed children. Then he made the statement that sent me reeling:

"The day I spent with Von was the closest thing I've ever experienced to walking with Jesus."

Dan explained that the whole experience was so eerie because he kept thinking to himself: "If Jesus were still walking on Earth in the flesh, this is what it would feel like to walk alongside of Him!" After that discussion, I kept wondering if anyone had ever said that about me—"The day I spent with

Francis was the closest thing I've ever experienced to walking with Jesus." The answer was an obvious "no." Would any honest person say that about you?

What bothered me was not that I hadn't "arrived," but that I wasn't even heading in the right direction. I hadn't made it my goal to resemble Christ. I wasn't striving to become the kind of person who could be mistaken for Jesus Christ. Isn't it ironic that a man can be known as a successful pastor, speaker, and CHRISTian, even if his life doesn't resemble Christ's?

1 John 2:6 "Whoever claims to live in him must walk as Jesus did."

When John made that statement, he wasn't speaking about how to be a church leader or even how to be a "good" Christian. He merely stated that anyone who calls himself Christian must live like Jesus did. So how did Jesus live? You could make a list of character traits to compare yourself to, but it would be far more beneficial to simply read through one of the Gospels. After you get a bird's-eye view of the life of Christ, do the same with your own. Are you comfortable with the similarities and differences?

It's easy to get caught up in the pursuit of "success" as American churchgoers define it. The thought of being well-known and respected is alluring. There have been times when I've been caught up in the fun of popularity. I've even mistaken it for success. Biblically, however, success is when our lives parallel Christ's. Truth is, there are many good Christs that you'll never read about in a magazine. They are walking as Jesus walked, but they are too focused and humble to pursue their own recognition.

May we make it our goal to someday have someone say of us: "The day/hour/15 minutes I spent with _____ was the closest thing I've ever experienced to walking with Jesus."

As Christians in America, we often complain about how antagonistic people are toward Christ. Personally, I'm not sure that Americans are really rejecting Christ. Maybe they just haven't seen Him.

Try to be COMPLETELY honest with yourself right now. Is the following true of you?

You passionately love Jesus, but you don't really want to be like Him. You admire His humility, but you don't want to be THAT humble. You think it's beautiful that He washed the feet of the disciples, but that's not exactly the direction your life is headed. You're thankful He was spit upon and abused, but you would never let that happen to you. You praise Him for loving you enough to suffer during His whole time on Earth, but you're going to do everything within your power to make sure you enjoy your time down here.

In short: You think He's a great Savior, but not a great role model.

The American church has abandoned the most simple and obvious truth of what it means to follow Jesus: You actually follow His pattern of life. I pray for those who read this article—that we don't become cynical or negative toward the church. Instead, let's make a personal decision to stop talking so much and begin living like Jesus. Then we can say as the Apostle Paul, *"Follow my example, as I follow the example of Christ"* (1 Corinthians 11:1). My guess is that you've never had someone say that to you, and you've never said it to anyone else. Why not?

7 Ways to Maintain Respect as a Leader

Ron Edmondson

As a leader, one of your most valuable assets is the respect of the people you are leading. If a leader is respected, people will follow him or her almost anywhere. If a leader loses the respect from the ones he or she leads, it becomes very difficult to regain that respect.

Often, a new leader is given respect because of his or her position as a leader, but respect can be quickly lost due to performance. Many times, it's the seemingly small things that cause the most damage to a leader's reputation.

I have found that a few simple (some not so simple) acts help protect the respect a leader enjoys:

1. Return phone calls and e-mails promptly.

2. Do what you say you will do.

3. Act with integrity.

4. Use fairness in your approach…not too harsh… not too soft.

5. Show others respect.

6. Learn continually and encourage growth in yourself and others.

7. Work as hard or harder than others.

Maintaining respect is a matter of acting in a respectable way. How are you doing in that area?

Why I Don't Believe in Christian Accountability

Mike Foster

Through the ministry of Deadly Viper, I get the chance to work with leaders on personal sustainability and living a life with no regrets. And though I champion the ideas of transparency, authenticity, and brutal honesty, I don't believe in Christian accountability.

The whole concept makes me cringe, and I don't think I'm alone in this assessment. It's horribly broken, ineffective, and doing a lot of people a disservice. In many ways, Christian accountability is facilitating a pathway to our lives being chopped up by character assassins.

So here are a few reasons why I don't believe in Christian accountability:

1. Lack of Grace

The primary reason Christian accountability doesn't work is because we are more interested in justice and fixing a problem. I've seen too many times great men and women get chewed up by this process. When we fail, what we need most is grace and a second chance, not a lecture.

We have all probably experienced or seen a harsh response to our struggles or failures. But there is a big problem when we respond with justice and not grace. You see, human beings are wired up for self-protection and survival. When we see others being hurt, rejected, or punished for their sin, we correctly conclude that it is better to hide, conceal, and fake it in the future. It basically comes down to this: *I don't want to get hurt, so I'm not telling.* When we lack grace, accountability breaks down.

2. Bad Environments

Let me be frank. If I were having an illicit affair with a woman, I'm not going to confess it to four guys at a Denny's breakfast. And yet, too often, Christian accountability is carried out in these types of environments. We meet in small groups in a weekly environment with a few of our friends. Ultimately, there is a lid on how transparent these conversations can be, and too often, we believe that if we are meeting weekly, then we are "accountable."

My best conversations about my brokenness and struggles have come in non-typical environments—places where I am completely relaxed, at ease, and feel removed from my daily life.

I have seen leaders every year go away for a week and meet with a coach or therapist and have this time be very effective. They dump a ton of junk, begin working strategies in their lives, and start dealing with significant character issues. I would rather have one week of brutal honesty than 52 weeks of semi-honesty at Denny's.

My point is simple. Find an environment that is going to allow you to open up and examine your current process.

3. The Results

Unfortunately, the results speak for themselves. If Christian accountability were a company, it would need a serious bailout. It's simply inadequate, and the results are sub par, at best.

The breaking down of our marriages, financial impropriety, egomaniacal and narcissistic behavior, sexual misconduct, and the bending of every rule we come across are simply signs of a failed system. Last week, I read a post from a pastor who had received e-mails from 33 other pastors who confessed to him of being involved in an affair.

4. We Game the System

If I wanted to, I could spend the next decade of my life convincing you how wonderful I am and how I have it all together. (Luckily, I have no desire to do that.) It bothers me that I'm clever enough to package Mike Foster in such a way that I could make you all believe what a swell guy I am.

The problem with Christian accountability is that you and I can game the system. I know how to beat it, and if you stick around the church long enough, you will figure it out, too. And that's a problem. We're the alcoholic that knows where the hidden key to the liquor cabinet is.

Gaming the system is not hard. We know the right words. We know the right things to talk about. We know how to frame things up to effectively keep everyone off course on who we truly are. I can do it, and so can you. And that's a big problem.

So that's why I'm not a fan of Christian accountability and truly believe it is busted. But please don't lose hope. I have something I want to offer up as a replacement to this flawed system of maintaining our integrity.

First off, I want to change the word from "accountability" to "advocacy." If we are going to redefine a process and introduce a new concept, I think it needs a new word. The word I use in this context with fellow friends and leaders is *advocacy*. The term can be described as active support, intercession, or pleading and arguing in favor of someone.

So let's take a look at what advocacy means:

Radical Grace Is the Foundation

Radical grace is the core engine for any healthy relationship. You cannot have true transparency or confession without it. I encourage people to make verbal commitments to each other and clearly state that they will stand by one another through the best AND the worst.

Most people live with the fear of rejection and allow this fear to dictate how honest they will be with others. In advocacy, we are constantly demonstrating that this relationship is a safe place. Through our response to one another's failures, our own deep confession, and reminding each other that we are in this for the long haul, we implement radical grace.

Focus on the "Yes," Not the "No"

Too often, typical Christian accountability revolves around long lists of what NOT to do. We spend way too much time discussing and managing the sin. Often, we lock on to the most minor unhealthy behaviors and think that's going to prepare us for success in life. Unfortunately, we operate on the faulty assumption that working on the symptoms will address the core problem. Bad idea!

Advocacy spurs us on to the "yes." It revolves around the crazy good things that we should be engaging in. It pushes us to live a life of positive risks, creativity, adventure, and significance. We rally around each other in this and focus our relationships around this theme.

I truly believe a large amount of moral blowouts flow from boredom and dissatisfaction. We become depressed and unsatisfied with our lives, careers, and marriages, and then we enter into dangerous territory. Why? Because we are not focusing on the "yes"!

I know that, in my own life, I become vulnerable when I have lost a sense of mission and purpose. Having an advocate in our lives is important in reminding us of our calling.

Priority on People, Not Organizations

When people fail or become involved in some scandal, too often we immediately consider the ramifications on the organization or company. I've talked to many Christians who are very concerned about how it impacts the cause of Christ when a pastor falls.

Unfortunately, we place more concern on the damage to the brand of Christianity or the church instead of the fallen individual. I've seen horrific and hurtful things happen to people in the name of protecting the organization instead of the fallen person. Quite frankly, that stinks!

If you haven't figured it out by now, Christianity's brand is failures and wrecked lives. Churches are places with messy people who do stupid things. I've certainly made my contribution to this effort with my mistakes. In advocacy, the importance is placed on the individual. It is about people, especially those who are most broken. The organization, church, or company should take a back seat.

Multi-Group Approach

Christian accountability is often accomplished in small groups that are too general or with just one person leading, which puts too much responsibility on one individual.

Advocacy embraces having multiple layers of transparency and connection. I have about 10 people who are involved in spurring me on to a life of integrity. They can actively speak into my life, and I will listen and make the necessary tweaks.

However, I have a deeper connection with about four people with whom I discuss harder things. I also have more structure with this group. This is what I consider to be the core.

But even beyond the core, I have one friend that has full access. We take complete responsibility for each other's integrity, purity, and sustainability. I refer to this person as my "first call." When the stuff hits the fan, I call him first.

I truly believe it is time to reinvent and rethink this very important component of our lives. I am deeply committed to all of us living a life of radical integrity and grace, and this is why a new discussion needs to happen around maintaining our integrity.

PART

1

PERSONAL
GROWTH &
LEADERSHIP

*People buy into the leader before
they buy into the vision.*
—*John Maxwell*

11 Ways You Can Serve the People You Lead

Perry Noble

I read Mark 10:35–45 the other morning and made a list of 11 ways that a leader can serve people (after all, Jesus said that is how to be a great leader).

1. Adopt the mindset that these people work with me and not for me.

2. Provide enough margin for the people who serve with you to be creative and brainstorm ahead. (The pastor that works "week of" in regard to his message really does a great disservice to those who support him in regard to creative elements.)

3. Make sure that the people you serve with have the resources they need to do the job they are expected to do.

4. Say "thank you" and "great job" A LOT instead of just pointing out all of the areas where a person came up short.

5. Try your best to make sure that if an area of the church is going to be impacted by a certain decision that someone from that area had input in the decision making process. (Learned this one from Andy Stanley.)

6. Make sure the expectations for the people you lead are both spoken and realistic. (We cannot hold people accountable for unspoken, unrealistic expectations.)

7. Don't confuse personal preferences with conviction from the Holy Spirit…if you tell the people you serve with that "God told me," then you had better be willing to bet your last Bible that you heard from the Lord!

8. Model what you consider to be important. In other words, when you are walking into the building and see a piece of trash on the ground, pick it up.

9. Listen to them!

10. Understand that your words weigh 1,000 pounds. Choose them carefully!

11. Understand that WHAT you say and HOW you say it matters. The people you serve with are human beings with hearts, minds, and souls—they deserve to be treated as such.

PART

1

PERSONAL
GROWTH &
LEADERSHIP

How Do We Measure Spiritual Growth?

Sarah Cunningham

In the field of education, measurements are crucial. Not measuring baking ingredients or 2x4s, of course, but measuring a student's progress. Tracking growth.

This is especially important for me as I'm hunkered down at the alternative high school—the last stop for the teens of Prison City. (We don't like to brag about it, but Jackson, my home base, houses the state prison. Please don't be jealous.)

Measuring *learning* in my context, like the spiritual one, is a tricky business. When it comes to internal processes—growth of the mind or the spirit, for example—there are no fancy growth charts to tack up against the wall.

To keep students progressing, then, good teachers ask themselves a guiding question: "How will we know when a student is officially 'educated'?" Or in other words, "What does a well-rounded graduate look like?"

This guiding question keeps the day-to-day operations on track. At the end of the day, the week, the month, is a student closer to being "educated"? Do they look and think and act more like a high school graduate than they did before?

With a million possible lesson plans to draw from, the guiding questions also help us choose the right classroom experiences. Does this presentation advance the learner toward being a graduate as we've defined it? If it does, roll forward. If it doesn't, cut the fat.

So the jump I'm about to make is probably pretty obvious at this point, right? How do we, in the faith arena, keep our faith fresh? How do we ensure that we continue to grow throughout life?

Now, no worries, we're not about to make a rubric for Christianity. Or advocate checking traits off a list to judge others' faith. Clearly not the point.

But I've found asking myself a similar question is not a bad idea. "How will I—or others—know if and when we are growing toward a more full experience of faith?" Or another way of saying it, "What does a lifelong follower of Christ—a person who has been devoted to Christ and his vision for years—look like?"

With a million possible devotionals to read, causes to take up, and programs to implement in our churches, these are the questions that help us set our course in the day-to-day, too. Does this sermon, this focus, this new program encourage us and those we lead toward becoming more like Christ? If it does, roll forward. If it doesn't, cut the fat.

At the end of the day, the week, the month, are we closer to embodying Christ and his vision for the planet? Do we look and think and act more like Jesus?

Questions like this make identity questions easier for me, too. Do I want to be influenced by and glean learning from the emergent church? The seeker movement? The house church explosion? Other Christian camps that will arise along the way?

Use the question as a funnel: What do the followers of those movements look like? Are they holy, prayerful, devoted to living out the way of Christ? Or after months of walking around with them, is the most prominent result the Urban Outfitter wardrobe and retro specs? (Or the American flag tie pin and fundy hair part?)

I'll give everything I have to becoming like the first (with or without the snazzy specs). But I hope to give absolutely nothing to the latter.

I've decided, while writing my new memoir, *Picking Dandelions: A Search for Eden Among Life's Weeds*, that I cannot afford the luxury of unchanged living. I have a feeling that anyone who claims to be following Jesus—really *following* him through all the places that he goes—would be different tomorrow than they are today.

So it's Christ or bust for me.

8 Things Pastors and Leaders Should Do on Facebook

Paul Steinbrueck

1. Listen.

James 1:19 NIV says, "My dear brothers and sisters, take note of this: Everyone should be quick to listen, slow to speak, and slow to become angry." Nothing could be more important on Facebook. Listen more than you speak. By listening, you'll get to know people better and learn what's going on in their lives. You find out who is hurting, who is frustrated, who is thriving, who is gifted in ways you never realized.

2. Pray.

James 5:16b NIV tells us, "The prayer of a righteous person is powerful and effective." Whether your Facebook friends post good news or bad, a success or a failure, you can always pray for them. When you do, ask God for guidance as to how to respond if at all. He may prompt you with the words to type in a reply. He may prompt you to pick up the phone. Who knows what could happen?

3. Engage/comment.

Of course, if all you do is listen and pray, you're not going to have much impact on Facebook. In fact, nobody's going to even know you're there. Show you care about your Facebook friends by engaging with them. Comment on people's updates. When other people comment on your updates, reply back to them. Respond promptly to messages and new friend requests.

4. Publicly encourage.

One of the best ways you can engage with people and show you care is to encourage them. It doesn't take a lot of time or effort, either. Posting a comment on someone's update with a simple "Congrats!" "That's awesome!" or "I'm praying for you," shows the person (and their Facebook friends) that you really are listening and you care.

5. Respond privately to sensitive issues.

Facebook not only provides the means to respond publicly to your friends but also privately. If someone posts an update alluding to a personal or sensitive issue—their relationship status changes, they've lost their job, they sound depressed—in addition to publicly encouraging them, you may want to send them a private message. Not only does it give you the opportunity to say something you might not want to say publicly, but by asking open-ended questions, you invite them to open up more privately about what's going on and how they're really doing.

6. Be human.

People are not connecting with you on Facebook so they can hear about God and church all the time. They want to relate to you as a human being. Post about what's happening in your life. Share photos and video of your family. Talk about your other interests and hobbies. Share links to articles you think are interesting.

7. Be authentic.

People are also not connecting with you so they can see how perfect people live. Don't just post the good stuff that's going on in your life. It's OK to express sadness, anger, and frustration. In fact, it's not just OK, it's necessary. We are all frail and sinful. People need to understand that as a pastor you are not better than they are. You are just blessed to be forgiven and have the Holy Spirit at work in your life.

8. Initiate friend requests.

Some people are afraid to initiate a friend request with a pastor. After you meet someone in the community or meet someone for the first time at church, initiate a friend request with them the next time you're on Facebook. Remember Jesus hung out with prostitutes and tax collectors, so you should be hanging out on Facebook with people who are not Christians, too.

The Problem with Pastors as Rock Stars

Ed Stetzer

A lot of kids grow up wanting to be a rock star. These days, the term "rock star" is applied much more liberally than the days of heavy metal. Athletes are rock stars, movie stars are rock stars, software designers are rock stars. The rock star aesthetic has been democratized.

You don't even have to live a rock-and-roll lifestyle to be a rock star. These days, even the most un-hip of occupations can achieve rock star appeal. Including pastors.

Somebody once said, "The Gospel came to the Greeks, and the Greeks turned it into a philosophy. The Gospel came to the Romans, and the Romans turned it into a system. The Gospel came to the Europeans, and the Europeans turned it into a culture. The Gospel came to America, and the Americans turned it into a business." And business is booming. Millions of churchgoers file into buildings each week, line up in rows like shelves at Walmart, and watch the stage. They come for one purpose: to see a show and hear a pastor.

This, by uncritical standards, is success. But while this phenomenon increases, I believe it can be damaging to the spiritual vitality of the American church.

Don't get me wrong, I am not saying pastors who look or act cool or who speak dynamically or who lead confidently or who have large congregations are the problem. I'd have to rebuke quite a few of my friends if that were the case. And I am not against large churches. It is not the look, following, or size of the church but the culture of the superpastor that can do great harm.

Furthermore, I think that any pastor of a church of any size can fall into the "rock star" trap. It is a sin issue and not just a size issue.

I see four general problems with the rock star pastor, and I will propose four fixes:

Personal Imbalance

No, not mentally. (Well, maybe mentally.) No, the problem of balance with a superpastor-type is the distance at which ministry is done. Superpastors tend to either fly high above and lord over their ministries like detached dictators, or they try lifting too much on their own. Both of these problems can stem from an enlarged ego. In the previous case, the superpastor thinks the normal work is for ordinary pastors, and in the latter case, the superpastor feels strong enough to handle it all.

Sometimes the superpastor is a passive sort who lets everyone else pass the buck to the pastor, afraid to delegate for fear of other people's failures tainting the ministry. In the case of the "lord on high" superpastor, the leadership culture is just as toxic, because staff and members tend to affirm aloofness and enable dysfunction. In either case, the biblical view of equipping others for ministry is absent.

Hindering Community

If the church life revolves around one person's speaking gift, it is incredibly difficult to move to community. A community "won" to a single voice is not won to community but to spectatorship. Thus, when pastors say, "It's all about the weekend," they tend to create an audience rather than a biblically functioning church community. This is still true if your church is an oft-criticized seeker megachurch or your verse-by-verse preaching point. Either way, if you get thousands sitting in rows but can't move them to sitting in circles, true community is hard to find.

As a guy who travels around speaking, I understand how quickly it can happen. For the last few weeks, I've spoken at a church close to my own house while the pastor is on a short sabbatical. But even in delivering biblical messages, I'm not engaging in biblical community with those people. It takes more than a stage to create a community. The temptation must be fought that a mass of people gathered to hear one person speak is equal to biblical community.

A gifted communicator can draw a crowd, but biblical community will sustain a congregation. A great orator is fun to have at worship but cannot build community during the other six days and 23 hours of the week. Great preaching will be used by God to bring others to faith and sanctify God's people, but it will also encourage the body to do life together on mission.

I'm not saying that every person in the community should have immediate access to the pastor. But I am saying that every pastor should be in some accountable biblical community.

Approval Addiction

Many rock star pastors enjoy having their egos stroked. When pastors become rock stars, it seems that they quickly learn how to strut while sitting down. But when they become the face of the church, the church becomes identified with the pastor. Thus, the measure of success is tied to the pastor's capacity to draw a crowd, sell books, and speak at the cool conferences. The scorecard of the church shifts from faithful growth to publicity ratings.

An approval-addicted pastor develops the split personality of an insecure bully. Paranoid that their reputation might be damaged by incompetency in others, the pastor resorts to pushing people around. Rock star pastors are addicted to measuring success by whether or not they get their way. Their measure of success becomes about meeting their personal needs, not submission to the mission of God. A rock star pastor is fanatical about approval, but not God's.

Selling Out the Church's Future

You can just check the headlines. When a rock star pastor falls, the church rarely recovers. When they do, it is through extricating their identity from that of the pastor's abilities and personality. No pastor is indispensable. It's good for pastors to remind themselves, "Others filled the role before you were born, and others will fill it after you're gone."

But the rock star pastor constantly needs more attendees, Facebook fans, and Twitter followers. In a twisted bit of logic, they work to make the Gospel well known through their own fame.

Some have pointed to the multi-site movement as an illustration of how the church has sold out to make rock star pastors famous. Personally, I am not anti-multi-site. When partnered with church planting, it has great potential. Nevertheless, while I'm not "anti," I do urge caution. At times, I've joked about "rock star celebrity pastors beaming their graven image all over the country." If you are a rock star pastor, perhaps you believe that the church simply cannot go on without you. You would be wrong.

Pride was inherent in the fall of Adam, and it rears its head whenever one person deems the church's future to ride on their shoulders or voice. Multi-site, or any program, as a necessity derived from the attention needed by a rock star pastor is idolatry.

So what can we do to counteract the superpastor tendencies? I think four simple ideas will help.

1. Focus on Equipping

A lot of churches talk a big game on this issue, but few play it. First Peter 4:10 tells us, "Each one should use whatever gift he has received to serve others, faithfully administering God's grace in its various forms." The lesson of 1 Corinthians 12 is even more extensive regarding the usefulness of all the parts of the body of Christ.

In a rock star pastor culture, only one is deemed capable for ministry. Maybe the rest of the staff can help, but they are secondary to the pastor. Only the pastor can proclaim God's Word and shoulder the decisions of the church. It sounds exhausting. Worse than that, it sounds unbiblical.

By focusing on equipping the saints, we move back to the biblical position that every believer is called to the ministry and mission of the local church. When ego is removed, the refreshed pastor can help believers fulfill their roles in God's kingdom.

2. Take a Sabbath

Rock star pastors are notorious for pushing themselves to the breaking point. The stories of depression, adulterous affairs, or just dropouts each month are heartbreaking. And they should be a wake-up call.

Not only should pastors take a permanent break from shouldering the entire weight of their church's growth, they should periodically just take a break. Sure, a few pastors are lazy and spend too much time goofing off, but most rock star pastors take it to the other extreme of non-stop labor. Pushing themselves beyond acceptable boundaries, these Type-A personalities cannot stand to not be doing something. They won't sit still.

Pastors: Sit still!

3. Adjust with the Economic Times

The recession has hit churches hard. Giving is down and, to adjust, churches are cutting back on programs and personnel. This is an opportunity for the church to abandon the "clergification" virus that plagues us. The mentality that only the professional clergy, especially the superpastors, can do ministry never shows up in Scripture. It is a holdover from pre-Reformation times and is damaging our ability to fulfill God's mission.

When the church relies on one or a few paid individuals to do all of the ministry, most is left unattended. Interestingly, the two-thirds world does not suffer from the malady of clergification. Not having the financial ability to pay superpastors, more believers do the work of the ministry.

Pastors can lead their churches toward a better stewardship of their resources. Rather than paying staff to shoulder the load, teach all believers to minister. Instead of employing people to speak for God in the community, lead all believers to be Christ's ambassadors.

4. Preach the Glory of God

Most rock star pastors don't mean to not preach God's glory. But they are, nevertheless, unintentionally preaching their own. For a pastor, being "out front" is a necessity that can become a danger. Their winsomeness wins over seekers; their way with words woos the weekly attendees. Charisma is an intangible gift but deceives one's own heart.

Once when preaching, cheering broke out for John Chrysostom. He responded, "You praise what I have said and receive my exhortation with tumults of applause; but show your approbation by obedience; that is the only praise I seek."

The decline in the church, perhaps, is caused by our satisfaction with earthly appeal. We should endeavor to present the glory of God instead of the cleverness of our abilities to edit movie clips, mimic the local CCM station, or engage social issues. People can walk away from all of that unchanged. But nobody can encounter the glory of God and live the same as they did before.

The glory of God is a good place to end this article. Pastors (of churches of any size) need to worry less about their status and be concerned more with God's mission and His glory. The glory of God should be your recurring song, and with that in mind, it's okay for rock stardom to fade out and the Morning Star to rise in your place.

The Gift of Rejection

Ben Arment

It's tragic how we become paralyzed by the fear of rejection. Before we take one step toward a goal, before we even try to see what's possible, we quit because we don't want to get rejected.

In his best-selling book, *The 4-Hour Work Week,* author Timothy Ferris describes how he challenged a Princeton University class to make personal contact with a seemingly impossible person to reach, such as Bill Clinton, Jennifer Lopez, or J. D. Salinger. The first student to do it would win a round-trip ticket to anywhere in the world.

Timothy was prepared to pay for the trip. In fact, the rules were such that anyone could have turned in a one-paragraph response and collected the prize. But no one even attempted the experiment. Timothy explained that the students didn't believe they could beat their classmates, so they gave up without trying.

Here's an important lesson: Never say no for other people. That's their job. In the pursuit of a goal, everyone has a job. Your job is to dream audaciously, act courageously, and make the ask. Their job is to say "yes" or "no." And this is their job and their job alone.

If you're a dreamer like me, you will have to make lots of asks. While writing this piece, I've made asks of four influential people, and every single one of them has turned me down. It's humiliating. So why do I persist in this self-punishing exercise? A long time ago, I learned that rejection is a gift. Let me explain.

Babe Ruth is known as the home run king. He was the first player to hit 60 homeruns in one season. Some say baseball became popular only when he started playing in the 1920s. When you think of Babe Ruth, you don't think of failure. But get this—from 1926 until 1964, Babe Ruth held Major League Baseball's career strikeout record. He swung at a lot of pitches and never connected on most of them. You've got to love that. The thing that brought failure to his career was the very thing that brought him success.

Rejection clears the playing field. If you can handle rejection, you'll become part of a small fraternity of dreamers who see their ideas become reality. When you make it past your first few rejections, the field of dreamers begins to thin out.

We've got to become people who are at ease with rejection. We've got to stop letting it deter us. At the risk of making a poor analogy, think about the difference between American men and Italian men when it comes to flirting with women. Italian men aren't crushed by rejection; they accept it as part of the game.

We must press through rejection, because there's a "yes" for us out there somewhere. And the only way to find it is by sifting through all the "no"s. I run a yearlong coaching process for 30 individuals called Dream Year. One of the participants, Justin Wise, told me he wanted to attend financial guru Dave Ramsey's EntreLeadership event in April 2008. This exclusive business conference hosts just 150 people in a prestigious location at a price tag of $4,000.

As a young ministry leader, Justin couldn't afford to go, but he believed there was a "yes" out there somewhere, so he decided to make an ask. He sent Dave an e-mail expressing his desire to attend but explaining that he couldn't afford it. He asked if he could come for free. One week later, Justin received a surprising response. Not only did Dave invite him to be his guest, but he also paid for his airfare and hotel room. I wonder how many of us in Justin's position would have said "no" for Dave before ever writing that e-mail.

As we go about making asks, God will open some doors and close others. But we have to persevere in asking. We have to keep trying doorknobs. We have to test our heels on the water's surface. Because when we press through rejection, when we sift through the "no"s, something amazing happens. Eventually, we get our "yes." And our goal becomes one step closer to reality.

What Makes a Great Leader?

Charles Lee

Leadership is often defined as influence.

In my opinion, everyone possesses the ability to "influence" or lead others in the general sense of the word, but not everyone is a leader (i.e., someone who functions in a publicly recognized role of guiding or influencing others). I have worked with several people who influence the lives of many people but didn't function well once given a key role of leadership in an organization and/or company.

The reality is that leadership in a formal sense requires a certain set of perspectives, values, and praxis that very few are able to carry out well. Over the years, I've had the privilege of working with some phenomenal leaders that are literally changing the landscape of our world. Here are a few insights I've picked up about what it takes to become a great leader:

Pain Frames Purpose.

Great leaders do not run away from pain but rather recognize that pain is what truly forms and informs their life purposes. It is not to say that they are sadistically seeking pain. Passion for one's purpose is often fueled in part by one's pain and suffering. Passion by definition is not only a reference to fervor but also the willingness to work with pain.

Collaboration Is Necessary for Creative Innovation.

Leaders recognize that they cannot and will not do it alone. Every great endeavor needs a team or community to help it flourish. Great leaders move from simply wanting collaboration to needing it. In addition, they welcome voices from unrelated fields to spark creativity and refinement of purpose.

Courage Guides Decisions.

Great leaders are marked by their courage in decision-making. They rarely lean toward the popular vote. Courage implies that there is often a deep presence of fear and obstacles. Courage is the ability to move forward in the presence of fear.

Compassionate Justice Provides Perspective.

No matter how tough a great leader may appear, deep inside they all care about the people they lead. Compassionate justice is a reference to a work that seeks to make things right with a posture of real care. Great leaders are leading because they feel they can change the environment or direction of something that could be better. People ultimately "follow" a leader because they sense that they have their best interest in mind, even if it means that they go against the grain.

Focus of Implementation.

Great leaders don't just talk; they do. They realize the hard work is in the implementation of their vision and courage. They don't make excuses nor choose to sit on their ideas. They simply move forward and figure things out along the way. Great leaders are focused on implementing better. They're not satisfied with a 30,000-foot view. They also want to see what's right in front of them. The focus is not just greater vision but greater action.

Living life as a leader is a noble pursuit. It takes a special person to move beyond the romanticized benefits of its role.

Are you a leader? If so, our world needs you at your best!

PART

1

PERSONAL
GROWTH &
LEADERSHIP

PART

2

CHURCH
LEADERSHIP

PART

3

PREACHING
& TEACHING

PART

4

CHURCH
GROWTH

PART

5

WORSHIP
& CREATIVE

PART

6

OUTREACH
& EVANGELISM

PART

7

YOUTH
& FAMILY

PART

8

SMALL GROUP
LEADERSHIP

PART

9

PERSONAL
GROWTH
& LEADERSHIP
TOOLS

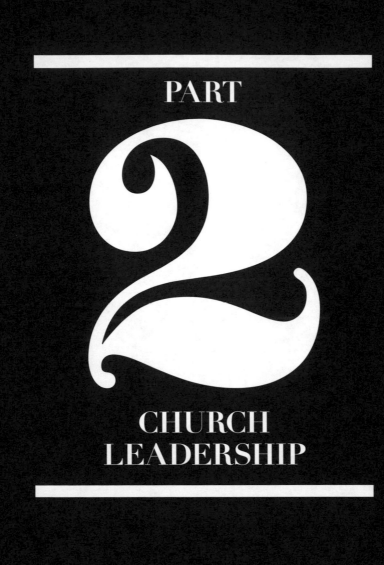

PART

2

CHURCH
LEADERSHIP

An authoritative church is very attractive, as long as that authority is used to shepherd and not to bruise. Sometimes, I have to talk to people very honestly, and that can be painful. But first, I have to make sure they know I love them. Leaders shouldn't wield authority; they should shepherd toward truth.

—Matt Chandler

3 Unspoken Promises Leaders Make

Hal Seed

Every Christian leader I know wrestles with the Romans 12:8 commission: "…If [your gift] is leadership, let him govern diligently." How can you measure whether you're leading with diligence?

At the time of this writing, there's a church that's thinking about joining my church, either as a merger or a satellite. This currently pastorless church needs leadership. I believe we can provide it. But can we? More specifically, what might it mean for me to lead this second congregation "diligently"?

Normally, when I invite a new staff or volunteer onto my team, I'm aware of the responsibility I'm assuming. With over 100 potential volunteers about to join my team, I've become acutely aware that every time I invite someone (in this case, many "someones") onto my team, I am making three unspoken promises to them.

The Unspoken Leadership Covenant

Stepping into leadership can be exhilarating. Newly minted leaders find themselves asking, "Will people follow me? Will they like me? Will I be able to accomplish anything?" Those and a dozen other questions run through their minds.

Meanwhile, followers are asking an opposite set of questions. They want to know, "Is this person trustworthy? Do I want to follow him/her? Do I like where they are going?"

Underneath this unspoken exchange is a covenant that all leaders make with everyone who signs up for their cause. Like the questions, this covenant is rarely verbalized and almost never brought to the level of consciousness. But it's there, and if you're going to be a great leader, you need to own it and live up to it.

The leader's unspoken covenant to their followers contains three promises:

1. If you follow me, I will make your life better.

2. If you follow me, I will care about you.

3. If you follow me, I will take you where you cannot go on your own.

When a follower decides to leave a church, cause, or movement, it's almost always because one of these three promises has been broken.

1. I Will Make Your Life Better

Years ago, a lady named Kelly asked me to pray that God would enable her to get pregnant. Lori and I had experienced several years of infertility, so we knew the pain she was enduring. I prayed often and fervently, but no baby. A year later, Kelly quietly slipped out the back of the church. Promise #1 was broken: I hadn't made her life better.

It didn't matter that I was incapable of making her life better. Only God could have repaired her reproductive organs. But a better life was the unspoken expectation. Without a baby, we had a breach of contract.

Had Kelly stayed at New Song, she would have experienced dozens of incredible events and moments with our church family. She would have seen countless marriages and families helped. She would have played a part in over 8,000 people coming to Christ. The one thing she wanted more than anything else was a child from her womb. I couldn't give it, so she didn't stay.

On the other hand, Ken joined the church when we were just in the start-up phase. He was a young Christian looking for an adventure. Did his life become better? Well, Ken met his wife at New Song. In fact, she came to Christ here. So did her daughter. So did Ken's sisters, and his father, his nephew, and a whole lot of friends. Ken has grown tremendously, led a Small Group, served in our Tech Ministry. Ken's closest friends are members of the church. Promise kept.

2. I Will Care About You

Leaders often feel stretched thin, but when a parishioner is in a crisis, they expect the leader to respond. A few years back, a longstanding New Songer lost her sister to spina bifida. Her sister (Diane) and parents had been members of Saddleback Church for almost three decades. I was impressed to learn that Rick Warren delivered on Promise #2. He showed up at Diane's hospital bed a few days before she died. He personally comforted and prayed with her parents. Promise kept.

As New Song has grown, I've found it harder to express care for everyone who's following. Sometimes, I don't hear about people's sorrows until long after the fact. But when I can look them in the eye within hours of their loss or pick up the phone and pray with them, those small acts of care go a long way toward fulfilling our covenant.

3. I Will Take You Where You Cannot Go on Your Own

One of my greatest joys is Scott Evans, a friend ten years my junior who two decades ago made the decision to follow me to San Diego and help me plant New Song. Today, he's the founder of Outreach, Inc., a company that serves churches and ministries nationwide. He agrees that if he had stayed at his computer-industry job, he'd be half the man he is today.

Another is Jim Britts, a man twenty years my junior who has served on our staff for the past nine years. Jim's passion is youth, and he's got a talent for screenwriting. He recently released his first film, *To Save a Life*, which is changing lives around the world. Jim would have been a success at whatever he put his hand to, but with the encouragement of the New Song family, he's achieved great things in both youth ministry and the film industry. Nothing could thrill me more.

Jesus promised that if we would follow him, he would make us fishers of men. I never set out to take Scott or Jim where we've gone together. Christ gets all the credit. When a leader follows the Lord, there's a good chance he or she will take some people on a few pretty cool adventures—adventures to places none of them could have anticipated. It's one of those unspoken promises that Jesus, the ultimate leader, has made to those who follow him.

Keeping These Promises

Faced with promises I may soon be making to a new church full of people, I have to speak the unspoken questions: Can I make these people's lives better? Can I care about them all? Can I take them where they cannot go on their own?

My honest answer is "no." I have no personal power to improve a human life. On my own, I am incapable of caring for them all. And by myself, I can't take anyone anywhere significant. Fortunately, I'm not on my own, and the Holy Spirit can do everything I cannot do. So I am confident of this very thing: that He who began a good work in the members of this church will carry it on to completion. And I will be there praying, encouraging, guiding, and caring to the best of my ability.

Every church leader goes through low moments and dark valleys where they're tempted to quit, slide, or take it easy and hope nobody notices. It's easy to get busy and forget the unspoken promises we've made. I know—I've been there, thought about doing that, and even priced out the T-shirt. To help prevent this, once a quarter I go through a list of my top leaders and ask myself the following questions for each:

1. How am I making his/her life better?
2. How recently have they seen that I care about them?
3. How well am I leading them to a place they could not go on their own?

I don't always get an "A" on every question or every person, but speaking the unspoken promises, even to myself, makes me a better leader. Hopefully, it inches me one step closer to being "diligent."

The Unspoken Promises Made to Me

Years ago, Jesus made these same unspoken promises to me. Without question, he has made my life better, cared for me incredibly, and taken me where I could not have gone myself. He's done all of this in ways that are exceedingly, abundantly above all I could ask or imagine. As a bonus, he's letting me do the same with others. I hope he's doing the same with you.

49

Are You Leading from the Front?

Greg Stier

The best leaders lead from the front. They don't delegate, abdicate, or relegate the heavy lifting to "subordinates." They dive headfirst into the hard work.

This is true of the best military leaders throughout history. Battlefield generals like Leonidas of Sparta, Alexander the Great of Greece, and George S. Patton of California fought side by side with their soldiers so that wars would be won. They didn't *direct and expect* from the back of the battle. Instead, they chose to *dive and drive* into the heat of it.

These warrior/leaders weren't afraid to get mud and blood on their uniforms. They knew that these condiments of battle were the real medals of honor in the sight of the troops who followed them.

But it's not just military leaders who knew this principle. Effective political and spiritual leaders throughout history have understood this as well.

Lincoln, the gangly 16th president of the United States, led the Union from the front by being a hands-on Commander in Chief. As a leader, he was immensely practical and accessible, so practical that he won the war, so accessible that he was assassinated at close range.

Ghandi, the bold liberator of India, led an entire nation from the front. He marched 240 miles of dirt roads over 24 days to protest the unjust English taxes on and rulership over his beloved country. His dust-encrusted act of courage eventually helped to emancipate an entire country.

The best leader of all time, Jesus Christ himself, led from the front. He boldly took on the religious establishment of his day without flinching. He stood up for the poor and oppressed when nobody else would. He challenged the stone-throwing hypocrites by protecting a scarlet-lettered woman, putting himself in harm's way so that she could be saved. He wrapped himself in a towel and washed the dirty feet of his disciples to show them how to lead from the front. He got mud on his "uniform," and then he got blood on it.

He led the charge for the transformation of the human race by picking up his cross and dragging it to his death. In the heat of battle, he lost his life and won the war. He taught us how to win by losing and how to live by dying. He showed us how to lead from the front.

Leading from the front is the most effective way to lead a family, a ministry, or a company. Let's not be afraid of heavy lifting. Let's not delegate the calluses or splinters. Instead, let us, like Jesus, fill our hands with both as we pick up our crosses and die to ourselves so that others can be victorious.

7 Habits of Behind-the-Back Leadership

Ron Edmondson

I was thinking recently about the "backside" of great leadership. Great leadership involves leaders who have matured in their approach to leading people. Leading well means that sometimes what a leader does when the team's back is turned is more important than what they do in the team's presence. The backside of great leadership is when a leader does what is best for the team and the organization, not for his or her personal gain.

Still not sure what I mean? Here are some characteristics of the backside of great leadership.

When a team member is doing good work, a great leader:

1. Protects your back when critics rise against you or your work.

2. Won't back you into a corner by holding you accountable for unreasonable expectations.

3. Welcomes you back to good favor after you make a mistake.

4. Backs you up when you attempt to make a thoughtful decision.

5. Gives back to the team more than he or she takes from it.

6. Never stabs you in the back with others on the team or in the organization.

7. Gets back to you when you need his or her input on a decision.

Why the Bible Is a Tough Book for Americans

Don Miller

I'm not a big fan of the "there are only two kinds of people" breakdown of
humanity, and yet in the past few years, I've found myself wondering if, well,
there are only two kinds of people. I'm not talking about people who either
like Neil Diamond or don't; I'm talking about *how* and *why* thinkers. Let me
explain:

We all live life asking questions, questions about how to get ahead, how to
make life more meaningful, questions about how to survive or help people
survive. The question *how* is an American question, and it rests on the
presupposition that we know what life is really about.

Some friends and I were walking down the street in Vancouver, British
Columbia last week, and I stopped our group and asked them to look
around and count the ads that they noticed. We were downtown in a major
shopping district, and even though we could see for blocks, we found only two
billboards or posters advertising stuff. If we'd been across the border in the
States, we'd have counted, perhaps, hundreds. The difference was striking.

Advertising is part of the reason we have become a *how* culture.
Commercials make us think we need things, and then the dominant question
(thus the story we end up living) is about how we get what we think we are
missing, so we wake up every morning wondering how we are going to get
ahead, how we are going to get paid, and so forth.

The problem Christians face is that the Bible is not attempting to
answer *how* questions. And if it is, it's a terribly written book and not
practical in any way in terms of addressing how to succeed, how to get
married, how to be more sexy, how to lose weight, how to organize your
finances, or how to build a business. Instead, the Bible is a *why* book. The
Bible is answering much larger questions: Why do we exist, why do we not feel
loved, why is there pain in the world, why has God left us, and so forth. Are

there exceptions? Sure. Proverbs has some wisdom on how to live, and there are other examples, but they are few.

So the question is, are you trying to answer small questions with your life or big questions? If you are trying to answer small questions (how do I turn Earth into heaven, because there is no greater epic for me), then the Bible fails. But if you are trying to answer larger questions (all of this will someday go away, and life is short, so what is really important in light of this) then the Bible is a book for you.

American culture is a *how* culture. We ask almost exclusively *how* questions because our commercialized culture is not interested in *why*. If we really started asking *why* questions, our entire economy would collapse, and honestly, we wouldn't care because once we answered the *why* questions, we wouldn't want all that stuff in the first place.

So what does the Bible say to the average American? Among other things, it says this: You are asking the wrong questions.

Bible Use and Ownership

According to the national Study of Christian Attitudes and Behavior
conducted by Christianity Today International and Zondervan in 2006, 95
percent of all U.S. people who label themselves as Christians have a Bible
in their home. Active Christians have an average of six Bibles. 25 percent
of Active Christians bought a new Bible in the past 12 months. 57 percent
of respondents say they have read the Bible, and 63 percent of professing
Christians make this claim compared with 98 percent of active Christians.
However, only 18 percent of respondents read their Bibles daily, 19 percent
2–3 times a week, and 39 percent once a month. Among active Christians, 35
percent read their Bible daily, 28 percent 2–3 times a week, and 37 percent
once a week.

Christianity Today 4/09

Who Are You Going to Offend?

Mark Batterson

One of the most important decisions you'll ever make is this: Who are you going to offend? You'll offend somebody; I promise you that. But will you offend man or God? That single decision will set the tone of your life. Either you'll become a people-pleaser because you're afraid of offending people. Or you'll become a God-pleaser because the last thing you want to do is offend the Almighty.

It's hard not to draw tremendous inspiration from the story of Shadrach, Meshach, and Abednego. King Nebuchadnezzar had shown them great favor and put them in positions of authority. It had to be difficult to refuse to bow to his ninety-foot statue. He was the second-to-last person that they wanted to offend. The first? God.

Daniel 3:16 says, "…O Nebuchadnezzar, we do not need to defend ourselves before you in this matter. If we are thrown into the blazing furnace, the God we serve is able to save us from it, and he will rescue us from your hand, O king. But even if he does not, we want you to know, O king, that we will not serve your gods or worship the image of gold you have set up."

It was their unwillingness to offend God that set the table for one of the most amazing miracles in Scripture. God delivered them from the fiery furnace.

Who are you going to offend? You need to settle it now.

The Foundation of Leadership

Scott Williams

When you read a statement like "The Foundation of Leadership," it draws out a wide range of thoughts. Those thoughts are derived from the various types of experiences you've had with other leaders, your leadership, and leadership in general. There are many leadership experts, authors, and professionals that define the foundation of leadership in varying fashions. I personally think the foundation of leadership is Trust—"The Trust of Leadership." People like to trust that their leader will get it done and lead them from here to there.

We can break "The Foundation of Leadership" down into two Trust categories:

1. The Team Trusts the Leader.

This is one of the most important aspects of leadership, ensuring that a leader earns the trust of his/her team. *Earn* is the operative word; positional equity will only get you so far. In order for a leader to be truly successful, they must have the relational equity in addition to the "Trust Equity" of their team members. Integrity, genuine care and concern for the team, proven track record success, boldness, no "yes man" syndrome… are just a few of the ways that a team will begin to truly trust a leader.

2. The Leader Trusts the Team.

This is probably the second most important aspect of leadership, and it's often overlooked and very rarely carried out. When I say trust your team, that means believing in them so much that you don't micro-manage, you get out of their way, you correct when necessary, you encourage them to lead up, you maximize their strengths, and you watch them soar. I was reading George Barna's new book *Master Leaders,* and in one excerpt, this question was asked of many leaders: "How does a leader gain people's trust?" Seth Godin responded: "You have to trust them." (That's simple, but brilliant!) Ralph Winter added to Seth's answer by stating this: "Trust is letting people have as much rope as they need to be sure they feel good and can deliver the goods." Actions speak louder than words; live out trusting your people.

I'm in no way saying I have all of the answers and I have this leadership thing figured out; however, I am totally convinced that the core of leadership is based on trust. I've always tried to lead with integrity, care, and concern, embracing the fact that if people don't trust you, they won't follow you. On the other hand, I truly believe in and trust my people. I trust them so much that they have no choice but to believe in and trust themselves. If I believe my team can fly, even if they can't, they will get darn close. Help your team to soar; TRUST THEM!

4 Kinds of Vision Idolatry

Will Mancini

I often remind people that I was a spiritual formation pastor before I started coaching leaders around clarity and vision. This often flavors how I see the world. Even though I have committed my life to helping leaders and ministries cultivate a clear vision, I am all too aware of vision idolatry, first and foremost from my own life.

1. Hardness: Loving the Vision More than the People the Vision Serves

On my first interview while still in seminary, an experienced senior pastor put a pie chart in front of me with three slices. The slices were marked "people," "tasks," and "ideas." His question is simple, "Which one of these do you like the most?" As a budding pastor, my response was quick and confident: "People first, and then tasks."

But some people are wired to love ideas. In fact, today I would answer the question differently with "ideas" at the top of the list. Many strategically minded leaders forge a ministry identity out of a love for people. But with success and growth, they learn to leverage their skills with ideas and tasks. The problem is when this natural ability trumps the essential motive of love and model of deep connection with others. Any vision you have is an idea. Therefore, gifted visionaries can idolize the vision idea itself, either above the God who gave the vision or above the people the vision serves.

The great commandment is to love God and others, not to love the ideas that God gives you.

2. Impatience: Wanting God's Vision on Your Timetable

A God-given vision can be beautiful in an intoxicating sort of way. When a leader experiences it and knows it's from God, it can pulsate through your veins with a

Spirit-inspired adrenaline rush. As soon as this happens, it opens the door for a form of indulgence—a holy sort of instant gratification that, in the end, isn't holy at all.

3. Entitlement: Using God's Vision as a Cover for Personal Gain

We never start out in ministry with this temptation or thinking that we will ever face it. However, as a ministry grows, a subtle and unperceivable mindset forms. Entitlement happens when the leader expects and demands certain benefits and "rights" as a leader. In essence, this form of pride layers over time with each "win" in the ministry. The leader loses the instrumental identity and assumes a cause-and-effect identity with them as the ultimate cause and not God.

4. Buzz: Allowing the Success of the Vision to Provide Emotional Sustenance

This final idolatry is nothing different than enjoying the process addictions (shopping, gossiping, pornography, etc.) or chemical addictions that provide a high that you can't live without. Being a part of a ministry that's growing is a thrill ride with a lot of emotional benefits. This blessing can easily replace the gospel as the driving force and power center of our days. The emotional fruit of success becomes the functional savior.

Are You Too Nice As a Leader?

Ron Edmondson

I was talking with a leader recently. She's an incredibly kind and gentle person. She's smart, hard working, and loyal. She's a relational leader and usually brings out the best in people, so she's had success in leadership. She is currently experiencing problems in a new position and asked for my help. In talking through the specific situation, it quickly became obvious that she has one weakness, and it is currently affecting her entire team. Her weakness? She is being too nice as a leader! It has made her well liked in the organization, but it also has made her team less successful than it could be.

A few team members are taking advantage of her niceness by underperforming in their roles. She hasn't challenged the problems, even though she knows she should. She's losing sleep over it but doesn't know what to do. The relational leadership she has used in the past is not working with these team members.

Perhaps you've seen this before in an organization. Maybe you've been on either side of this issue. If this is your situation, you have probably even thought or said things such as, "I gave them an inch, and they took a mile." I am not suggesting one become a mean leader. I am suggesting one become a wise leader. Wisdom learns to guide people in the direction that's best for them, the leader, and the entire team or organization. In the situation above, I advised my friend to take off her "nice hat," at least temporarily, to address the few people causing the majority of the problems that are impacting the entire team. As hard as it will seem at first, in the end, it will be a blessing for the entire team.

Here are three problems with being too nice as a leader:

It's bad for the leader.

The leader ends up stressing over the wrong things. Instead of worrying about the big picture, the leader is focused on a few problems with usually only a few people. The leader feels unsuccessful, even like a failure at times as the team achieves less than desired results.

It's bad for the organization.

The team suffers because a few people mess up the system and progress for everyone else. Those on the team who wish to do the right thing lose respect for the leader. Others will follow the example of those taking advantage of the leader and lower their performance standards.

It's bad for the person.

Enabling bad behavior is never good for the underperforming team member. It keeps him or her from identifying their full potential and from realizing personal success. They may be a superstar if they are given structure and held accountable to complete their work.

Leader, have you become too nice as a leader? Are you allowing problems to continue out of a fear of not being liked? If you are not careful, you can become everyone's friend, but nobody's leader. The sooner you handle the problem (and the problem people), the sooner things will begin to improve on your team for everyone…and the sooner you can get a good night's rest.

What Every Pastor Should Know Before They Start

Mark Batterson

I recently received an e-mail from a pastor asking my advice: *What are the top things every person should know before they senior pastor their first church?* Here's my list of the things every pastor should know before they start.

1. Be Yourself.

Even more important than being a pastor is being yourself. Be authentic. Be real. Share your weaknesses and struggles. Remind your congregation that you are a work in progress just like they are. Be true to the unique passions and giftings God has given you. Develop core values and core convictions.

2. Put Your Family First.

I limit my church-related meetings to one evening per week. Establish those boundaries early on. If there is ever a conflict between family and ministry, it's a no-brainer. Family first.

3. Have Fun.

Church ought to be the most enjoyable hour of the week. Don't take yourself too seriously. The healthiest and holiest people laugh at themselves the most. Let your congregation see you laugh at yourself. A lot.

4. Keep Learning—Readers are Leaders and Leaders are Readers.

Once you think you have it figured out, it's the beginning of the end. There are ways of doing church that no one has discovered yet. Keep experimenting. Realize that if a 100 people give you 30 minutes of their time to listen to your sermon, your message better warrant 50 hours of listening time. Study to show yourself approved, and make sure you're doing both biblical exegesis and cultural exegesis.

5. Hire People You Like Hanging Out With.

How much you enjoy ministry depends on who you're doing ministry with. Hire people you can laugh with. Hire people who love God and love life. Hire people who go the extra mile. Hire people who work hard and play hard. Hire the right people then let their portfolio conform to them like a new shoe conforms to your foot.

6. Do Recon.

You've got to do everything within your power to keep from going into maintenance mode. Stay in growth mode. Remain an open-source system. Go to conferences and visit other churches.

7. Be a God-Pleaser.

I remind myself of what Abraham Lincoln said all the time: You can please all the people some of the time, some of the people all of the time, but you can't please all the people all the time. Don't worry about offending people. Worry about offending God. Stay true to the vision God has given you. Don't waver when people want you to conform to their vision of what the church should be. You'll spend the rest of your life contorting yourself and your church into a thousand shapes. Make sure you're doing ministry out of the overflow of what God is doing in your life. Make sure you allow God to work in you before you ask Him to work through you. The church will never outgrow you! If it does, it's dangerous!

8. Keep It Simple.

Less is more. We have two goals: Plug into a small group and plug into a ministry. Don't try to do too much. Be really good at what you do. Know who you are. Know who you aren't. Develop a kingdom mindset. Learn to appreciate the unique role that other churches play in your community. Then play to your strengths.

9. Paint Your Church Purple.

Either you are remarkable or invisible. Too many churches are ignorable. The good news ought to make the news. You've got to do things to get the attention of your community. Do what you do with an excellence that makes people do a double take. Make sure your print materials are aesthetically pleasing. Do outreaches that bless the socks off your community. Find the needs in your community and fill them. Dare to be different. Add a touch of creativity to everything you do!

10. Enjoy the Journey.

If you're a visionary, you'll tend to live for the future, but enjoy the moment. Be the best pastor you can be during every stage.

Spiritual leadership is knowing where God wants people to be and taking the initiative to get them there by God's means in reliance on God's power.

—*John Piper*

15 Gut-Check Questions for Leaders

Perry Noble

I have always found it interesting that I Corinthians 13 is sandwiched in between a chapter having to do with spiritual gifts and speaking in tongues. I know that all of us have probably heard it read at a wedding, but what if we took this same passage and applied it to our leadership? (Which, honestly, I think it was written more for church leaders and not wedding ceremonies!) Here we go...

1. "Love Is Patient"—Am I giving others the same room to make mistakes as I want them to give me?

2. "Love Is Kind"—Do the people I lead actually like being around me? (If you want to know the answer to this question, just ask yourself how much they ask to hang out with you outside of work!)

3. "It Does Not Envy"—Am I automatically jealous of anyone who has a great idea, and do I constantly perceive others as a threat to my position? (Another leader struggled with this; it didn't go well with him—see I Samuel 18:6–9.) By the way, this is why some young leaders can't thrive in their current conditions, because the more "mature" leader perceives them as a threat.

4. "It Does Not Boast"—Do I feel like I always need to remind people of my previous victories? (If we are obsessed with the past, then we're not advancing toward the future!)

5. "It Is Not Proud"—Do I feel that I am the only one in the organization that has all of the answers?

6. "It Is Not Rude"—Am I always cutting people off mid-sentence as soon as I discover that I do not like their idea, or am I willing to hear them out? (People don't always have to be right as long as they feel like they've been heard.)

7. "It Is Not Self Seeking"—Who is this about—really?

8. "It Is Not Easily Angered"—Are people afraid to bring me information that is true and accurate because they know I will lose my mind and begin to yell? (Don't shoot the mailman!)

9. "It Keeps No Record of Wrongs"—Do I remind people of their past failures or encourage them in their current condition?

10. "Love Does Not Delight in Evil but Rejoices in the Truth"—Can people be honest and open with anyone in the organization, including me? (When a leader does not have people around him who will share the truth, he becomes the Emperor who had no clothes!)

11. "It Always Protects"—Do I have the back of my staff? It's very discouraging to work for someone who demands loyalty but will not extend it.

12. "Always Trusts"—Do I believe the people who lead their assigned areas can make day-to-day decisions without my input?

13. "Always Hopes"—Do I always automatically assume the worst or the best about people? It is amazing what can happen on a staff when the leader believes in the people he leads.

14. "Always Perseveres"—Am I quick to give up on people after they make one mistake, or am I willing to teach them through it?

15. "Love Never Fails"—Do I have a high turnover OR a low turnover in the number of people who work with me/for me? (If the number is high, then maybe it isn't the people failing.)

Escape from the Turtle Cage

Mike Foster

Zoo visitors are supposed to be fixated on the animals. Yet, during our recent family trip, it wasn't the Galapagos turtles—the world's largest tortoises—that captured my attention. In fact, it was the cage the zoo was building for them that I found so fascinating.

A sleek sign highlighted features of the coming tortoise exhibit: a state-of-the-art barn with heated floors, specially selected cactus, and an interactive area for visitors. The project would take months to complete at a price tag of $1.2 million.

Clearly, this was an impressive project. Yet, one thing struck me.

IT WILL STILL BE A CAGE.

Don't get me wrong. It's going to be a nice exhibit. Guests will probably love it. The turtles may feel like they've scored a penthouse suite. But the fact remains, if the tortoises trek through enough exotic plants, they will run into a wall and a reality check. Despite appearances, they haven't been freed. They're just being confined behind fancier bars.

The turtles' scenario prompted me to reflect on my own situation.

Over the course of my life, I too have sunk energy and resources into upgrading my cage. I've slightly improved my social or financial condition. I've worked to ensure things that represent me—my appearance, job title, the way I carried myself—pleased others, outdid those around me, or at least kept me even with the next guy.

Along the way, I imagined I was moving closer to being free. But a few steps in, I'd slam into reality; I hadn't found freedom at all. I'd just increased the personal pressure to perform at a higher level, to achieve greater numbers, and to be accepted by the right people. I'd dressed up my weaknesses and imprisoned myself behind fancier bars called "success."

If anything, my "improvements" often made my journey harder. I ended up with more to prove, more image to manage, and more anxiety about the future.

Unfortunately, all of this soured the warm feelings I was actually chasing. And in the end, what we will find is the same truth the turtles did: You can't experience real freedom while imprisoned.

So how did I escape my turtle cage? How did I free myself from this paralyzing system that I was trapped in?

The key that unlocked my cage was grace. When I clearly understood who I was in God's eyes, I was freed. When I found my identity in how he saw me, the prison doors miraculously opened.

My value wasn't based on my performance, success, or how many followers I had on Twitter. I found no pleasure in the typical benchmarks of leadership success and was truly at peace with being loved and wanted by him.

So how does this play out practically in my life?

Well, over the past few years, I have worked very hard at becoming a "person of no reputation." I've discovered when you give up your reputation, you don't have to spend so much time and energy defending and proving it.

For most of my adult life as a leader, I used my skills to create cover-ups to hide my failures and dysfunctions. The problem with this plan, of course, was that maintaining a publicly acceptable version of Mike Foster became my full-time job on top of my actual full-time job. Over time, this became one too many full-time jobs.

In hiding my weaknesses, I eventually realized I had been denying something really important: the real me. And as much as I hate to admit it, the less desirable parts of myself are still me.

In fact, those traits are just as much me as any of my strengths or accomplishments. Trying to cut free of my flaws, then, was no more logical than trying to saw off a broken arm. Sure, a broken limb isn't necessarily pretty or fully functional but, with some healing, it still holds potential to contribute. Good or bad, it's still connected to the whole; it's still a part of the story.

Becoming a person of no reputation has allowed me to risk more, take greater pleasure in my work, and to discover true community with friends and team members.

So what about you?

You know it is never too late for any of us to escape from our turtle cages. Maybe your first step is to become a person of no reputation. Or perhaps it means getting on the phone, swallowing your pride, and healing a messy relationship. Your escape might involve you overcoming your fear of failure and pursuing a new venture or job.

Maybe it means saying words we've never said before, refusing to dwell on our checkered past, or simply beginning to tell the truth of who we really are. Each of us knows what issues we've been dressing up, the fancy bars we've installed to imprison ourselves.

I've decided I'm through upgrading my cage. I'm taking a jackhammer to its walls and setting out after real freedom.

PART

CHURCH
LEADERSHIP

Long Distance Leadership

Brady Boyd

Can you leave your church for the weekend and not fret? Can you not show up one Sunday and the worship services continue? Are most Sundays built around your charisma, your strengths, and your talents, or can someone different than you lead a weekend service? Do you have to be at every public gathering so people will feel the meeting is important?

I believe the real test of a leader is not so much when they are up front but when they are away and someone on the team is leading. Too many churches are built around one set of spiritual gifts and around one personality. The healthiest churches I know have empowered a diverse group of people to lead so that many spiritual gifts and many perspectives can be on display to the congregation.

This is one reason I have not embraced the video campus model, and instead, I am experimenting with another pastor leading a Sunday night campus who preaches my message live instead of asking people to watch me on a screen. There is nothing wrong with the aforementioned model so I am not challenging the leadership of many of my friends who do this at multiple campuses. What I am saying is there is another option that may work just as well.

My model is messier, requires a lot of relational equity with the campus pastor, and demands loyalty and trust from one another. But in the end, it allows me to mentor young communicators and helps build our fellowship around a multitude of gifts and personalities and not just one. I am still the primary leader, and I have final say on the sermon topics. We preach the same main points and use the same Scriptures, but a team is formed, and many players get in the game.

This is just one way I am purposely leading New Life while purposely staying away from many of the gatherings. I want to lead, at times, from a distance.

Have you empowered people around you to lead, or does everyone look to you to oversee every gathering? Are you preaching in your own pulpit more than 48 times a year? If so, can I suggest you immediately begin mentoring your replacement, because unless you are spiritual Superman, you are headed for burnout.

Step away and lead from a distance. You will find rest for your soul, and the church will get to feed from a buffet of teachers and not from just one menu item. Your team will rise to the challenge, and your church will become healthier than ever. Try it for a year and let me know if I am right or wrong.

PART

3

PREACHING
& TEACHING

*Life is too short
and hell is too hot
to just play church.*
—*Larry Osborne*

4 Steps from Good to Great Preaching

Kent Anderson

Most people can recognize a good sermon when they hear one, though they might have difficulty articulating why. For those of us who try to preach those "good sermons," it is useful to understand what it takes to get those positive responses from our listeners.

Of course, listeners vary and have different things that they are looking for in a preacher. A listener's *theology* will determine his or her sense of the sermon. Those who are committed to a high view of Scripture might expect something different than one committed to a more active view of the work of the Holy Spirit. *Learning style* is a factor in considering the effectiveness of a sermon. Some listeners learn best through reflection; others prefer a more active and participatory approach. *Culture* will affect one's evaluation of a sermon. Where we come from, what generation we belong to, our denomination, our economic situation, and our gender all play a part in determining the kind of preacher we best respond to.

Still, if preaching is preaching, there are certain things that can be said across the board. If the following things are in place, we can be fairly confident that our sermons will be well appreciated and lead to the kinds of responses we expect. These, then, are the factors that result in "good" and maybe even "great" preaching.

A good sermon is rooted in the Bible.

A sermon ought to find its footing in the Word of God. Many fine things could be said by a preacher, but if the listener doesn't feel that the sermon has been helpful in engaging the Bible, it falls short as a sermon. This means that the Bible will be used as more than window dressing or as a jumping-off point. The Bible will govern the sermon and be the source of its big idea if the sermon is any good. Good preachers understand that God still speaks through his Word. The Bible is the one instrument that God has promised to bless. When it comes to good preaching, the Bible is where the power is.

A good sermon helps people hear from God.

This is as helpful a definition of preaching as I know. Preachers work to connect people with the voice of God. If a listener does not sense that she or he has been in the presence of God and heard something meaningful from him, then the sermon could not have been that good. As such, the sermon does not have to fit any particular pre-fab form. The sermon as a medium can flex to respond to the interests and concerns of any culture and situation. If it helps people hear what God is saying, it is a good sermon, regardless of the preacher's style. This underlines, of course, a dependence on the Scriptures.

A good sermon will be easily understood.

Some preachers seem to confuse complexity with depth. In my experience, it is the simple truths that are the most profound. Listeners can understand good preaching. Good preachers work to understand the language, the culture, and the interests of those to whom they preach. They work hard to clarify and unify the presentation so that there will be no confusion about what they are trying to say. In most cases, good sermons offer one idea—an idea big enough yet simple enough for listeners to appreciate and apply to their lives.

A good sermon exalts the person of Jesus Christ.

We are Christian preachers, which means that every sermon we preach will exalt the person of Jesus Christ. While not every text is directly Christological, I believe that every sermon ought to be. What are we saying that a Jewish priest couldn't say? What are we offering that goes beyond what people hear on Oprah? At the end of the day, Christian preachers offer Jesus Christ as the hope of mankind. A good sermon will be sure to make that clear.

These four principles apply to any good sermon I have ever heard. A good sermon will integrate the person and presence of God with the person and presence of the preacher. The divine and the human collaborate in the mystery that is good preaching.

Making the Message Memorable

Larry Osborne

Like most pastors, I learned early on that if my preaching was to be *powerful*, it had to be *memorable*. That sounded simple enough—until I had to pull it off week in and week out.

All too often, I'd spend hours putting a sermon together hoping to change lives only to find out later that the only thing anyone remembered was the funny story about my kids or the illustration about getting lost in Seattle instead of the biblical principle it was supposed to drive home.

So-called communication experts told me I needed to use more props and compelling stories. Other people told me to get rid of the gimmicks and stick to the meat of the Word. Some warned me to shorten my messages in light of shrinking attention spans, while others pointed out that most of the best-known and most listened-to pastors were seldom brief in their remarks.

Over the years, I've tried all kinds of things to drive home a point and make it stick—from shorter sermons to lengthy discourses, from narratives to hyper-practical "Five Steps to Whatever," from verse-by-verse to hot-button topics. For a while, we even stopped in the middle of the sermon to allow time for questions and discussion (something the extroverts loved and the introverts absolutely loathed).

I also made use of a cottage industry of illustration services, books, tapes, and seminars that were available to help. And nowadays, you can add to that a host of online sermons and websites offering outlines and downloads full of fresh ideas and insights.

Some of the stuff was pretty good and helpful. Some was pretty goofy. But frankly, none of it came close to approaching the impact of something I stumbled upon years ago: *Home Bible studies built around a discussion of the previous weekend sermon.*

Now, I know that small groups are nothing new. And here at North Coast Church, they've been the hub of our ministry since the mid-1980s. But combining the sermon and our midweek small groups into a lecture/lab combo was not only new, it was risky.

We'd always offered choices. Tying everything to the weekend message meant we were bucking our own tradition and the conventional wisdom that said people want more, not fewer, choices. To some of our folks, asking everyone to use the same sermon-based curriculum (and writing it ourselves) felt like we'd suddenly gone high control—especially to those who'd thrived in a free-market of self-selected topics and book studies.

Still, we went for it because we liked the potential upside. We thought it might offer significant *educational benefits* to study one thing and study it well rather than studying lots of things, none of which we ever covered in depth. We also hoped it would positively impact our *shared sense of unity and mission*. And finally, it seemed like it would be a lot easier to find people who could *facilitate* a discussion of the sermon than *inductive Bible study leaders* who could lead a traditional Bible study.

But one thing I didn't expect was that it would make me a better preacher; maybe not a better preacher in the eyes of the homiletics connoisseur—but a far better preacher in terms of my messages being memorable and life changing. Here's why.

Increased Attentiveness

The first thing I noticed was that once we started connecting our small group questions to the sermon, people were noticeably more attentive. I wish I could take credit for improved material, delivery, or style. But I hadn't changed. What had changed was the congregation's awareness that they were going to discuss the message later in their small group. As a result, they were much more attentive.

And to my surprise, I discovered that attentiveness is contagious. When everyone else in the room is dialed in, it seems to send a subtle, perhaps subliminal, message that this is important stuff—don't miss it. So most people work a little harder to hang in even during the slow (should I saying boring?) parts of the message.

Increased Note-Taking

The most obvious sign of the congregation's increased attentiveness was a marked increase in note taking. That alone had a significant impact upon the memorableness of my sermons.

Educational theorists have long pointed out that we forget most of what we hear unless we also interact with the material visually, verbally, or physically. In short, taking notes dramatically increases recall. And tying small groups to the sermon dramatically increases note taking.

It's not just the neurotic note takers who benefit (you know the kind, the folks who get a nervous twitch if a blank is left unfilled or a point skipped). We found that the note-taking bug also bit folks who would have normally sat back and listened. But aware that they would be discussing key points in the message later in the week, they began to take notes as a way to "lay down some crumbs" to find their way home again when their group met.

Spirited Discussion

When I first entered the ministry, I dreamed of communicating God's Word so powerfully that people would discuss it during the week. I envisioned impassioned discussions of deep truth leading to radically changed lives.

But if truth be known, for most of our congregation, the frantic pace of a typical week quickly pushed Sunday's sermon to the background. The thought of sitting down and carefully reviewing what they'd heard on Sunday never entered their minds. They were too busy. Shoot, so was I!

But once we started tying our small group questions to the weekend message, nearly everyone took the time to review their sermon notes because it was an essential part of their preparation for their small group's meeting. Even if someone rushed through the homework a few hours before the meeting or even on the way to the meeting, I was still far ahead. The stuff we talked about on Sunday was no longer on the back burner of their subconscious. For a few short hours, it was once again front and center. And I'd become a more memorable preacher!

This process has worked so well we've never gone back. Twenty years after our first sermon-based small groups, we still have 80 percent of our weekend attendance meeting to discuss in greater depth the meaning and application of the previous weekend's sermon. And it's a concept that has scaled easily with our growth, from 180 more than 6,500 in weekend attendance.

Many of you may have tried something similar if you worked your way through *40 Days of Purpose* or any similar study. The good news is that you don't need to go through the hassle of making video presentations to be shown in the home. It can work just as well to put together a series of questions that review, dig deeper, and look at a parallel biblical passage or two. That's all we do. We put a note sheet and the questions in the weekend bulletin and let people prepare for their group meeting at their own pace.

It's become the core of our ministry's health—and the secret to making my preaching more memorable.

PART

3

PREACHING
& TEACHING

6 Tips for Preaching to a Hard Audience

R. Larry Moyer

Speaking to a broken heart is like giving nourishment to a starving child. Speaking to a hard heart is like correcting a rebellious teenager. So how do you do it?

If you're looking for an easy answer, it's not there. But here are some helpful ideas—ones that may crack open the most callous heart.

Start on your knees.

Remember, not only can you not do it, God doesn't expect you to. You are the instrument; you're not the power. An employer once told an employee to attempt the breaking of a rock with a pickaxe. After a half-hour of severe blows, the rock showed no signs of breaking. The employee threw the pickaxe aside. The employer asked him why he had stopped. The man answered, "Because I obviously have had no impact on the rock." The employer answered, "The job of using the pickaxe is in your hands. The results are not."

Only God can break the "rock" of a hard heart. If the heart is that of a callous non-Christian, only God can show him his need. John 16:8 NKJV refers to the Holy Spirit of God not the human spirit of the preacher, when it says, "And when He has come, He will convict the world of sin, and of righteousness, and of judgment…" If the heart is that of a cold Christian, prayer remains the starting point. If Jesus prayed for them, we should too (John 17:20).

Watch your attitude.

If a speaker doesn't admit that a hardened heart can invite frustration or even anger on his part, he is probably not being honest with himself. Preaching to a hardened heart can make us feel like we are wasting our time. "Why try?" we are tempted to explain. "If they want to ruin their lives, why not let them ruin them?"

But humility, not hostility, cracks a hardened heart. Paul says to Timothy, "...in humility correcting those who are in opposition, if God perhaps will grant them repentance, so they may know the truth..." (II Timothy 2:25 NKJV). Paul was writing a pastoral epistle, so the context would indicate that "those who were in opposition" may be unbelievers who have never come to the truth or believers who are walking from the truth. Either way, it's the attitude behind what you say that penetrates. If I am a hardened person, I may argue with what you say, but it is hard to refute the proper attitude in which you've said it. Does not Ephesians 4:15 admonish us to speak the truth in love?

One speaker I know attempts to break a hardened heart with what many have observed as harsh and blunt statements. He defends his position by pointing out that Christ said of the Pharisees, "You are of your father the devil..." (John 8:44 NKJV). He further points to John the Baptist, who refers to those listening to him as a "brood of vipers" (Matthew 3:7). My response is three-fold. To use those particular accounts as a pattern for breaking hardened hearts is not in keeping with the intent of the paragraphs. Why not go instead to what Paul tells his disciple Timothy as found in II Timothy 2:25? Second, to liken ourselves to Christ and John the Baptist is a bit arrogant. We are certainly not the Savior, or even the forerunner of the Savior, as we speak. Third, it must be noted that they are the exception, not the norm. Christ Himself was noted for being "gentle and lowly in heart" (Matthew 11:29 NKJV). We ought to ask ourselves, "Does my attitude have the same reputation?"

Rely on truth, not emotions.

Your thoughts could matter less and, frankly, may have no authority. Christ's thoughts could not matter more, and they have full authority. This is why preachers need to be expositors—ones who, each time they stand before the people, unfold the meaning of a particular text of Scripture, first to the people of that day and then to the people of our day. That way, a hardened heart has to struggle with God, not you. You may become the scapegoat, but the hearer's problem is really with the Author of the Scriptures, not the communicator of the Scriptures. A seasoned pastor once told me, "The first book any pastor ought to preach through, a paragraph at a time, is I Corinthians. It speaks to every problem in the church." If you attempt to use emotion to convince, it distracts from the authority of the Word. If you use the calm (yet enthusiastic) preaching of the Word and allow a passage such as I Corinthians to convict, it respects the authority of the Scriptures.

Use humor.

Tell me I'm in a wretched condition—callous to spiritual truth, uncaring about anyone except me, unteachable in spirit—and I'll likely get mad at you. Tell it to me in a way that makes the hardest heart grin, and I'm likely to reflect on what you say. Be careful, though, how you enter and exit the humor; it can make a big difference. For example, suppose as you are preaching you say, "Sometimes, we find it hard to admit where we are spiritually and how great our need is, how far we have walked from Him and how much we need His mercy. A woman who had her picture taken was totally disgusted with how it looked. Storming mad, she walked into the photographer's office, slammed the picture down on his desk, and said, 'That picture doesn't do me justice.' He responded, 'Madam, with a face like yours, you don't need justice, you need mercy.' Now, wait a minute, before you laugh, have you ever thought about how much we, too, need mercy? If He gave us what we deserve, we wouldn't stand a chance. We deserve His justice, but we receive His mercy." This kind of humor, I'm not easily going to forget. You make me laugh, but the Holy Spirit may use it to make me listen.

Use "we" more than "you."

A hardened heart, whether it is a non-Christian who hasn't come to Christ or a Christian walking from Him, grieves the heart of God. But so does impatience, unkind thoughts, and selfish thinking on the part of any growing believer. Sin of any kind is offensive to God. Furthermore, as D. L. Moody once said, "But for the grace of God, there be I." Had it not been for His grace, we too would be lost. Any believer stands the danger of walking from God if he ceases to grow as a Christian. Therefore, as we speak to hardened hearts, "we" has to be a big part of our vocabulary.

"We" in speaking has three advantages. For one, you don't come across as "holier-than-thou." Listeners understand that you not only see them as sinners, but you see yourself as one. Secondly, "we" helps you speak as a caring friend, not a scolding parent. When my heart is hardened, I need such a friend. The scolding is deserved, but the care is more needed. Thirdly, it lets me know you are speaking with me, not at me. This is particularly effective in reaching hardened hearts because by speaking with me, you come up underneath me; while speaking at me, you come down on top of me.

Is there a place for "you" language in preaching? Most definitely. But "you" should be used prominently in the end of your message and "we" used at the beginning. As you come to the end of your message, "you need to come Christ" is in order. After all, you as the speaker have already come to Him; the listener is the one in need. If I'm a Christian with a hardened heart, "you" is also in order as you close your message. You as the speaker have already dealt with the truth of the passage you are speaking from. You are now asking the listener to do so.

Develop your communication skills.

Hardened hearts need to hear from a communicator, not a speaker. What a speaker says may go in one ear and out the other. What a communicator says tends to have an impact. Why? Communicators look at several things: "How can I say this in different words than they have heard before?" "How can I use illustrations to drive home my point and cause them to identify with it?" "Where would humor be effective?" "What kind of analogy would help?" "How can I keep my message to thirty minutes?" "How can I speak in a way that causes them to want to come back?" "How can I say this in truth, but also in grace?"

Communicators are difficult for a hardened heart to turn away from because they present the truth of the Scripture in a way that penetrates. If my heart is hardened, truth communicated well allows me to leave your presence, but it makes it more difficult to leave your message.

Conclusion

Are these ideas guaranteed to penetrate a hardened heart? No. But that, again, is not our business. Our assignment is to do our part and let God do His. I dare say, though, millions of hardened hearts have been broken through these six principles. They have caused more than one person to admit, "Oh, wretched man that I am..." (Romans 7:24 NKJV).

7 Questions to Ask Before You Preach

Francis Chan

1. Am I worried about what people think of my message or what God thinks? (*Teach with fear.*)

2. Do I genuinely love these people? (*Teach with love.*)

3. Am I accurately presenting this passage? (*Teach with accuracy.*)

4. Am I depending on the Holy Spirit's power or my own cleverness? (*Teach with power.*)

5. Have I applied this message to my own life? (*Teach with integrity.*)

6. Will this message draw attention to me or to God? (*Teach with humility.*)

7. Do the people really need this message? (*Teach with urgency.*)

(Taken from a message at the Desiring God National Conference)

Megachurches, Growth, and the Art of Pastoring:

A ChurchLeaders.com Q & A with Eugene Peterson

PART
3
PREACHING
& TEACHING

Eugene Peterson has influenced the faith of thousands through his writings on spiritual formation. He has written more than thirty books, including his contemporary translation of the Bible, *The Message*. Peterson's most recent book is a memoir of his life and ministry titled, *The Pastor*. In this interview, Peterson shares his thoughts on church models, spiritual growth, and the art of pastoring.

ChurchLeaders: Eugene, in your book *The Pastor* you describe how important your childhood was in forming you for ministry—specifically your father's butcher shop—can you elaborate on the importance of your childhood and how it impacted your view of the church and pastoring?

Eugene Peterson: Well, in the sectarian world in which I grew up, there was a very sharp distinction between the saved and unsaved in the church world and the other world, and in that butcher shop, there was no division. It was all one world, and pastors kind of represented for me an alien world or a world that was very circumscribed. It just felt tiny to me, and the butcher shop just took in the whole community and all kinds of people in the community. So I think that was it. There was sense that God so loved the world. It's something embracing, and I got that. That kind of penetrated my imagination and never left it.

CL: What kind of church models did you experience growing up?

EP: I grew up in a culture that was very entertainment centered. Pastors were really good storytellers, and they were attractive people, glamorous. And then I transitioned to a mainline denomination when I was in university, in seminary, and I wasn't very attracted to that world either. It was more religion is a business and keeping good records and making sure everybody was keeping the rules. So in neither place did I find a model. I guess I experienced anti-models or non-models, and when I became a pastor, I thought this is what I was born to do, but it didn't have anything to do with celebrity or entertainment. It had nothing to do with organization and such. I had the whole world, the whole field to myself to figure out what was going on, and I did find allies, most of them in the cemeteries. Pastoral work that has been done for two thousand years that didn't fit those two stereotypes that I had grown up with or that I experienced.

CL: You often talk about the need for pastors to avoid the pressures of "fast" growth. I'm curious, what do you think about the "church growth" model for ministry? Is it helpful or potentially hurtful to the life of the church?

EP: Well, I don't want to be too harsh or dismissive. These are my brothers and sisters doing this, and they're doing good things and doing things I could never do. But I do think that the commercialization, making just this slight twist on things so that religion becomes a consumer commodity, really changes the way you look at the church, and it makes you dependent upon money and numbers, and that's very addictive. It's really hard to get out of that. But it also means a terrific loneliness in the pastoral life. The pastors who give themselves to this, and many of them, not all of them, but many of them end up with pretty thin lives. That just grieves me.

CL: You talk about the consumer commodity aspect of church, could you give me a tangible example—something specific that creates more of the consumer mindset that you're talking about?

EP: Well, when the Gospel is presented as a way to get what you want, have peace, have success, that's introducing a very distorted view of what Biblical revelation is, and it has become much more American than Biblical. And so that's what I was hoping, in writing *The Pastor*, or after I got started writing it, that I could get some dignity to a pastoral life which was modest and non-competitive and personal and local, and those are not qualities that are much in evidence.

CL: You talk a lot about the importance of "place" and ministry context in pastoring. How would you encourage young pastors to better embrace their ministry locale as a part of their formation as a pastor?

EP: Well, this is where most of the satisfaction comes in being a pastor, in being local and being personal. The vocation of the pastor is one of the best in which you can learn to find out ways to be intimate with people and to understand the actual location where you live. This Earth is glorious, and we're not disembodied—we don't levitate. We're people with our feet on the ground, and who else gets to do this in quite the way a pastor can do? You know, a doctor deals with bodies who are disembodied from place and relationships, and the businessman is dealing with commercial transactions that have nothing to do with relationships as far as he's concerned. But a pastor gets to do it all; the whole thing comes together, and the pastor knows whole entire families and neighborhoods and gets to see the whole thing: the good, the bad, the indifferent, the sick, the healthy. I think it's a glorious vocation to get called into, and it saddens me when pastors eliminate so much of it just by ignoring the actual circumstances in which they live and try to plant something that's disincarnate and using programs instead of relationships in order to cultivate the Christian life.

PART

3

PREACHING
& TEACHING

CL: You've written more than thirty books, many of them on spiritual formation. In your opinion, does church size matter when it comes to spiritual formation? Are megachurches healthy places to grow?

EP: It's very difficult to develop maturity in a place where the size is so huge. I'm thinking particularly about pastors. How can you preach to people you don't know? The sermons become, and the church is run, primarily through programs, which are inherently depersonalizing. And so you're choosing a way to have church that makes it very difficult to be at church. Of course, there are many good things that happen. You can have mission projects and world influence in what's going on, and you can certainly say what needs to be said. You know, our primary theological tenant is the Trinity. God is personal, and He's interpersonal. There is nothing God does that doesn't come from a Trinitarian sort of an operation, and when we start to develop strategies that bypass the personal, the local, then it seems to me we're just hamstringing ourselves.

CL: What are the major things you would encourage young leaders and pastors to be involved in on a daily and weekly basis in their ministries?

EP: I think one of things I think I'd like to convey is that there are twenty hundred different ways of being a pastor, and there's probably no other vocation in which you're able to be yourself, with your whole self as a pastor. And I think it's important for each of us to say, "What's gone into the making of me as a pastor?" and use the strengths that I've been given, the experiences I've been given to be a faithful servant of Jesus Christ. But I think local and personal is very important. There are a lot of different ways to preach a sermon or teach a class or visit somebody in the hospital, but if we try to take somebody else's mantle and put on us, it's like Saul's armor. It just doesn't work. It might look really good, but we can't move in it. It keeps us from being ourselves. So I think that's what I'd say. Pastors I've known and who have been important to me have kind of done it out of their own skin, have tried to be modeled by somebody else.

5 Purposes of Preaching

David Padfield

Many great sermons are recorded in the New Testament, such as the Sermon of the Mount (Matt. 5–7), Stephen's history of the Jewish nation (Acts 7), Paul's address on Mars' Hill (Acts 17), and Peter's first sermon under the new covenant (Acts 2). Men today have very little respect for preaching—maybe it's because they don't know the purpose of preaching. Why *do* we preach?

1. Explain the Scriptures

This sounds so simple, yet it is often forgotten by men today. In Acts 7, one-third of Stephen's sermon was from the Old Testament. His audience knew what the verses said, but he had to explain what they meant and how it applied to them.

When Philip preached in Acts 8, he explained Isaiah 53. The eunuch wanted to know "of whom does the prophet say this, of himself or of some other man?" (Acts 8:34 NKJV)

After Artaxerxes released the Israelites, Ezra, a scribe and priest of God, read the "Book of the Law of Moses" to the people. With aid from the Levites, Ezra "helped the people to understand the law" (Neh. 8:7 NKJV). "So they read distinctly from the book, in the law of God; and they gave the sense, and helped them to understand the reading" (Neh. 8:8 NKJV). Does your preaching explain the Scriptures?

2. Hold Up the Scriptures As Light

In Apostolic sermons, no appeal was ever made to modern theological thought. Men of God simply proclaimed God's word. Jesus said, "You shall know the truth, and the truth shall make you free" (John 8:32 NKJV).

The Apostles never claimed an emotional experience as the basis for salvation. They presented God as having revealed His will to man (1 Cor. 2:6–13). This revealed will was placed into written form, "by which, when you read, you may understand..." (Eph. 3:4 NKJV) Do you consider the Scriptures sufficient to light men's lives?

3. Disturb People in Error

Peter did not soft-pedal the truth in Acts 2. He accused his audience of killing the Son of God. As a result, these people were "cut to the heart" (Acts 2:37). Cutting a man to the heart is not a task to be relished—it is the end result of freedom, joy, and salvation for which we seek.

The way some men preach today, a lost man might never know his condition. Sinners will never cry out, "What must I do to be saved?" while listening to the preaching done by some today: what about your messages?

4. Present Christ as the Only Hope of the World

The first thing Paul did in every city he visited was to lift up Christ and set Him before men as their only hope. Paul told the Corinthians he "determined not to know anything among you except Jesus Christ and Him crucified" (1 Cor. 2:2). Salvation does not come by the preaching of politics or moral platitudes—our hope is in heaven, not in earthly capitals.

5. Tell About the Church

Some advise, "Preach the Man, not the plan." But we can not preach the King without His kingdom, nor the Groom without His bride. When the gospel was preached in Acts 2, men were added to the church (Acts 2:47). This is the church Jesus promised to build (Matt. 16:18), and the only one which He will save (Eph. 5:23).

Let us not put our trust in institutions built by men, for they will be uprooted (Matt. 15:13). As the hymn goes, "The kingdoms of earth pass away one by one, but the kingdom of heaven remains."

This checklist can help determine whether your messages place the focus on the King and His kingdom: What are your purposes for preaching?

Pastors & Prayer

Pastors vary widely in what they're praying about. In an Ellison study, pastors said they prayed about the following during the preceding seven days:

Needs within the congregation **98%**

The congregation's spiritual health and growth, wise leadership **94%**

Personal spiritual growth **86%**

What to say in a sermon **82%**

The country as a whole **82%**

Personal needs **81%**

War, disaster, global events **76%**

Local outreach efforts **71%**

Individual government leaders **68%**

Overseas missions **62%**

Local churches or pastors **61%**

Numerical growth of their church **56%**

Financial health of their church **56%**

Personal financial needs **50%**

Christian leaders **50%**

Persecuted Christians **46%**

Their denomination (among denominational churches) **39%**

Other topics **11%**

Ellison Research, May 23, 2005

The Importance of Moving People

Steven Furtick

Great preachers and leaders know how to **move** people.

As soon as I say that, I know that the first thing that comes to many people's minds is emotional manipulation. After all, when unchurched people say they really liked your sermon, they usually say that it really *moved* them. And in their minds, they're probably talking about pure emotion. Maybe intellectual curiosity.

But that's not what I mean. Anyone can do that, and it doesn't guarantee any kind of positive growth in the lives of the people you're preaching to and leading.

What I mean is the concept of moving people further along in their lives. Advancing them beyond their current level of development. Beyond their current walk with God.

I like that concept. That image. And it's something that I think all pastors should strive after. **Pastors have to know how to move people.** And they have to know how to move them on two tracks: **1) individually** and **2) corporately.**

The words you speak should move people on a personal level. It should grip their hearts and make application to their lives personally. If you don't move the individual and you're only casting broad vision to the church as a whole, you're only going to preach to the highest commitment level people, and your church isn't going to go very far.

For example, you can make the greatest pitch for the greatest capital campaign in church history. But if the individual people and families in your church aren't moved to live lives of generosity, the thermometer on your stage is going nowhere.

You have to move the people to move the church.

But you also have to move the church as a whole in the right direction. You should always have a direction the church needs to move in corporately. A common goal that you want the collective efforts of the individual people in your church aimed at. If you don't, the church won't advance.

Going back to our example, it's not enough just to move people to tithe. What you have to do is figure out where God wants to take your church. What it's going to take financially to get there. And then cast a compelling vision that moves individual people to get on board to make it happen.

You have to move the church to move the people.

Good preachers and leaders are great at moving individuals.

Good preachers and leaders are great at moving churches.

Great preachers and leaders are great at *both*.

PART

PREACHING
& TEACHING

5 Reasons to Preach the Tough Stuff of Prophecy

Hal Seed

As a preacher, I'm called to proclaim the whole counsel of God, yet for years, I shied away from the prophetic books.

After all, most of them are confrontational, controversial, and confusing. Then, one Labor Day weekend, I invited one of my board members (not even a staff member, mind you) to do a message on the end times. Our attendance usually flags a bit on holiday weekends, but that weekend it surged. I decided it was time to face my fears and tackle the perils of prophecy head-on.

Okay, maybe not exactly head-on. I decided to start by preaching the book of Daniel. Ask any small group what they'd like to study next, and a substantial number of them will say, "Either Revelation or Daniel." Daniel is the shorter of the two, and besides, one-half of it is history, not prophecy. I titled the series "Future History," and scheduled it to begin December 1. It allowed me to use Christmas Eve to talk about Daniel's influence on the Wise Men.

To my surprise, the church filled up during that series! We grew by 17 percent over the next ten weeks. People were so hungry for more, I ended up writing a book on Daniel. Was that series a fluke, or had I tapped into something?

I am not a prophet or the son of a prophet (I work for a non-profit institution), but I've discovered five reasons why you and I ought to preach through the prophets.

1. People are curious about prophecy.

People everywhere want to know what God says, and some of his most direct communication comes from the pens of prophets. People especially want to know about what God says about the future, which makes books like Daniel,

Zechariah, Revelation, and passages like Joel 2 (The Day of the Lord), Isaiah 65–66 (The New Heavens and The New Earth), and Ezekiel 36–48 (The Valley of the Dry Bones, Ezekiel's War, and The Millennium Temple) particularly palatable to them.

2. People need help understanding prophetic literature.

Personally, I need help in understanding biblical prophecy. I have years of formal education in Biblical Studies, yet I still find myself consulting commentaries every time I open apocalyptic literature. I need to be reminded of the context in which the prophets spoke. I need help from smarter men than I to decipher the word-pictures and references from that day. If pastors need help understanding prophetic literature, how likely is it that the average layperson will dig into it unless we teach it to them? More than 20 percent of Scripture is prophetic in nature! Surely, preachers should not skip over more than a fifth of the Bible!

3. People need assurance about the future.

In uncertain times, people need to know the certainty of God's victory. Isaiah 40:1 says, "Comfort, comfort my people." With all the unrest in our world, people are looking for the comfort of God's clear teaching about the future of planet Earth.

I suspect that some communicators feed their churches a low-fat prophetic diet because they're afraid they'll drive people away with higher doses. My experience shows that prophecy is actually one of the great draws of the 21st century. A year after I preached "Future History," I led our church through a series on the book of Jonah. With four short chapters, the story's over almost before it's begun. But the church grew by 18 percent over those four weeks.

4. People need to hear what God says about things that displease him.

Personally, I love living in this day and age. In sheer variety of worldviews, the early 21st century rivals 33 A.D., and options for ethics and standards of right and wrong run the gambit. People can believe anything (and sometimes they do). But at the core of our beings is the image of God (Genesis 1:26), and inside our hearts is eternity (Ecclesiastes 3:11). When we use pointed passages of prophecy to describe God's displeasure at sin, our words cut to the core and resonate with God's image-bearers. People need to hear what God says about chasing lesser things, lack of care for the poor, manipulation of the truth, perpetuating social injustice, and the like. When God says, "Turn to me now, while there is still time. Give me your hearts" (Joel 2:12), those words can pierce cleansingly, effectively, and life-changingly into the tender places of our souls.

5. People need to experience the mystery of God.

In no other type of literature is God's mystery and wonder on display as it is in the books of the prophets. Daniel's description of the Ancient of Days (Daniel 7:9–10) is one of the most awe-inspiring glimpses of God in the Bible. Isaiah 6:1–5 rivals it. Where in the Epistles can you find this same level of mystery? Flip through the Minor Prophets (the ones you've been avoiding), and you'll see what I mean.

I make no claims that I have mastered the art of preaching the prophets. But now, when I'm praying about what God would have us study during the coming year, I consider all sixty-six books, and I make a point of remembering the prophetic books. We've got the whole playbook available to us, and the less-common plays can be just the ones that turn the game around and win one for the Kingdom.

The true shepherd spirit is an amalgam of many precious graces. He is hot with zeal, but he is not fiery with passion. He is gentle, and yet he rules his class. He is loving, but he does not wink at sin. He has power over the lambs, but he is not domineering or sharp. He has cheerfulness, but not levity; freedom, but not license; solemnity, but not gloom.

—Charles Spurgeon

Why Preparing Sermons Takes Me So Long

Joe McKeever

When a pastor friend confessed that he frets before preaching a series in another church—"Should I preach this? Or that? Or the other?" —I smiled in memory of doing the same. I must have given myself ulcers from the anxiety of those days.

What cured me? Prayer. I'm not in the least implying my friend does not pray sufficiently; I'm only confessing that prayer changed everything for me. Once I know what the Lord is telling me to preach, I do not ask again but get on with the preparation.

Second is doing the Bible study. Let me illustrate from a real-life example of preparing a message from Romans 12. I already had the basic outline: This chapter, I am fully convinced, is a well-rounded description of a healthy church. The first two verses—"present your bodies a living sacrifice"—deal with the most basic of considerations, the personal commitment of every person to Jesus Christ. Verses 3–8 describe a congregation in which the members all have spiritual gifts, know what they are, and are exercising them well. And verses 9–21 present the various kinds of relationships between the members. I aimed to intertwine and interrelate these themes so the listener could easily see how God's people are to be related to Him and to one another.

Clearly, just the Bible study portion of this sermon could easily take an hour. However, a pastor simply cannot tell everything he knows about a text in a single sermon. Otherwise, the pastor's preparation will extend beyond reckoning, and the actual sermon will extend into Sunday afternoon.

As I reflected on the Romans 12 text each morning during that sermon's preparation, it occurred to me that I am the product of a healthy church, which was the role model for the seven churches I've served over nearly a half-century of pastoral ministry. What's more—and this was the insight which made me realize it was from God—I was present the night that church began to self-destruct. I actually witnessed my home church beginning to die, and even today, the memory of the experience saddens my heart.

Telling these two stories in a sermon could take 15 minutes each, easily. And I did plan to tell them. These two experiences were crucial in the formation of my heart's burden about this message—and that's often something that does not appear through the fog of my brain until a couple of weeks into the preparation. Only with this realization could I settle on the message's focus of helping the congregation treasure, work for, and protect the health of their internal relationships.

I should interject here that this was not the only message I was working on at the time, nor do I usually work on only one sermon at a time. Each morning after working on the Romans 12 sermon, I would move on to other messages, all of them in various stages of preparedness.

Finally, on the Thursday before the Sunday I preached the sermon, the Lord showed me the outline for the sermon. (I am not saying loosely or casually that "the Lord showed me." I believe He is in charge of every detail of a sermon, if the preacher will lean on Him sufficiently.) He gave me three points to illustrate the themes from Romans 12: Foundation, Framework, and Finishing. I organized the supporting statements from the passage for each of the points, and only then did I begin to craft the actual text of the sermon.

Now, was the sermon ready to be preached? Not even close. If I had stood at that moment and preached the sermon as it existed in my head and heart, it would have easily taken two hours. I was a long way from preaching it.

At this point in the process, I typically take some walks or a drive—solitude in the car is a great time to go over a sermon—and preach through the message several times. Each time, I get a better feel for what needs to be included, emphasized, or omitted in the sermon. I also comb the books in my study looking for supporting insights, in this case on church health. Some were helpful, but most were not. This research does not comprise a great deal of time; it is frequently done in spare moments when I am taking a break from something else. This last portion of the preparation—practicing and refining the message—is just as Holy-Spirit-dependent as any other part. "Unless the Lord build the house"—and that's what I was trying to do in this message with the Foundation, Framework, and Finishing—"its builders labor in vain" (Psalm 127:1).

Suffice to say, preaching is hard work and not for sissies. It's definitely not for the faint of heart or couch potatoes. Now you see why we keep encouraging churches to pray for their pastor!

4 Essentials to a Great Sermon

Artie Davis

I'm a firm believer in learning from others and not re-inventing the wheel unless there is no wheel! I want to share some tools and strategies I have gleaned from others and by trial and error.

1. Team

A great tool in preparing a great message is having others to bounce ideas around with. At Cornerstone, we have a teaching team, and we meet on Monday mornings. We brainstorm about passages, illustrations, transitions, and translations. It's great fun, and a huge time saver. It really allows the teaching pastor for that week to focus more on prayer and delivery. (Side note: It also is good if for some reason the scheduled speaker has an emergency and can't speak, it is very easy for one of the other team members to step in; they helped to craft the message!) If your church isn't large enough to pull a teaching team from your staff, you can team up with other pastors online or by Skype. If you build it, they will come!

2. Tech

Using good technology is a must if you desire to save time and increase the quality of your messages. There are several good ones out there; some work only or better on certain platforms, i.e., Mac or PC. Whichever you prefer, you really need a good stand-alone program that is NOT Web based. You never know when you will be caught with your wi-fi pants down! I have used Word on a PC and Logos on my Mac, and there are others. They vary widely in price and content, but start with something!

3. Time

Schedule your time when you plan to do your sermon prep. Put it on your calendar like an appointment, and let nothing save Jesus Himself pull you away from that appointed time! There are many distractions, people, and "emergencies" that the enemy will use to pull you away; don't fall for it! At 11 on Sunday morning, you WILL regret it.

4. Prayer

Schedule prayer time! This is the most important time, even more so than prep time! Remember, you are to speak as one speaking the very words of God. In order to speak His Words, you better take the time to listen to His voice! Schedule it, put an alarm on your cell phone, that's what I have to do!

5 Keys to Sticky Preaching

Larry Osborne

Whether your church is 50 or 5,000, your congregation has far more diversity than you might think. Now before you say, "Wait a minute Larry, our congregation is homogeneous, too homogeneous as a matter of fact," let me remind you that diversity isn't only about ethnicity. It's also about age, length of time as a believer, socioeconomic status, special interests, learning styles, and a wide array of cultural subsets.

And as if diversity is not enough, everything keeps changing at the speed of the Internet. If you feel like you're preaching to multiple moving targets each weekend, you probably are! No wonder some of us feel stressed. It's hard to preach sticky messages or tightly Velcro people to a ministry when everything and everyone keeps moving all the time.

For the past 25 years, I've pastored the same church. But it's hardly been the same church. We've grown from an overgrown Bible study, to a small church struggling to break the 200 barrier, to a multi-site megachurch. We hit our stride as a boomer-focused, seeker-friendly ministry only to wake up in a culture bored with boomers and enamored with hip-hop, subwoofers, and missional focus. By my count, we've gone through at least five distinct seasons and iterations of ministry. We've been in the latest one for the past four years or so.

In a hyper-change world, sermons that hit it out of the park just ten years ago—okay, five years ago—no longer cut it. It's not that God's word no longer has power; it's that the cultural language of my congregation and yours keeps changing. And when the target audience keeps moving, it can be hard to hit the mark, much less make anything stick.

So what can we do?

Over the years, I've discovered some things that have helped me (and my church) navigate the mounting complexity and ever-increasing rate of change in our culture. They've enabled me to grow and change as a preacher—and they've allowed our church to become larger, more diverse, and demographically younger without losing the boomers and builders who got us started.

From a distance, many people think the key has been our pioneering work in offering multiple venues and styles of worship. No doubt, that's helped. But just as important (perhaps more so) are a series of things we've consistently done from the pulpit to help make sure our messages remain applicable to an ever-widening and fast-changing demographic. Here are a few of the most important ones we try to bring into the planning and delivery of every sermon.

1. Set Aside the Commentaries.

Don't worry. I'm not suggesting that we set aside the hard work of study, faithfulness to the text, and theological precision. I am suggesting that commentaries and the podcasts of our favorite preachers are not the best place to *start*.

The one thing that plays well in every age group and cultural subset is *authenticity*. It's a key to unlocking the hearts of the widest audience possible. The more diverse our communities become, the more important this trait will be. It's the one thing no one can argue with. It's hard to write off.

Yet, the only way to preach authentically is to start with what God told *you*, not what God told someone else at some other time. That means the starting point in sermon prep needs to be: "What does this passage say to me...today?"

At North Coast, we have a preaching team, a real preaching *team*. No one in our congregation knows who they are going to hear on any given weekend. Whether it's me or our other teaching pastor, Chris Brown, we both start our study of the text by asking, *What does it say to me today, and how does it fit with what I'm observing in the life of others and our congregation?*

Only *after* we've finished with that process do we begin to check out what others have said and done with the passage. We check commentaries to see if we're on-target or off-base theologically. We might listen or read the sermons of others to pick up some helpful insights and applications. But it's always second, never first.

Here's the reason why: If we start with our favorite commentary or teacher, it's hard not to be overly swayed by their observations, insights, and illustrations. Everything is seen through their lens. It's hard to remain authentically and personally engaged with the text or a topic.

You can see this principle at work in any small group discussion. No matter what the question, the first person who speaks usually frames the answers for the entire group. Even if my initial response was to take the question in an entirely different direction, I'll almost always segue into the flow of their initial answer.

Preparing my messages in this order not only raises their authenticity quotient; it also helps me keep up with the fast-paced changes in our culture. Commentaries, my favorite preachers, and even my old notes can quickly lock me in the past. Frankly, the burning questions of 10–15 years ago are often not very relevant today. This also goes for the burning theological debates and the cultural hot buttons of yesteryear. And I'm not the same person either; so all things considered, the same passage can garner radically different insights if I give it the opportunity.

As an aside, this also helps with longevity. If I were to preach the same applications to the same text every time, after 28 years, I'd have some rather bored parishioners. It's hard to be sticky when you're boring.

That doesn't mean there isn't great value in commentaries, my favorite preachers, or even my old preaching notes. But the value is in balancing, correcting, and nuancing what God is teaching me today, not regurgitating what he taught me in the past.

2. Think Buffet, Not Banquet.

I was taught that every sermon should be tied together by a golden thread. It should have one primary point, and everything should help drive that point home. A great sermon is memorable when people can easily recall all the main points. Done right, it is akin to a spiritually themed banquet, a feast to be savored and easily recalled.

This strategy may have worked in a one-size-fits-all culture. But today, it will limit the breadth of your ministry. Here's why.

A tightly knit, single-point sermon plays well on the speaking circuit. It wins awards from homileticians. But by its very nature, it best fits a narrowly focused group of people. It's like a great Thanksgiving dinner: well themed and delicious to Americans who like turkey and dressing. But it's rather unappetizing to a Vietnamese immigrant—or a Seattle vegan.

In the same way, the more diverse our communities and churches become (again, not just ethnically, but socially, generationally, and in special interests), the more a narrowly focused banquet risks missing large segments of your congregation altogether.

Because of this, I switched years ago to a buffet model. Unlike a banquet, a buffet offers lots of entrées. In most cases, none of the entrées are as elegantly prepared or presented as they would be for a grand banquet. But unlike the banquet, the goal is not to create a great meal and a lifetime memory. Instead, the goal of a buffet is simply to offer a good meal with lots of options. It does its best to have something for everyone, in contrast to the banquet that offers one thing for those who like it—and nothing for everyone else.

As a pastor with a diverse flock to feed each week, I try to prepare a buffet of wisdom and insight from God's word, knowing that not everyone will eat or need the same thing. I intentionally ask myself, *What's in here for the long-time Christians who have heard it all? What's in here for the window-shopper who doesn't know Job from job?*

I no longer worry if every transition is picture-perfect. I no longer approach preaching as if it's an art form. It's a meal. And it has to feed a diverse group of picky eaters who don't always want what's good for them. So I spend most of my time finding ways to get as many nutritional dishes on the table as possible. The more I can offer a wide variety of insights and Scriptures, the greater the likelihood that they will find something they want and need.

3. Never Underestimate the Power of the Sound Bite.

Sound bites are important, not for memory but for clarity. That's because the more diverse our audience is, the greater the likelihood for a large gap between what we mean to say and what they hear.

Good sound bites transcend different demographic distinctions. They increase the odds that what I say will be understood and remembered accurately.

While proper exegesis, faithfulness to the text, solid Biblical concepts, and transitions are all crucial, without a sound bite, most of what we say will be lost. There's just too much information flying at people today. The battle for mental shelf-space is intense. By Sunday afternoon, even the "ah-has" can be lost.

So I work *really hard* at boiling my main points and principles down to a few sound bites. These sound bites capture the essence of what I'm teaching in a memorable way that people can take home. They help make the message stickier to more people.

Good sound bites are *principle-driven*. As such, they are much more likely to transcend age, spiritual background, and educational differences than simple prose or even a narrative.

Here are some examples:

- Instead of simply saying, "During times of discouragement, don't assume you are outside of God's will," the sound bite might be: *A valley doesn't mean a wrong turn.*
- When stressing the need to flee sexual temptation rather than trying to stand up to it, I might sum up the principle this way: *We can't resist what we're supposed to flee.*
- Rather than merely warning people to guard themselves against the little compromises that can eventually lead to a larger spiritual failure, the sound bite might be: *Spiritual failure is seldom an explosion; it's usually an erosion.*

4. Like Your Congregations.

Yes, I mean *like*, not love—and *congregations*, not congregation. Sometimes, we can love people in the Lord but not like them in the flesh. And all of us have more "congregations" than we realize.

I've found that it's critical for me to cultivate a genuine appreciation of the various mindsets and subcultures in our church. That's not always easy to do. It's one thing to preach about the body of Christ; it's another to genuinely embrace the differences and idiosyncrasies of the real people who populate all the tribes within our church.

Relating well to a wide cross-section doesn't mean I have to BE LIKE them. But I do have to LIKE them. Truth is there will be times when people move to a place we don't understand or like. It might be the younger generation's body art, piercings, and music, or the older generation's struggle with change and new wineskins. It doesn't matter. When people know we don't like them, they can smell it. And they stop listening.

Both Chris and I have our natural comfort zones. But we each work hard to get into the world of those we understand least and would most naturally avoid. I find that as I begin to understand any group of people, I almost always begin to like that group of people. And once I like them, it's easy to communicate and reach them.

It's when I fear, ridicule, or write-off a group of people within the body that I lose my ability to bring God's word to them. Then, instead of being sticky, my messages and our church become more like Teflon than Velcro.

One way that I know I've broadened my ability to understand and appreciate the diversity within our congregation is when I can hear their "yeah buts" in my head as I prepare a sermon. Every sermon and every point rises a "yeah but" with somebody somewhere. The more I'm aware of those "yeah buts" and address them, the more likely it is that my sermon will hit the mark with more than only those who are "just like me."

This has become such an important part of our message preparation process that every Tuesday, Chris and I meet with a group of other staff members for what we call a sermon prep meeting. In reality, it's a "yeah but" meeting.

In it, we go over the basic points of the message (at least as far as it has come together at that point, which sometimes isn't much). We find out what resonates and what doesn't. In particular, we decide what points, verses, or statements might raise potential questions for those who are new Christians, not-yet Christians, biblically illiterate or well taught, young or old. It's a powerful exercise that helps make our messages stickier with a broader audience. It also helps us address the "yeah buts" in our sermons rather than in the foyer.

5. Create a Common Anchor.

Finally, the most powerful tool for pulling a diverse and moving target together is to tether everyone to a common anchor. Spiritually, that's Jesus Christ; but organizationally, it's needed as well. Without it, ministries and programs tend to become silos. And over time, diversity becomes disunity. Our organizational anchor is something we call Sermon-Based Small Groups. We launched them when we were less than 200 in attendance because we could already see that our individual programs and ministries were pulling people in different directions.

For over 25 years now, we've maintained an average of 80 percent of our adult weekend attendance in one of these groups. They are simple and organic, basically a lecture/lab approach to the weekend message. But they make the message and our church sticky. They keep the ever-widening diversity of our congregation from splintering into a cluster of factions, each with its own view of what our church should be and do. Whether a small group is made up of tattooed and pierced twenty-somethings or blue-haired senior citizens, the experience of discussing the sermon and trying to apply it is remarkably similar, and it bonds our congregation together at a cellular level.

These five principles have helped make North Coast a much stickier place. I encourage you to consider filtering some of your next sermons through these lenses. They aren't a magical fix-all formula, but they have been powerful tools in my own preaching and ministry. By adhering to them, my messages have been able to stay fresh and sticky, despite the fact that I'm often preaching to a target that not only seems to be moving, but moving in every direction all at once.

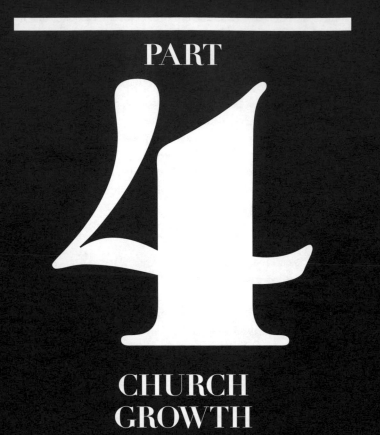

PART

4

CHURCH
GROWTH

As believers, as followers of Jesus, if we're not chasing after something that is so much bigger than we are, and there's no way we could ever accomplish it without God, then we are playing it too safe.

—Brad Lomenick

7 Secrets of Healthy Churches

Thom Rainer

In an issue of *Outreach*, I wrote about the seven sins of dying churches. The response to the article was significant, but one response was recurring: "Thom, now that we've heard about the characteristics of dying churches, can you tell us about the characteristics of healthy churches?" I went back to my research of over 2,000 healthy churches in America to find unifying features, and I am excited to share them with you.

Let me offer a few disclaimers. First, I'm not going to bore you with all the data we have. Second, my list of principles is by no means exhaustive. I am sure you'll wonder why some were not included. My research team and I did the best we could to determine seven of the major principles that healthy churches follow, but some were likely omitted. Finally, these "secrets" are not really secrets. It just sounded good in the title.

Secret 1: The church's leadership and the laity hold to a high view of Scripture.

While holding to a conservative and evangelical perspective of the Bible does not guarantee health in a church, we don't find health in congregations where Scripture is not held as authoritative. This so-called secret has been revealed by many researchers beyond our own work.

Secret 2: The churches and their leaders seek to be relevant.

It's a dangerous word in today's churches. "Relevant" carries with it a multitude of meanings, and the meaning is positive or negative depending on one's perspective and philosophy of ministry. I should clarify at this point that relevancy does not and cannot mean biblical compromise.

Many church leaders long for the day when church members will be first concerned about biblical fidelity and reaching a growing unchurched world with the Gospel. Sadly, too many members are more concerned about their own comforts than making the necessary sacrifices to be relevant and reach out to those who are not followers of Christ. Most of the church conflicts I have witnessed or heard reported dealt with peripheral issues: the style of music, the length of the sermons, the physical facilities.

Secret 3: The churches and their leaders hold to the primacy of preaching.

In some churches, preaching has lost its power and emphasis. It is perceived to be an irrelevant ministry and style of communication. Or it may be a central part of the worship service, but the time and study involved in sermon preparation is lacking. There is preaching, but it has little power.

Among the churches we studied, preaching was primary for those with healthy conversion growth and meaningful discipleship ministries. Pastors who preached each week spent five times as much time in sermon preparation as those who preached in unhealthy churches. There is a powerful correlation between sermon study time and health of the church.

Of course, if the preachers are to spend significant time in the preparation of sermons, the church members must give them the time to do so. There cannot be an expectation that they attend every meeting, meet every pastoral care need, visit everyone, and provide hours of counseling. The members must give the preacher time to focus on prayer and the ministry of the Word (Acts 6:4). In other words, the laity must be unleashed to do much of the ministry of the church.

Secret 4: The churches have a healthy small group structure.

For some churches, the primary small group was Sunday school; for others, it was home groups or small groups that met in diverse locations. The churches that emphasized moving as many members as possible into a small group assimilated those members five times better than those who attended only worship services.

Another sign of a healthy small group structure was the involved leadership of pastors and senior pastors. They see the critical importance of members and guests connecting in a smaller setting.

Secret 5: Healthy churches emphasize corporate prayer and church prayer ministries.

They do more than give lip service to the importance of prayer. My team and I once worked with a church of 250 that had someone praying in an intercessory prayer room every hour of every day. That means 168 members committed to pray in that room one hour every week. Since the leadership of the church began emphasizing prayer three years ago, attendance has more than doubled.

Another common element in healthy churches' prayer ministries is that members pray for non-Christians by name. They are unashamed and unafraid to be vocal about the greatest need any person could have: salvation through Jesus Christ.

Secret 6: Churches that are healthy take membership seriously.

There seems to be two major trends away from responsible membership. The first and most common trend is to have inflated membership rolls that have little integrity. Church membership means little or nothing and has no level of accountability. The second trend is found in churches where the leaders do not believe that membership is an issue. A casual attendee has the same level of accountability as a long-term leader. These churches think the concept of membership is antiquated, if not unbiblical.

Secret 7: The healthy churches are highly intentional about evangelism.

They have ministries, programs, and emphases that lead members to reach out with the Gospel to their unchurched friends, relatives, co-workers, and acquaintances. As a doctrinal note, the leaders in these churches believe in a literal hell. Their evangelism is thus motivated not only by the good news of the Gospel, but the bad news of rejecting the Gospel.

Has your church had a health exam lately? How would it fare in your honest assessment of the seven secrets you just read? As a whole, the American Church is not healthy. May God provide your church with all she needs to be effective and healthy for God's glory. And may you hear these words of encouragement: "Everything looks good."

This article originally appeared in the Jul/Aug and Sep/Oct 2006 issues of Outreach *magazine. Visit Outreachmagazine.com to learn more.*

It's Probably Not the Worship Style

Kevin DeYoung

I was at a denominational meeting not too long ago, sitting at a table
with a half-dozen other pastors and elders. At one spot in the agenda, we
were supposed to take 10 minutes to talk about vision and direction of the
denomination. This led to a conversation about our churches and why so
many RCA congregations keep losing members. An older man at my table
lamented that his church continues to shrink. What used to be a rather large
church has declined to a shadow of its former glory. He quickly offered an
explanation, "People just don't like traditional worship anymore. We have the
hymns and the liturgy and the organ. The growing churches have guitars and
drums. Our style just doesn't work anymore."

I wasn't sure quite how to respond. There can be a hundred reasons for a
church's decline—some of them the fault of the church, some of them not.
But I knew a little bit about the church this man was from. It's a church with
classic worship and liberal theology. They have hosted pro-gay events before
(to cite one example). Knowing this, I asked the man if he thought the gospel
was faithfully preached each Sunday. Of course, he said he was certain it was.
I suggested that the reasons for their decline were probably more complex
than simply their worship style. I didn't get far in the conversation except
to add that there are plenty of examples of thriving churches with classic
worship, and we shouldn't assume our church problems can be fixed by a
simple change of instrumentation.

I don't share that story to suggest that liberal churches always shrink and
robust gospel-centered churches always grow. But I do wish church leaders
would stop assuming that their problems boil down to a certain worship style
and can be fixed with another. I run into church leaders fairly often who
struggle to make sense of their declining numbers. I feel for these brothers
(and sometimes, they are sisters in my circles). I don't know all the reasons
for church growth or church decline. Growth does not equal faithfulness
any more than decline equals failure. Sometimes situations, histories, and

circumstances are outside our control. Regenerating human hearts always is. So we should be slow to judge another church's fruitfulness.

And yet, we can ask better questions. I'm not against changing worship styles. There may be good reasons to do so in some circumstances. But I doubt very much that's usually the real problem. Instead of assuming that young people will flock to our churches if we drop the organ and plug in the guitar (and we have both at our church), declining denominations and shrinking churches should ask deeper, harder questions:

- Is the gospel faithfully preached?
- Is the Bible taught with clarity and passion?
- Are the sermons manifestly rooted in a text of Scripture?
- Do the elders/pastors and deacons meet the qualifications for church office laid out in the New Testament?
- Are the sacraments faithfully administered and protected?
- Is church discipline practiced?
- Do the elders exercise personal care over the flock?
- Are there good relationships among the staff and other leaders?
- Is the worship service put together thoughtfully and carried out with undistracting excellence (as much as possible)?
- Do the people in the congregation sing the songs with gusto, or are they going through the motions?
- Is a high bar set for church membership?
- Are the people of the church engaged in personal ministry?
- Is the congregation marked by increasing prayer and evangelism?
- Do the pastors believe in the complete trustworthiness of all of Scripture?
- Do they take adequate time for study and preparation?
- Do they truly believe and eagerly rejoice in their church's/denomination's statement of faith, creeds, and confessions?
- Are their lives examples of personal holiness?

There are scores of other questions you could ask. These are only a sample. It may be after facing these questions that a church decides to change a few programs or alter a few songs. But until a congregation asks these tough questions, the quick fixes will not fix much of anything. Don't assume the style is the thing. Check your substance first.

3 Kinds of Church Complexity and What to Do About It

Will Mancini

Unnecessary complexity lives to some degree in every church. Effective leaders know how to identify it and deal with it because complexity always drains energy, attention, and other resources from the mission of Jesus. Be aware of these three kinds of complexity:

1. Decision-Making Complexity

The first kind of complexity is the classic "How many people does it take to change a light bulb?" Every decision in your church has a "people count." The people count is how many folks are given permission to speak into a decision. And every decision in your church has a "decision weight." The decision weight is a measure of the decision's importance. Is the decision a small, medium, or large decision? Are we buying copy paper, selecting the color of the carpet, or purchasing property? Using these two variables, you can discern the complexity of decision-making.

How many people are involved at what level of decision-making? The higher your "people-count-to-decision-weight" ratio, the more dramatic the complexity you let in.

2. Doctrinal Complexity

Every ministry has a theological conviction. The question is what defines the core? Do you have a simple "pail of orthodoxy," or do you wheel around a heavy metal toolbox with dozens of "critical issue" compartments? Remember, when Pharisees tried to stump Jesus, they steered Him into the complexity of 613 laws of the Torah (as traditionally numbered). They literally tried to set verbal traps for Him by asking Him which commandment is the greatest. But He evaded their sting with stunning clarity—the entire Law and Prophets hang on two love commands (Matt 22:37–40).

3. Programmatic Complexity

Although many churches are waking up to the problem of the program paradigm, this kind of complexity inhibits the mission and vision of our best churches. Churches in North America are over-programmed and under-discipled. We raise up program managers instead of disciple makers. We think that more programs attract more people, when in fact, fewer, more meaningful initiatives engage people. Engaged people, then, attract people, inviting others to know Christ and to follow Him together. One simple diagnostic question is, "If I stood in your primary ministry environment (usually worship), how many 'doors' of possible next steps or programmatic ministry options would be presented before me?" If you have three or more doors, you probably have too many. It's not uncommon for churches to have 8–13 "doors."

What should the leader do about complexity?

The answer is found in the axiom "do more by doing less." If you don't see complexity as the addition of the unnecessary, then you will never receive the "less is more" principle in your leadership heart. There are three logical ways to do less: reduction, combination, and elimination.

Reduction. Many times, the first step is looking for ways to do less of some dynamic that created complexity. For example, you reduce the number of people involved in a decision, or you might reduce the word count in your statement of beliefs as a church. Even in an over-programmed environment, you can simplify without eliminating a program just by reducing the number of programs advertised in the Sunday worship guide.

Combination. Combining things is an often-overlooked strategy for battling complexity. Sometimes two teams, two belief statements, two programs, or two initiatives are not so different. Two can and should become one. With a little more work and conversation, the synergy of a good combination will be well worth it. One church took a separate Wednesday night men's ministry event and combined it with the primary strategy of Adult Bible Fellowships. At Auxano, we wanted to launch both a coaching network (called co::Labs) and a Church Unique Certification process at the same time. After developing them separately, we decided to scrap the certification model and use the co::Labs as the primary step of certification.

Elimination. The most obvious step to remove complexity is to just flat out cut stuff. Gardeners know to prune the branches for maximum health and growth. My mentor, Howard Hendricks, used to say, "The secret to concentration is elimination." Jim Collins recommends a "stop doing list." Right now, you could probably be more effective by eliminating 20 percent of what you are doing as a church. What would that 20 percent look like for you? Don't be afraid to stop doing things, but make sure you have the right conversations and look for ways to reduce and combine first.

Top 5 Ways to Burn Out Your Staff

Brian Kaufman

While working at a church, have you ever thought to yourself, "This wouldn't fly in the corporate world"? Oftentimes, churches have their own set of rules when it comes to organization, processes, administration, etc. Seminaries do a great job of corn feeding the best theology and education to pastors and church leaders, but they tend to skip the part about the business of running a church. Combine that with the ADD + OCD + Type A pastors that typically go along with a quickly-growing megachurch setting, and you've got yourself the perfect storm for staff burnout. So let's explore together the top five ways to burn out church staff—guaranteed!

5. Espouse "Family First" but Expect "Church First"

How many times have you heard, "We really encourage you to make your family first…" followed by, "Hey, I realize this is last minute (or maybe they don't), and you've got to get home, but can you…?" There is unnecessary pressure applied to staff because, in my opinion, church leaders continuously fail to plan, create unrealistic expectations, and ultimately are poor at time management. At the end of the day, a "family-first" church feels more like a "family-later" when the staff suddenly has new tasks, the pressure of a deadline, and a fear in the back of their minds that they either get this done or they lose their jobs.

Or perhaps they don't fear losing their jobs, but the leader requesting the task has grossly overestimated the critical nature of the task to the point where the staff member feels that if they don't get it done then people won't know Jesus…and that's on them. Try choosing to go home an hour early to play Legos with little Susie and Johnny with that kind of stress.

4. Job Creep, Pay Fixed

Have you ever heard of "scope creep"? It's when you agree to a set of expectations only to have those expectations slowly grow outside the original scope. Eventually, you look back and wonder where the project you signed up for went. Because of the unique nature of a church, staff often wear several "hats" to the point of being comical. Try asking someone that has worked for the church for more than a year what they do, and you'll usually get a little chuckle followed by a list of roles that would never fit neatly on a business card.

There is nothing really wrong with wearing several "hats." Giving/tithing at churches is so pathetic that church leadership must constantly walk a tightrope between payroll and the responsibility that comes with managing a growing church. As a result, staff feel the pressure of getting things done that are well outside the scope of what they signed up for.

Here are the steps to burnout in the above scenario:
- Hours/responsibilities increase
- Staff become mediocre at their jobs because they can't do any one thing really well
- Sense of value decreases
- Stress level increases
- Spouse/children start noticing
- Pay stays the same
- Appreciation decreases (because everyone else is stressed and too busy)
- Hours/responsibilities increase again
- Burnout

3. Poorly Cast Vision

This one is simple. Choose any or all of these:
- Don't remind staff why they are there
- Completely avoid talking about where the church is headed
- Never discuss the reason your staff is a critical part of moving forward
- Offer no reasons for why you do things or make decisions. In fact don't filter any decision through any vision—that way your staff are kept guessing

- BONUS: Start to openly compare your church to the bigger, shinier, rock star church down the street

That should do it.

2. Don't Empower Your Staff

There is nothing more rewarding for a staff member than to feel unable to make decisions. Whoops! Of course, that's not right. If the staff is engaged in the church's vision, it is likely that they are there (giving up a higher salary) to continue moving forward in that vision. They were hired because, ideally, they add tremendous value. They stay because they feel empowered to use their abilities and passions to continue to add value. They feel that they matter.

If you want staff to burn out, simply give them expectations to get things done with no empowerment to get them done. And for giggles, add some red tape (more typical in older churches) they have to get through. Then start questioning and/or overriding every decision they make, and they'll soon be on their way out the door—head hanging, knots in the stomach and neck, and completely frustrated.

1. Lead Pastor: Micromanage

Boom! Yeah, I said it. Here's the thing—large, fast-growing churches typically have a lead pastor personality-type that compliments that pace of growth—Type A, OCD. This isn't necessarily a negative until the lead pastor is up in everybody's business about every detail.

You've got to give the lead pastor grace. Here's the deal; the church wasn't always big. You've probably got a story where the church started with 10 couples in a living room, clubhouse, or gymnasium—that's the nature of church growth. The lead pastor, like a small business owner, was the CEO AND the guy that cleaned the toilets. He did everything, managed every detail, and made sure things got done. If a ball was dropped, it was his fault. Fast forward to today—he feels the same pressures and responsibilities. But now, everything is bigger; there are more people involved and much more to do. It's in your lead pastor's nature to want to control and hold onto everything. Back in the day, this is partly how the church moved forward.

So what was once necessary to move forward is now completely annoying, frustrating, and sometimes hurtful. To a staff member, micromanagement equates to distrust. Staff think, "Why did he hire me if he questions everything I do?" For men, this is emasculating, and for women, it creates insecurities, frustrations, and resentment. He/she feels less valued, less empowered, and even begins to question her core identity.

Conclusion

Pastors and leaders: let go and breathe. Your church will continue to grow; your people will continue to grow. Newcomers will get connected if they really want to (they aren't cattle, but that's another article). Your staff are capable... trust them. Continue to cast vision, continue to teach, continue to connect with your church—that's what you love to do anyway.

If you must, hire an executive pastor to bridge the gap and run the day-to-day. If you've already got an exec, ask yourself if you are burning them out—take them out to lunch, get a feel for where they are at, and then (if necessary) ask for forgiveness. And while you're at it, do the same with your staff. Help them recharge their batteries, create a healthy, dynamic, creative, empowering work environment, and watch your staff take on new tasks with excitement!

6 Tips for Church Revitalization

Tom Cheyney

Incredible changes have taken place in the past hundred years. We are experiencing more change than ever in history. The rate of change is so great that we barely catch our breath before another blast of change slams into us. The starting point for unfreezing a stuck church is the development of a solid community of faith that includes spiritual leaders, the absence of major conflict, trust in one another, and a desire to connect with the unchurched world.

Everything we are acquainted with is changing. If you are sensing you might be facing a little stuckness in your church, perhaps some of the following ideas might help you.

1. Realize you are trapped in a habitual routine.

Become aware of what you have tried in the past that has not worked. Become willing to let go of what has not worked while honoring previous attempts. Often as a church planter and then a revitalization restart leader, I would take three steps forward and two steps back at times. But I was still gaining one forward step even in those times where we were breaking with routine.

2. Become more open to other points of view.

Focus on the solution, not the problem. Iron sharpens iron so allow others to assist you with big ideas that might help the revitalizing church to continue to advance. Remember that even your lay leaders have a vital stake in the renewing church's continual growth. Often, they are closer to a possible solution due to less of the responsibility for leadership being on their platter. While you are up to your ears leading, they often can step back and think about those things that might bring further growth to the church in need of revitalization.

3. Examine your daily thinking and how it has or has not served you.

Realize there is a choice of which path or action to take. Sometimes, revitalization leaders just need to readjust their strategy a little as they move forward from the various phases of growth in the renewal effort. I personally often reflect on why the Lord would not allow me to do the same thing in one church that I had just done in another. God is about the new, and often, the old has passed by, and He desires to create something so new in you and your church that you need to let go of the old thinking that has not worked or is no longer working.

4. Assess your next steps for change.

Ask the question: Am I doing these things out of preference, practice, pattern, or panic? Many a church planter and pastor have said to me, "I do what I do!" and then wonder why it is getting harder to see growth and advancement. That is a preference! Others just keep on trying an idea and keep driving it, hoping that practice will eventually make it perfect. It often does not! Still I see all over the country revitalization pastors who get locked into a predetermined pattern and just cannot see a way out to do something else. Finally, renewal leaders can get so fearful of the lack of growth or advancement that they just panic and try to settle into a comfortable maintenance mentality. Assessing your next steps will greatly help you and your work of church renewal. As you are doing so, be sure to check your ideas out with others.

5. Understand that if you make a blunder, it is all part of the journey.

See what your part of any blunder is and apologize where and when necessary. Good church revitalization leaders are not free from mistakes so don't try to be perfect. When you do make a blunder as the solitary leader, acknowledge it, learn from it, and seek to discover the life lesson in it. Many times in my ministry, I have done a dumb thing that was not well thought out (I could lead a conference on the dumb things church renewal leaders do and never use anybody else's ideas)! What I have learned from it, though, is if you are transparent enough as a revitalization leader to admit your mistakes and your people sense it is a heartfelt confession, they will indeed forgive you and even respect you much more because many pastors and planters just cannot admit when they make a mistake! If you take risks as a church-renewal pastor during times of needed change, sometimes things will not work out the way you had envisioned they would, and a strong renewal leader acknowledges it and then moves on. Blunders are sometimes part of the journey so don't beat yourself up over them. Also, don't expel these blunders as not important to the fellowship so make the apology and reconnect with your membership before it is too late! If you wait too long to do this, by the time you realize you need to do this, it will be too late, and your apology will ring hollow, and your leadership as a church revitalization leader will come into question.

6. Appraise your revitalization plans by whether they fit your beliefs and core values.

Then act accordingly. What are core values? They often are unwritten statements that guide who we are and what we do. They inspire our words and actions. Gerald Colbert reminds us, "They are convictions about how a church operates, not doctrinal statements about what it believes. They are the foundation for developing relationships, church systems, ministries, and strategies. They are the four to seven key statements that distinguish a church." Remember what core values do? They clarify expectations. They clarify roles and relationships. Core values offer a compass for strategic planning. They help in sharpening your church's mission statement. Take a minute and consider: are your beliefs and core values reflective of the beliefs and values of Jesus? Ask yourself: How do these beliefs and values reflect God's Word?

Revitalization transformation is difficult—if it weren't, you would already be doing it. That is why we need support and guidance along the way as we prayerfully seek to revitalize the local church.

Momentum Builders for Ministry

Alan Danielson

It's not only important to understand what stops momentum but also to know what builds momentum. Here are a few of my thoughts.

1. God's Guidance

Although this is obvious to most of us as church leaders, it astounds me how often we miss it. I'll never forget planting a church in Santa Fe, New Mexico. I had a New Testament and a copy of the *Purpose Driven Church* as my two favorite tools. Sadly, the *PDC* often won out over the NT. I had a tendency to read about Saddleback's success and then copy what they did. Ironically, Rick Warren clearly says in the book NOT to do that! What I didn't understand back then was context. Every church has a unique context and calling. The first and best thing every ministry should do is not look to successful programs and strategies elsewhere, but seek God's will. I love how simply Perry Noble puts it: "Listen to God and do what He says." Nothing will build momentum greater than that!

2. Systems

Systems determine outcomes. If you want staff to turn in reports by a specific time, create a system that makes it happen (i.e. automatically generated e-mail reminders). If you want your volunteer sound technicians to deliver consistent results, create a system that makes it happen (i.e. training and a checklist they complete before each service). To me, systems are evidence of "smart work." Most volunteers and staff work hard, but only the best work smart. They create systems that require tons of effort to create, but they yield residual results. Hard work doesn't always yield residual results, but smart work does it every time. Spend time with your team determining how you can work hard for a season to create systems that will get results long after.

3. The Right People

Sadly, some people depend too much on systems. They create a system and then get lazy. These are definitely not the right people. Finding the right people for your team is a difficult challenge, but it is of primary importance. Hiring mistakes and high staff/volunteer turnover kill momentum. Doing the diligent work necessary to find, recruit, and hire the right people MUST be done.

Your networking skills and gut-checks are not enough; you must have a system in place to help you find the right people. My own approach to hiring is two-fold: 1) Test for aptitude and ability, 2) Interview for character and culture. Use a series of tests (Myers-Briggs Type Indicator, CDAT, APT, Triple-Threat Leadership, and Strengths Finder are some good examples) that objectively determine whether or not a candidate has the skills, temperament, attitude, and raw ability for the job. These tests cost money, but it's better to spend $100 or less to determine that someone is not the right person for the job than to spend thousands hiring and firing the wrong person.

If the testing indicates that the person shows promise, move on to the interview. There you should focus your interview questions around determining whether or not the candidate has the personal character necessary and whether or not the candidate fits your organization's culture. While it may not be feasible to use a process this thorough for recruiting volunteers, it's a good idea to incorporate some of these steps for high-profile and high-capacity volunteer roles.

4. Clear Communication

Communication is non-negotiable. People won't move with you (thus halting momentum) if they don't understand where they are moving. Everything necessary should be communicated multiple times and in multiple ways. Different people hear things differently, so variety in communication is a good thing. The repetition that comes from this variety is good, too. The old marketing adage states, "People don't get the message until they've seen or heard it seven times." Remember, you've been chewing on your next big idea for weeks, months, or years. You aren't going to get your entire church to embrace the idea if they've had all of three days to consider it. Set a date for any change that needs to be implemented then communicate, communicate, communicate. That way, the change won't be as difficult or painful when the date arrives. Trying to make changes without communication halts momentum.

5. Consistency

Nothing keeps momentum going like consistency. Delivering consistent quality results and making consistent quality decisions will accelerate momentum every time. Consider two athletic teams with the same record of six to one. The first team lost their first game but has gone on to win their last five games. They are now the league's favorites to win the championship. The second team started out strong, winning their first four games. Then they lost a big one. They won their most recent game, but just barely. Most people believe they are a solid team, but it's doubtful they'll win the championship. The difference is consistency.

No team can win all the time, but great teams win consistently. Many churches aim at having an amazing Easter and Christmas. Those two weekends every year are absolutely stunning! The rest of the weeks are just "good" though. Those churches don't experience much growth. Then there are churches that treat every weekend like Easter and Christmas. They strive for consistently excellent results...every...single...week! Those churches seem to explode. The moral of this story: Aim your team at consistency, and you'll enjoy momentum. Aim at the occasional win, and you'll struggle to grow.

7 Characteristics of Prevailing Churches

Shannon O'Dell

Prevailing churches are on the rise, and God is growing His Kingdom all over the world. In my limited travel, I have seen these qualities apparent in each local church. Note this: The qualities are there, but the approach, style, and way of executing these attributes are extremely unique.

1. Leadership

A growing church ALWAYS has a great, called leader. Leadership that is directed through a sensitivity to the Holy Spirit. This leadership is developing leaders, and their staff is developing leaders. I believe many churches will never experience God-growth because the leader is not called…food for thought (1 Timothy 3).

2. Evangelistic

The Gospel is shared, taught, and illustrated through the life of its leadership. I am even watching a comeback of "come forward" invitations and series built on evangelism. Not "walk an aisle and pray a prayer," but true repentance and lordship.

3. Exciting Children's Ministry

Focusing on the next generation is a church preparing its future.

4. Concerned About the Poor

God is shouting to His Church, "Meet the needs of the poor, oppressed, needy, orphans and widows." Prevailing churches are listening and acting.

CHURCHLEADERS.COM

5. Generous

Giving is priority.

6. Great Worship Experiences

Music, preaching, lobbies, volunteers, kids' areas, offerings, and even the announcements are prepared, creative, and excellent.

7. Doing More with Less

Churches that are growing are cutting the fat and producing even greater results. Budgeting is fluid and lean. This is creating more preparation and utilizing the gifts within the church more than counting on money and a couple of staff members to accomplish tasks.

PART

4

CHURCH
GROWTH

Why Church Hurts

Matt Appling

Have you noticed all the Christians apologizing for the church?

It's kind of the thing to do these days. It just seems better to assume *everyone* out there has been hurt, wronged, isolated, burned, or ostracized by the church. It's almost the battle cry of my generation. *"We've been emotionally wounded by the church!"*

When Donald Miller wrote *Blue Like Jazz,* making public apologies on behalf of all Christianity seemed novel and refreshing to many readers, and many of us have run with that idea in the years since. Some Christians just can't resist telling everyone what jerks we've all been. Don't get me wrong, there are some things to apologize for. (And I'm not talking about cases of serious *abuse.)*

When you stack up all the apologies, it might make a passer-by think that maybe the church is just an agent for *pure evil.* I'm not here to apologize or take back apologies that have been made. If anyone should feel hurt by the church, it's me. I'm here to ask why does it happen? Why does the relationship people are supposed to have with the church break down?

A Low-Maintenance Friend

Think about the *least* important relationship in your life, the person you have the *lowest* maintenance friendship with. The person you talk to once every few months or even years. Most people probably have at least one of those friends. I've had several. One even told me he valued how low-maintenance we were. It was weird. It was also probably the last time we talked. No hard feelings.

If that person were not in your life, would it make that much of a difference? Probably not. You already have the lowest possible investment in that person. If they decided not to talk to you or call you in six months, it wouldn't hurt you that badly. I dare say, it's probably nearly *impossible* to be hurt by that person.

There are some people who have that relationship with their church. It's very low-maintenance. There's no emotional investment, no risk. They sit on the fringes. If you don't want to *ever* be hurt by the church, this is where you want to be.

A High-Maintenance Friend

Now think of the *most* emotionally risky relationship in your life; the one where you've invested the *most*. Probably the most emotionally risky thing anyone can do is have children. Right behind that is getting married. With either of those, you're putting your heart and soul into that relationship.

That's where any good church leaders are with their churches, and that's where people need to be with the church. It needs to be an *emotionally risky* relationship. Any relationship that's worth keeping has some level of emotional risk to it. That's the only way you get anything out of it. Has anyone ever benefited from an emotionally distant marriage or an absent friend? Same with church. People get out of it what you put into it.

Irreconcilable Differences

The unfortunate thing about emotionally risky relationships is the people involved eventually are hurt by the relationship, one way or another. People put their heart and soul into their marriages and children. Thus, their hearts and souls can be crushed by their spouses or kids. Spouses and children can hurt you, disappoint you, burn you. Or you can just *lose* them, one way or another. Any way you look at it, you're going to get hurt, sooner or later.

I have come to believe that the people who are hurt the most by the church are the ones who care most about the church. How can you be hurt by something you don't care about? Why would you be wounded by the thoughts or opinions of someone who you don't value?

The more you become emotionally invested in the church, the more vulnerable you are to disappointment and hurt. It's the people who pour their hearts and souls into the church who can *most* have their hearts and souls completely stomped on by other Christians. Why did I get hurt by my church? Because I cared about it. If I were sitting on the fringes, I wouldn't have cared what happened to it. I would've moved on.

The church relationship breaks down for the same reason any high-maintenance friendship or marriage breaks down. The love or friendship turns out to be *conditional*. Married people love each other, until they have *irreconcilable differences.* Isn't that a trite reason for divorce? It just means those two people had love for the other that was *conditional*.

The relationship breaks down because one person didn't meet the other person's *conditions* for being loved.

Church breaks down because Christians decide their love for others is *conditional.* Or their love for their church is *conditional.* So maybe you're the person who didn't meet Christians' conditions for love. Maybe your church didn't meet *your* conditions for love. It disappointed you, and you walked away. Either way, the result is the same.

In fact, I might say that given enough time, a person who is truly emotionally invested in the church won't be able to *not* be disappointed or hurt by the people inside. Just like any other relationship, it's inevitable.

Maybe making apologies for the church is quickly becoming a cliché. But it will never become obsolete so long as people continue to emotionally invest in it.

10 Reasons Why Small Churches Stay Small

Part 1

Joe McKeever

First, an explanation or two, then a definition.

I know more about getting smaller churches to grow than larger ones. I pastored three of them, and only the first of the three did not grow. I was fresh out of college, untrained, inexperienced, and clueless about what I was doing. The next two grew well, and even though I remained at each only some three years, one almost doubled, and the other nearly tripled in attendance and ministries.

By using the word "grow," I do not mean numbers for numbers' sake. I do not subscribe to the fallacy that bigness is good, and small churches are failures. What I mean by "grow" is reaching people with the gospel of Jesus Christ. If you reach them and start new churches, your local church may not expand numerically, but it is most definitely "growing." If you are located in a town that is losing population and your church manages to stay the same size, you're probably "growing" (i.e., reaching new people for the Lord).

These are simply my observations as to why stagnant, ungrowing churches tend to stay that way. I send it forth hoping to plant some seed in the imagination of a pastor or other leader who will be used of the Lord to do great things in a small church.

I have frequently quoted Francis Schaeffer who said, "There are no small churches and no big preachers." I like that. But it's not entirely true. We've seen churches made up of just a few people and stymied by lack of vision and a devotion to the status quo. And here and there, we may encounter a preacher with the world on his heart and the wisdom of the ages on his lips; that, for my money, is a "big preacher."

But this is not about being such a preacher. We're concerned with not being one of those churches.

The "ten reasons" that follow are not necessarily in the order of importance or prevalence. This is the way they occurred to me, and the order seems right.

1. Wanting to stay small.

"We like our church just the way it is now." While that attitude usually goes unspoken—it might not even be recognized by its carriers—it's widespread in many churches. The proof of it is seen in how the leaders and congregation reject new ideas and freeze out new people.

The process of rejecting newcomers is a subtle one, never as overt as snubbing them. They will be greeted and chatted with and handed a printed bulletin. But they will be excluded as clearly as if they were—as I was once— the only man in a roomful of sorority women at a state university. (I was an invited guest, about to bring a message to them. They couldn't have been nicer, but alas, they did not invite me to join!)

"Bob's class is meeting this week over at Tom and Edna's. Come and bring a covered dish." "The youth will have a fellowship tonight at Eddie Joe's. We're serving pizza and you don't want to miss it."

Unless you know who Bob, Tom, Edna, and Eddie Joe are and where they live, you're out of luck.

Pastors who want to include newcomers and first-timers in things should use full names from the pulpit. "I'll ask Bob Evans to come to the pulpit and lead us in prayer." This allows newcomers to learn who people are.

"For those who need directions to Eddie Joe Finham's house for the youth fellowship, he's the guy with the crew cut wearing the purple shirt. Raise your hand, Eddie Joe. He has printed directions to give you."

No one can promise that if a church wants to grow it will. However, I can guarantee you that if it doesn't, it won't.

2. A quick turnover of pastors.

A retired pastor who had served his last church some 30 years was supplying for a small congregation south of New Orleans. That week he told me of a discovery he made. "On Sunday afternoon, no one invited me to their home, so I had several hours to kill before the evening service. In the church office,

I was reading their history and discovered that in their nearly 50 years of existence, they've had 22 pastors."

He was aghast.

"Think of that," he said. "If they had around six months between pastors, that means the average tenure was less than two years."

He was quiet a moment, then said, "They didn't have pastors. They had preachers."

It takes at least a couple of years to become the real deal for a church, a pastor in more than name only, one who has earned the right to lead the congregation. With larger churches, the time period is more like six years.

Again, no one will promise you that keeping a pastor a long time guarantees the church will grow. But I can assure you that having a succession of short-term pastors will prevent it from growing as surely as you took a vote from the congregation to reject all expansion.

3. Domination by a few strong members.

The process by which a man (it's almost always a man) becomes a church boss is subtle and rarely, if ever, the result of a hostile takeover.

The pastor of a small church leaves for another town. The pastorless congregation looks within its membership for leaders to rise up and "take care of things" until a new pastor arrives. There will be pulpit supplies to line up, a search committee to form and train and send forth, and a hundred details to see to for the operation of the church. So two or three faithful and mature members (we assume) are chosen. They do their job well.

If the next pastor leaves after an unusually short tenure for whatever reasons, the congregation resorts to the fallback position: They enlist the services of those same two or three mature—and now experienced—leaders.

That's how it happens that one of them or possibly all three began to look upon themselves as the church itself. They make important decisions for the body, and everything works out. When the new pastor arrives, they let him know that anything he needs to know, he should call on them. He quickly sees that they have set themselves up as the board of directors, a layer of authority between the hired man (the preacher) and the congregation.

The bosses explain that they are protecting the congregation. "We don't like to upset them with matters like this." "These things are better off handled by just a few."

The longer this situation continues this way, the more entrenched these men become in their dictatorship. Pity the young idealistic pastor who walks into that church unsuspecting that they lie in wait for him, to—ahem— "give direction to his ministry." Or, as one said to me, "We thought you would like to have some help in pastoring this church."

In almost every instance, such self-appointed church bosses exist to frustrate the pastor's initiatives, block his bold ventures, and control his tendencies to want the church to act on (gasp!) something he calls faith!

Result: The church stays small. No normal church family coming into the community would want to join such a church.

The remedy: The congregation must see that key lay positions in the church rotate, that no one stays chairman of deacons for thirty years or church treasurer for a generation. Members of the congregation must stand up in business meetings and ask questions: "Why was this done?" "Who made the decision that our church would do that?" "Why was the congregation not informed on this?"

The one thing church bosses cannot stand is the light of day shown on their activities. Even though they convince themselves what they are doing is in the interests of the congregation, they don't want others to know about it. "They wouldn't understand."

Oh, we understand all too well. (Read about Diotrephes in the little Epistle of III John. He "loves to have the pre-eminence.")

4. Not trusting the leaders.

A phenomenon which I've seen in small churches and never in a large one occurs at the monthly business meetings, which incidentally, is also a custom a lot of growing churches have found they could do without. (They choose excellent leadership for the deacons, finance committee, and other key groups, and ask them to keep the congregation on course.)

In the small-and-determined-to-stay-small church, the treasurer passes out the monthly financial statement, which accounts for every penny spent this month. The discussion centers on why 35 cents was spent for call forwarding and two dollars for paper for the office.

The director of the vacation Bible school, the Sunday school director, the children's choir leader, and of course, the pastor—all are frustrated that the congregation doesn't trust them with 20 bucks, let alone 200, for some task.

The small-and-determined-to-stay-small church is far more concerned about the dollars and cents in the offering plate than in the lost souls in the community.

"I want to know what that revival cost the church," said a disgruntled deacon in the monthly meeting. The pastor rose and cited a figure.

"And what did the church get out of it?" the plaintiff said. "Only one person saved, and a child at that. Poor stewardship of our resources, if you ask me."

With that, another deacon walks to the front and takes something out of his pocket. He writes in his checkbook, tears out the check, and hands it to the treasurer.

"Gentlemen," he says, "that one child that was reached is my son. And he's worth every penny of it."

The tiny-and-deadset-on-remaining-tiny church would never step out on faith and do something so bold as to have an aggressive evangelism campaign to reach the lost and unchurched of their community. And if they did, unless their mindset changes, they would then harass their leaders into the grave demanding an accounting of every dime spent.

When the pastor search committee announced plans for the candidate to spend the following weekend at their church, a member stood to raise a question. "That's not long enough for us to get to know him. How do you expect us to be able to vote on him if we only have a weekend with him?"

Another member stood. "May I respond to Mr. Alan? We can't get to know him well enough in a weekend to make this kind of decision. That's why we have elected good leaders for this search committee. Let's trust them."

Elect good leaders and trust them to do their work. It's a faithproof system for growing a church.

5. Inferiority complex.

I was a seminary student when called to my second pastorate. Determined to figure out how to grow that church—they had been stuck at 40 in attendance for years—I read everything I could find in the seminary library. Fortunately, they had quite a few books on pastoring the small church.

What I discovered was something I was beginning to notice in my people. Small churches often are stymied by inferiority complexes. "We can't do anything because we're small. We don't have lots of money like the big churches in town."

So they set small goals and ask little from their members.

One day, I was visiting in the First Baptist Church of a nearby community. In no way was it what we would call large, but it was three or four times the size of mine. The pastor and I were chatting about some program or other. He said to me, "My people won't attempt anything like that. They say, 'We're not large like the First Baptist Church of New Orleans.'"

That's when it hit me: feelings of inferiority can be found in all size churches.

I wouldn't be surprised if the members of FBC-New Orleans were excusing themselves for their inaction by saying, "We're not Bellevue in Memphis or the FBC of Dallas."

I don't know who the members of Bellevue or FBC-Dallas look at with envy. But I'll bet it's some church bigger than them somewhere.

The remedy is to put one's eyes on Jesus Christ. "Lord, what do you want us to do?" That's the best prayer one can ever pray, and it has nothing whatever to do with what another church is doing.

In that seminary pastorate, I encouraged our people to set the goal high for our annual Christmas offering for foreign missions. One day, a member told me she was chatting with a neighbor who belonged to my friend's First Baptist Church in the next community, who asked her about the size of our mission offering goal.

When she told her, the neighbor sniffed, "Why, ours is double that!"

Thankfully, my member said nothing. She could have responded, "It should be triple since your church is three times the size of ours." But she didn't, and I was pleased.

Peter said, "Lord, what about John here? What do you want him to do?" Our Lord said—and thus set a wonderful pattern for all of us for the rest of time—"What is that to you? You follow me!"

Want your church to reach people and expand and grow? Get your eyes off what others are doing. Most of them, to tell the truth, are declining at a rate so fast it can hardly be measured. You do not want to take your cues from them.

Ask the Lord, "What would you have us to do?" Then do it.

If We Build It, Will They Come?

Carlos Whittaker

Somewhere in the past 20 years, a slew of churches have grabbed a hold of a new "outreach" strategy: If we build it, they will come.

So we create attractional services to attract people to see God for the first time. Which…happens. Which…works.

I can't help but imagine what would happen if we took the "attractional service" budgets and began to dump them into the "attractional Christ follower" budget. I think some HD projectors might disappear. I think some subs might disappear.

In the end, I think that having 200 "humans" outside the walls of a church building—who are more attractional than any programmed hour—could literally multiply your efforts 200 fold.

Or am I crazy?

I'll answer that.

I am.

But Islam is not the fastest growing religion in America because of their services. It is because of its followers. We have to stop thinking that our Sunday services will reach America.

They will reach part of America.

A very small part.

And the rest of America will be reached by the Christ followers we build in our churches.

10 Reasons Why Small Churches Stay Small

Part 2

Joe McKeever

6. No plan.

The typical, stagnant small church is small in ways other than numbers. They tend to be small in vision, in programs, in outreach, and in just about everything else.

Perhaps worst of all, they have small plans. Or no plans at all.

The church with no plan—that is, no specific direction for what they are trying to do and become—will content itself with plodding along, going through the motions of "all churches everywhere." They have Sunday school and worship services and a few committees. Once in a while, they will schedule a fellowship dinner or a revival. But ask the leadership, "What is your vision for this church?" and you will receive blank stares for an answer.

Here are two biblical instances of church leaders who knew what they were doing.

In Acts 6, when the church was disrupted by complaints from the Greek widows of being neglected in the distribution of food in favor of the Hebrew widows, the disciples called the congregation together. They said, "It is not right for us to neglect...(how they would fill in this blank reveals their plan)... in order to wait on tables." And then, as they commissioned the seven men chosen, the disciples said, "We will turn this responsibility over to them and give our attention to...(fill in the blank)."

In the first instance, the disciples saw their plan as "the word of God" and in the second as "prayer and the ministry of the word."

CHURCHLEADERS.COM

How do you see your ministry, pastor? What is your church's focus?

Earlier, when Peter and John were threatened by the religious authorities who warned them to stop preaching Jesus, they returned to the congregation to let them know of this development. Immediately, everyone dropped to their knees and began praying. Notice the heart of their prayer, what they requested: "Now Lord, consider their threats and enable your servants to... (what? How they finished this is how we know their plan, their chief focus)."

"...To speak your word with great boldness" (Acts 4:29).

When the Holy Spirit filled that room, the disciples "were all filled with the Holy Spirit and spoke the word of God boldly" (v. 31). Clearly, that means they spoke it into the community, the world around them, and not just to one another.

When I asked a number of leaders for their take on why so many small churches do not grow, several said, "They need to focus on the two or three things they do best. Not try to be everything to everyone."

Some churches need to focus on children's ministry, others on youth or young adults, young families, or even the oldsters. (Tell me why it is when a church is filled with seniors, we look upon it as failing. It's as though white-haired people of our society don't need to be reached for the Lord.)

Some will focus on teaching, others on ministry in the community, some on jail and prison ministries, and some on music or women's or men's work.

One note of explanation: this is not to say that the church should shut down everything else to do one or two things. Rather, they will want to keep doing the basics but throw their energies and resources, their promotions and prayers and plans, into enlarging and honing two or three ministries they feel the Lord has uniquely called them into.

7. Bad health.

It's no surprise to anyone who has spent time in more than a few churches to learn that some are unhealthy. And by that, we do not mean just because they are small, they are sick. You can be small and healthy; behold the hummingbird.

An unhealthy church is known more by what it does than by a list of characteristics and attributes. A church that runs its preachers off every year or two is unhealthy. A church that is constantly bickering is unhealthy. A church that cannot make a simple decision like choose the color of the carpet, adopt the next year's budget, or accept changes in an order of worship may be unhealthy.

So what is a healthy church, and how do we get from here to there?

Entire libraries could be filled with books written on the healthy church, and consultants abound, ready to assist congregations toward that purpose. But here it is in shorthand.

Romans 12 is God's blueprint for a healthy church. It divides into three parts: verses 1–2 call for each individual to make a personal commitment to Christ ("present your bodies as a living sacrifice"), verses 3–8 call for each one to find his/her place of service where they can use their spiritual gifts, and verse 9 through the end of the chapter describes the relationships within a healthy, loving fellowship of believers.

Show me a congregation where everyone is committed to Jesus Christ, each one is using the God-given spiritual gifts in the Lord's service, and the fellowship is sweet and active—and I'll show you a healthy church.

8. Lousy fellowship.

This overlaps with the last point, but it deserves a spot by itself.

For my money, the best thing a church has to offer individuals and families in the community—other than the saving gospel itself—is a place they will be loved and welcomed and made part of an active, healthy family. It's what we mean by "fellowship."

There are ways to tell if the fellowship in your church is unhealthy. Here is a brief rundown.

First, regarding the visitors to your church, the fellowship is unhealthy if:

a. Visitors are basically ignored.

b. In some places in the church, visitors are even resented.

c. No one follows up on visitors to let them know they are wanted and give information on the church.

d. There's no attempt to get people to visit your church in the first place.

Second, regarding the worship services of the church, the fellowship is probably unhealthy if:

a. Everything is orderly, but it's the same order you've used since forever.

b. The singing is lifeless and any departure from the norm is verboten. A new hymn or chorus, a different kind of musical instrument, a testimony here, an interview there, a short drama or video—no, sir. Not in our church.

c. There's no laughter, nothing spontaneous.

d. The invitation time is tacked on, lifeless, and without any response, ever.

e. The prayers are stale and filled with platitudes.

When the Old Testament prophets called on God's people to "break up the fallow ground"—Hosea 10:12 and Jeremiah 4:3 (NKJV)—they wanted to see evidence of brokenness, a willingness to change, a desire to bear new fruit.

Fallow ground is soil that has lain unproductive for several seasons. The hard crust requires a deep turning plow to open it up, and even then, the soil may require more preparatory work before it is productive.

A church with poor fellowship or essentially none is not failing to have enough socials and dinners. The church is failing in the most basic of areas of disciples: a failure to love.

Jesus said, "By this all men will know that you are my disciples, if you love one another" (John 13:35).

My observation from my own heart and nearly a half-century of ministry is that the disciple who is close to Christ loves the brethren. So a congregation that is unloving toward one another may be said to be far removed from the Lord and in a backslidden state. It's a simple deduction.

"Draw near to God and He will draw near to you!" (James 4:8 NKJV)

9. A state of neglect permeates the church.

Not always, but often, a dying church shows signs of its weakening condition by the disrepair of its buildings and the neglect of its appearance. The interior walls haven't been painted in years and bear the collective fingerprints of a generation of children. The carpet is threadbare, the piano's keys stick, the pulpit chairs need reupholstering, and the outside sign is so ugly it would be an improvement if someone knocked it down.

I received a vivid lesson on neglect early in my ministry when we received word that a high school student had taken his own life.

Although the family were members of another denomination, our youth minister and I called at their home to express our sympathy and offer our services. Along the way, my colleague filled me in on the family's situation. The dad was said to be having an affair, he and his wife bickered constantly, they were heavily in debt, the children were without supervision, and the brilliant son who had taken his life was rudderless.

As we parked and walked up the sidewalk, we were struck by the disarray of the yard. The grass was knee-high, and clutter was everywhere.

Inside, the father calmly brushed aside our condolences. "The way I look at these things," he said, "is that they all have a way of working out for the best." I was stunned. I thought, "Sir, your child is dead. Tell me how that is going to work out for the best."

We left sadder than when we arrived.

Dying churches do not tend to their business. They let problems fester and divisions go unaddressed. Listen closely and you will hear a leader speak those infamous words: "These things have a way of working themselves out."

And so they do nothing, and the church drifts on toward the grave. No one gets saved, no one joins, people drift away, the community becomes less and less aware of the existence of that little church, and the remaining members complain that people just don't love the Lord the way they used to.

10. No prayer.

It's tempting to make a little joke here and say, "Such churches do not have a prayer," but they could if they chose to.

When King Saul was bemoaning the woes that had descended upon him as a result of his rebellion against God, one of his chief complaints was that God no longer heard his prayer. "He inquired of the Lord, but the Lord did not answer ... " (I Samuel 28:6).

Luke tells us, "Then Jesus told his disciples a parable to show them that they should always pray and not give up" (Luke 18:1).

Pray or quit. Those seem to be the alternatives.

Want to give your congregation a little test, Pastor? Next Sunday, call for your people to meet you at the altar for a time of prayer. Do not beg them or cajole them. Just announce it, then walk there yourself, kneel and begin praying. See if anyone joins you. Notice who comes and pay close attention to who does not.

It won't tell you everything you'd like to know about your church, but it will say a lot.

A friend on Facebook requested prayer for his new ministry. When I asked what he was doing, he responded privately that in addition to pastoring his church, he is working for the state convention in his region. He said, "Almost all our churches in this part of the state are dying. We have buildings that were constructed for hundreds now running 15 or 20."

The plan, he said, is to get things in place to re-evangelize those regions as these old-line churches die off.

I hope they don't wait until those churches actually close their doors. A lifeless church can take a long time to give up the ghost.

The best approach would be for that stagnant, dying congregation to awaken and get dead serious about becoming vibrant again. This would mean taking the unprecedented step of doing anything it takes to re-establish their witness and presence in the community.

In almost every case I know personally, that is not going to happen. The leaders would rather see their church disappear from the Earth than to do anything new and different.

That is as sad a sentence as I've written in a long time.

That's why the only approach most of us have ever seen work is to bring in church planters from outside and start afresh.

The leadership of the dying churches will resent it. "Why are you spending money on starting new churches when we already have churches here? You could invest a fraction of that to help bring our church back, if you were thinking straight."

Stay the course, church planters. Not only will you do a good work in your own new congregation, but you might just build a fire under that old bunch. Their resentment may awaken them to fan the flames of the dying embers of their own faith.

PART

CHURCH
GROWTH

The pastors who arrive to begin new congregations will use innovative methods, almost always leave the suits and ties in the closet, set up guitars and drums and install screens and projectors, and come up with names for their churches that seem unchurchlike: Sojourn, Mosaic, Praiseworthy, Koinoia, Maranatha, Celebration, Vintage, and River.

God bless 'em.

But know this, church planter. A generation or two from now, if Koinonia and Sojourn and River and Celebration have not changed their methods and have become set in their ways, they too will be left behind as the ever-creating Holy Spirit seeks those who want to be new wineskins for the new things He is always up to.

Now, let us pray.

"Father, we do like our routines and ruts. Forgive us for limiting you by asking you to adapt to us instead of the other way around. Lord, in the words of the old hymn and the older Psalm, 'Wilt thou not revive us again that thy people may rejoice in Thee?' We ask this for Jesus sake. Amen" (Psalm 85:6 KJV).

Why We're All About the Numbers

Steven Furtick

I get asked all the time if Elevation is all about the numbers.

Let me just clarify something:

Our church is all about the numbers.

The number of **lives** that Jesus can permeate and penetrate with the gospel.

The number of **marriages** that can be restored.

The number of **teenagers** following the Lord.

The number of **depressed people** that can find hope in Jesus.

The number of **dads** who don't give their kids any attention who will learn to order their lives by the Word of God and start prioritizing their families.

What else matters? What else should we be about?

This might come as a shock to a lot of people, but measuring numbers and putting an emphasis on them isn't a new phenomenon.

Two thousand years ago, Luke by the inspiration of the Holy Spirit wrote:

Those who accepted his message were baptized, and about **three thousand** *were added to their* **number** *that day…And the Lord added to their* **number** *daily those who were being saved* (Acts 2:41, 47).

Apparently, God is all about the numbers. So I want to be, too. And so should you.

It's unacceptable to me as a pastor that we would stop growing when the Lord wants to add to our number daily those who are being saved. And in order for that to happen, we need to track every scrap of statistical data at our disposal. We've got to make sure we're measuring ministry numbers to measure our effectiveness and enlarge the Kingdom of God. I don't want to waste a single dollar or second on a program, piece of equipment, or ministry position that isn't the best option for reaching the most people.

You might be averse to numbers for a number of reasons.

Maybe you don't like the idea of big crowds. If that's the case, you wouldn't have liked the New Testament Church. And you *really* won't like **heaven.**

Maybe you think it steals away from discipleship. It's possible. But it's just as possible for that to happen in a church of 10 people as it is in a church of 10,000.

Whatever your reason is, remember: **Every number is indicative of a story.**

Personally, I don't want to put a cap on the number of stories God wants to redeem. Especially when I read this:

... I looked and there before me was a great multitude that no one could count... And they cried out in a loud voice: "Salvation belongs to our God ... " (Revelation 7:9–10).

Now that's a number worth shooting for. And I don't know about you, but I don't want to wait until I die to see this. I want to see this partially fulfilled in my lifetime. More people worshipping Jesus than I can count.

I want to see a little heaven on Earth through Elevation Church. Through every church. I think it's what God wants, too.

And that's why we're all about the numbers.

PART

5

WORSHIP
& CREATIVE

Missions is not the ultimate goal of the church. Worship is. Missions exists because worship doesn't.

John Piper

Cheerleading vs. Worship Leading

Glenn Packiam

"Jesus rose from the grave, and you, you can't even get out of bed!"

It's been a few decades since Keith Green sang those words, but the sentiment is alive in worship leaders all over the world. Every Sunday, when our eyes happen to catch the lazy stares of hollow faces with folded arms, we feel a not-so-holy anger rise up. As much as we try to resist it, some version of the "I can't believe you're not more into it" speech comes out. Blank looks turn into offended smirks, and the worship moment is effectively lost.

Even when we don't give in to the urge to smack people around for not being more fervent in their worship, there is still this underlying belief that we owe God something in response to His extravagant love. Call it a gratitude ethic. Put it on a bumper sticker as the catchy "Live for the One Who died for you" phrase. It's the same core belief: God has done much for me, now I've got to do much for Him. Because of this theology of a God who acts and then awaits our action, pastors often berate sinners and lecture the lazy.

Much has been made of how worship is a response to what Christ has done for us. Certainly, there is truth in that. It is "in view of God's mercy" that we offer our "bodies as living sacrifices," our "spiritual act of worship." Worship is a response. But it is more than our response.

Offered in the One

In the Old Testament, there were three primary pieces of Jewish worship: temple, priest, and sacrifice. All the way up until the Exilic Period, the way God had instructed Israel to encounter Him was through priest and sacrifice and in a temple or tabernacle. In the New Testament, the book of Hebrews serves as our chief expositor of Old Testament worship and how it is fulfilled in Christ. Hebrews argues that Christ is now our great High Priest who offered up His life before heaven's mercy seat as a perfect sacrifice once for all (Heb. 7:27). Jesus, speaking of His body, talked about the temple being destroyed and then rebuilt in three days (John 2:19–21). So, Jesus is Temple, Priest, and Sacrifice.

But there's more. Paul calls us "God's temple" (1 Cor. 3:16), Peter calls us a "royal priesthood" (1 Pet. 2:9), and Paul urges us, as mentioned earlier, to offer our "bodies as living sacrifices" (Rom. 12:1). But we are not these things on our own; Jesus is at the heart of it. Because Jesus is *the* Temple, we are a temple. Because Jesus is *the* Great High Priest, we are priests. Because Jesus is *the* perfect Sacrifice, our sacrifice is acceptable. Because Jesus *is* and because we are in Jesus, we *are*.

It Goes Both Ways

Christ does more than mediate God to us; He mediates us to God. God demonstrated His love for us *in* Christ by paying for our sins and making us new, alive to God. But it's not as if we say, "Thanks, I'll take it from here." *We* demonstrate our love for God as we offer our lives in Christ.

So how does this change the way we think and talk about worship? How does it change the way we lead worship? Here are a few thoughts:

1. Speak of Christ's work in more than the past tense.

The mediation of Christ is not merely something we look back to as a past event. The Living Christ is in our midst. In worship, we are not simply responding to Christ's work on the cross; we are responding to Christ's work in us presently.

2. Remind people that even our response is hidden in Jesus.

We do not stand on our feet before Christ. We are not temple, priest, or sacrifice on our own merit. We are those things because we are in Christ. Our songs, our prayers, our lives become acceptable and pleasing to God because they are being offered up to God in Jesus.

3. Focus on calling attention to Christ (not on how people are responding).

First of all, you congregation's response is not your main concern. As worship leaders, our role is to call attention to Christ—His work in the past, His work at the present, and His work that will culminate in time to come. How people are or are not responding is not our concern. Anything we do to elicit response usually ends up leaving people trying to muster up something on their own, ratcheting up emotion, or white knuckling their guilt-driven devotion to God.

So the next time our congregations seem bored and aloof, perhaps instead of cheerleading them into giving their all, maybe we can find ways to call their attention to the Living Christ, present in our midst, ready to take our broken lives and turn them into beautiful offerings to God.

4 Lessons for Managing Creatives

Phil Cooke

Everyone loves what creative people do, but many find their lifestyles and behavior a little strange. Just hire an advertising agency or glance at MTV to confirm that there are some pretty odd creative people out there. But for the Church to reach its real potential, we have to learn to maximize our creativity and cultivate our relationships with original thinkers. There's no question that creative people are wired differently. Their perception of the world, their reactions to events, and even the way they sleep is often dramatically different from most. Therefore, much of that behavior comes out of biological differences. So trying to change their behavior is often a futile and impossible task.

They even have different priorities. Instead of political battles over a corner office, access to the boss, or a bigger title, creative people are more interested in the color of their office or being able to listen to music while they work. Few creative people care about the same things other workers care about.

Creative people see different ways to achieve the same goals. Most pastors or ministry leaders want to achieve goals, but often they are overly concerned about how to reach the goal. They are interested in rules, procedures, and paperwork. One Christian TV station executive I know has a "flow chart" for the station that looks remarkably like Dante's journey through hell. Just reading it gives me the chills.

On the other hand, creative people are just as driven, but much less concerned about "how" they reach the goal. That's why "breakthrough" thinking often comes from creative people. They see the world differently and are more concerned about achieving the goal than rigid, specific ways to get there.

The fact is if you have creative people in your office, you need to make a conscious effort to deal with them differently. Here are a few suggestions:

1. Within reason, don't let their habits, appearance, or style bother you.

Sure—there are unavoidable office rules for smoking, suggestive clothing, breaks, etc. But if it's not absolutely critical to the mission of the church or ministry, cut them some slack! Let them have a little fun with their hairstyle or clothes, and you'll see their motivation dramatically increase.

2. Give them flexibility in their schedules.

Who cares if they do their best work at night? In most creative functions, you can easily measure their output and the quality of the work, so worry less about how many hours they put into it. As long as they keep up and are doing great work, what does it matter when they do it?

3. Learn the art of compliments and motivation.

Most creative people are easily hurt by criticism—it's part of their make-up. But if you can compliment and motivate them, you won't believe how the level of work will improve. Remember, a carrot always works better than a stick.

4. Finally—learn to value creativity.

If we're going to impact this culture with a message of hope, we need the most creative people doing their best work. Can your church, ministry, or organization do things in a more creative way? Are you reaching this generation in a language and style they understand? Are you always on the lookout for creative people to help you achieve your vision?

Learn to manage creative people, then stand back and watch the difference it makes.

17 Common Worship Leading Mistakes

Marie Page

1. Including too many new songs in the set

Your congregation is there to worship—most will find it difficult to do so if they spend most of the time learning your latest masterpieces. Vary your set list to include a variety of older, recently introduced, and brand new songs, and be ready to make changes on the fly if you sense your congregation is becoming weary.

2. Pitching the songs too high

Remember that a comfortable range for a woman is about five semitones (half steps) lower than for a man. Change the key down to avoid going above top D, particularly if you are playing in a small church situation.

3. Clunky moving from song to song

Playing a song once it's underway is fairly straightforward so make sure you concentrate on rehearsing how to start and end a song. Practicing a seamless flow from one song to the next is worthwhile to focus on. It will help if both are in the same key with a similar groove, and if you are using music, make sure the sheets are side by side on your music stand.

4. Poor band dynamics

Conflicting rhythms, one instrument speeding up/slowing down, vocalists overwhelming the sound with too many ad-libs or vibrato. Exercise leadership in directing your singers clearly, and if necessary, get them some vocal training. Get them to listen to each other's parts and possibly film or record a service to help with some constructive criticism.

5. Lack of leadership

Without clear guidance from the worship leader, it's difficult for the band to know what they are meant to do, let alone the congregation. Give a good clear brief in practice and use vocal cues and body language to communicate during the set.

6. Overly complex vocals

Congregations get easily confused when the lead vocalist slips into harmonies, trills, and ad-libs. Simple clear melody is always the easiest to follow. Leave the harmonies for the backing vocalists.

7. Poor phrasing and blending by vocalists

Make sure that all your singers are phrasing each "musical sentence" in the same way. It can help to have one backing vocalist leading the others so that everyone finishes their words at the same time. In the studio, singers are often asked not to finish the last consonant in a line so that the ending doesn't sound jagged.

8. Wrong keys or wrong capo positions

Make sure all of the band is playing in the same key. Issue your set list in advance with instructions for keys. And if you change your mind, make sure that everyone knows.

9. Tuning

Are all your instruments in tune and are they staying in tune throughout the set? Even the right notes out of tune sound far worse than the wrong notes in tune so buy yourself a decent tuner like the Boss TU2—cheap tuners can be so frustrating.

10. Lack of rhythm and togetherness by the band

This can be caused by many things including poor musicianship and lack of overall direction. Try to generate a sense of team where everyone plays their part to contribute to the whole without any one musician standing out. Also, ensure that you have the relevant instruments in your foldback, i.e., the kick drum and other instruments responsible for rhythm.

11. Winging it

Either the result of poor preparation or trying something new out on the spot. Be sure you can accomplish what you have in mind. Are you trying to sing a song without the lyrics in front of you, and you've forgotten the words? Does your AV guy have the words for the congregation, or do they have to remember them, too? Do you and the rest of the band know all the chords you need?

12. Technical problems

The sound gremlins can happen to the best of us but try to get there early, set up methodically, and make sure your technicians are well trained in the system they are using.

13. Problems with pitch

You're starting a new song, and you've suddenly realized you've started on completely the wrong note. Try to identify the problem songs in advance and quietly play the note you need to hit on your instrument. Hold the note in your head while playing the intro and then hit it with confidence. Alternatively, ask one of the other (confident) vocalists to lead on that song.

14. Overemphasis on the melody line

Make sure your backing vocalists and single melody instruments are playing harmonies. The lead vocalist and congregation are all on the melody line—create some contrast.

15. Worship crash

These are often caused by trying something complicated that hasn't been practiced enough. Never try anything complicated until you, the band, and the congregation are really familiar with the song.

16. Starting the song in the wrong tempo

Either invest in an in-ear click or sing the song through in your head first so that you can pace the tempo properly. Generally, the chorus is the fastest part of the song.

17. Audiovisual failure

This happened to Matt Redman one time. Matt just shifted his set list to songs with simple lyrics and gave spoken vocal cues to the congregation at junction points in the song.

*A man can no more diminish
God's glory by refusing to worship
Him than a lunatic can put out
the sun by scribbling the word
"darkness" on the walls of his cell.*
—C. S. Lewis

PART

5

WORSHIP
& CREATIVE

How to Cue the Congregation in Worship

Bob Kauflin

A while back, I received an e-mail asking this question:

One of the central roles of a worship band is to help the congregation to sing. Do you have advice on how a worship band can best cue the congregation? What kinds of things could I tell my instrumentalists and singers to do to help the people come in on the first words of a song or verse? How would you in general encourage congregational singing?

This question highlights one of the differences between leading a group of people to praise God from their hearts and simply playing and singing music for them. While people can certainly join along as we play our songs, it's helpful when we make it obvious we expect them to sing. If you sing songs the exact same way every time, cuing the congregation isn't as much of an issue. But if you regularly switch things up as you sing a song (repeat a verse, sing the chorus twice, go back to a different part of the song, etc.) people need to know where you're going. Cuing them is one way to do that. Here are a few thoughts.

Give cues clearly.

In discussing the benefits of prophecy vs. tongues, Paul writes in 1 Cor. 14:7–8, "If even lifeless instruments, such as the flute or the harp, do not give distinct notes, how will anyone know what is played? And if the bugle gives an indistinct sound, who will get ready for battle?" In other words, clarity matters. The less time people spend trying to figure out where we're going in a song, the more time they'll be able to give to exalting Christ in their minds and affections. That means I don't want to mumble or speak too quickly. It also means that if different parts of a song begin with the same phrase, I have to say something other than the initial words to let people know what we're going to sing. Generally, if I don't say anything, people (including the projectionist) should anticipate me going to the next part of the song.

Make sure you have enough time to give cues.

Trying to squeeze in a verbal direction at the last minute not only makes me sound frantic, but it doesn't really help anyone. I should have a feel for how long the spaces in the song are. Also, I don't have to say the whole first line to let people know what we'll be singing. Saying two or three words works, or even simply, "Verse 2."

Don't give cues too early.

I've been guilty of giving direction immediately after a section of a song has ended, leaving people eight bars to figure out when they should come in. By that time, they've usually already tried to come in or forgotten what I said.

Don't cue the band without cuing the congregation.

Some leaders develop elaborate signals to let the band know what's next, while leaving the congregation clueless. That's why I generally give verbal cues rather than visual ones. An exception is when I'm signaling to the band that we're going to sing a cappella or end the song, neither of which the congregation has to know in advance.

Vary the music to indicate when you want people to sing or not sing.

Instrumental cues can work as well as verbal cues. You can increase the volume of the band, ritard slightly, or vary the harmonic changes to indicate it's time to sing. For instance, you can lead into first chord with a walk-up on the bass. If you want people to wait to come in, keep the instrumentation subdued and sparse.

Vary your cues.

Most of us tend to do what's most efficient. "Efficiency" can suck the life out of a congregation's singing. To vary it up, you can make a comment on what you're about to sing. Before the fourth verse of "In Christ Alone" ("No guilt in life, no fear in death"), I might say, "This is the effect of the gospel." You can also sing a cue rather than speak it. Or just move up to the microphone.

Think tone as well as content.

Some leaders sound like they're barking out military commands when they give cues. Cuing a congregation can be an opportunity to impart faith and understanding to people as well as give direction.

Don't cue too much.

Leading is like giving directions on a trip. You only need to say something when there's a turn. You don't need to highlight every store, gas station, or landmark that you pass by. Give people a break from your interruptions (a lesson I continue to learn). But be sure you're there when they need to make a turn.

10 Ways to Grow As a Creative Leader

Brian Orme

How many times have you seen a killer series graphic, a fresh design, or a video that breaks all the rules (and still works) and found yourself jealous for not creating it yourself? If there's one universal among creatives, it's this: We all have an insatiable desire to create better things. We want to push ourselves beyond our current boundaries in skill and talent to become stronger designers.

This drive for excellence and growth is consistent with a God who charged his people with high standards when it comes to design. God never commanded anyone in Scripture to do shabby work. In Philip Ryken's amazing little book *Art for God's Sake*, he says, "God took whole chapters of Scripture to explain what to make and how to make it." In short, design matters to God.

What does that mean for today's church creative? It means that what you create matters. When we begin to see the things we create as a way to worship the Savior, suddenly, even that haphazard graphic, logo, or website copy becomes highly important because we're creating for the glory of God.

With that in mind, here are ten ways to challenge yourself as a creative to design better things and become more skilled in your craft, no matter what it might be, for the glory of God and the building up of the saints.

1. Pray.

I know, I'm starting off with the pat Sunday school answer. But seriously, your life as a creative isn't disconnected from your life with Christ. The more you pray—and truly connect with God—amidst your work, the stronger your creative vision for worship will be. Remember, whenever anything in

Scripture was created, the Holy Spirit was there. Bottom Line: God wants to empower you for the work He's created you to do. Stay connected to Him.

2. Be Your Best (or Worst) Critic.

Evaluate your work. Be willing to throw away good design to pursue the best. Don't settle for done. Also, don't worry about the time you feel you've wasted in an unsuccessful project. That time is valuable. Which leads me to me next point.

3. Fail Better.

Samuel Beckett once said, "Fail. Fail again. Fail better." If you don't make mistakes, how will you ever make anything of value? Want to create better things? Get cozy with failure. Make him/her your friend.

4. Make Sticky Designs.

Stephen Brewster says, "Really good creative pieces are sticky, tell stories, and carry the conversation beyond the reach of the creator." If your design doesn't move those who view it, chances are it's not telling a compelling—or sticky—story. We have the most amazing story to tell; let's do our best to make it just as compelling (from whatever angle) in our creations.

5. Find What Moves You.

Be careful not to distance your designs from real life. In a recent article for *Entrepreneur* magazine, Bruce Mau says, "The difference between great design and design that misses the mark is empathy—the ability to make the human connection." Find out what moves you and embed that emotion into your design. Make the human connection one of your design filters and you will grow as a creative.

6. Be Disciplined.

Don't fall for the myth of inspiration. Creativity is hard work. Anything worth its salt in design will probably have a long trail of pain, frustration, passion, and pursuit. But the journey is worth it.

7. Break the Rules.

It's good to remind yourself that sometimes the rules of design are meant to be broken. If you find yourself at a creative roadblock, try painting outside the lines. Get out of your creative comfort zone, stop using your go-to tricks, and do the unexpected.

8. Challenge Yourself with New Media.

Paul Arden once said, "If you get stuck, draw with a different pen." If you want to grow as a creative, the need to expand your skills on new platforms is essential. This takes time and can be extremely challenging and complex, but learning a new media will make you a better artist.

9. Study the Best.

As a creative, Ernest Hemingway studied the best writers and tried to defeat them at their strengths. He was cocky at times, but his goal was to beat every writer, living or dead, at their craft. Seek to be the best at what you do. Be competitive. Don't be a wimp. (Don't be a jerk either, but you get the idea.)

10. Join the Community.

Break the stereotype for creatives that says we like to work alone. Joining a community of creatives will give you an outlet to share your work, view what others are doing, and engage in the conversation. Commit yourself to a creative community. Be vulnerable. Share your work. Grow.

Why They're Not Singing with You

Brian Taylor

The songs are selected, rehearsal is done, and everyone is ready to go. The clock strikes, the band kicks up, and you get ready to pour your heart into the next twenty minutes. Everything is going great until about four minutes in, when you look out into the congregation and see that there are only about eight other people singing with you. Some are staring, others are texting, and a couple seem to still be sleeping. All you can think is, "What is going on here?! C'mon guys!"

Unfortunately, this is an all too familiar scene on Sunday mornings. And we have all been there and experienced it. It's discouraging. It's frustrating. It leaves you feeling inadequate and disappointed. Getting the congregation to sing with you is one of the most difficult tasks of the worship leader. Sometimes, it involves moving people beyond their cares to magnifying the Lord. Other times, it's battling personal preferences. We even have to deal with how the weather affects people's attitudes. However, sometimes the silence is simply a result of some very practical problems. The good news is that these problems have very simple solutions!

If you find this is happening to you regularly, here are six things you can do to begin to break the code of silence:

1. Check your keys.

There's a current trend in worship music right now that involves keying songs really high. That's great for solo stuff, and it even works for many churches. However, at our church, we've found that our best scenario is when men and women can split between their choice of two different octaves, as opposed to what I call true unison (which is everyone on the exact same pitch). We have defined our "congregational range" as keys where the melody does not drop below a low A and doesn't rise above C or D, an octave higher. Of course, we have times where we go outside of this, but the goal is not to spend too much time at either end. Otherwise, you alienate those that aren't skilled at singing because they can't reach the high highs or the low lows. Remember, you don't have to sing the song in the same key they do on the original recording, and you might have to sing it in a key that's not necessarily the most comfortable for you! If you're having a problem with people not singing along, the first step is to check your keys.

2. Make sure the melody is clear and strong.

Once you're sure your songs are in singable keys, you have to make sure that the melody rings through nice and clear. The vast majority are going to sing during worship like they sing when they listen to the radio—they're going to match what they hear. If they can't hear the melody, then they don't know what to sing. Make sure that your team knows and sings the same melody (this includes phrasing and timing), and that your sound team is focusing in on the people carrying the melody of a song. Another point on this is that every worship leader needs to learn how to be content singing the melody of a song. People don't need an ad-lib every five seconds, nor do they need a display of your vocal abilities. You're a worship leader, not a soloist. They need you to be their guide. Keep the melody strong and default to singing it. You'll be amazed at what happens.

PART

WORSHIP
& CREATIVE

3. Take the time to teach them the song.

People sing the most confidently when they are sure of how a song goes. A tool that we utilized and had great success with is the "mini-choir rehearsal" when introducing a new song. The goal is to create a worship learning environment with minimal pressure. I take about two or three minutes during the set with the piano and run through all of the main parts (a verse, chorus, bridge, etc.) of a song. I play and sing the melody to them and have them sing it back to me, while our vocalists sing with them. I even use my hand to guide them up and down the melody like I would our choir. Then we start the song from the beginning with the full band, and I continue to use the hand motions through the first round of the verse and chorus or any of the more difficult parts throughout the song. And in case you're wondering, yes, the Holy Spirit still sticks around while you're learning songs. The results to this "call and response" time have been great, and our song learning curve has drastically changed. (Also, you may find that doing a new song two weeks in a row helps increase retainment.)

4. Simplify and build.

Sometimes, the issue is that there are too many things going on in a song. Maybe there are too many different verses or melody changes. Maybe the chord progressions don't clarify the route of the melody. Many things contribute to a song not working well during a worship time. A key to remember when selecting songs is that the majority of your members are not musical. What you or I can pick up in one or two listens takes them significantly longer. Choose songs that are intuitive. If you really want to do a complex song, don't be afraid to simplify it some to make it more digestible. You can change the rhythm of the lyrics to make them more consistent. You can alter the melody line to keep it within the appropriate range. Tailor the songs to your congregation.

Also, don't feel like you have to do the entire song at once. Remove parts like "Ohh's" and "Whoa's," until the congregation is more comfortable with the basics of the song. If a song has a lot of parts, first teach the verse and the chorus. Then in a couple weeks, after you've done the song a couple times, teach the bridge or other parts. Build on the foundation you've established and continue to facilitate a no-pressure learning environment.

5. Make sure that your entire team is engaged.

One of the most important keys to congregational engagement is making sure that everyone on the platform is engaged. You will lead best when you are leading by example. People are not just looking at the worship leader; they're looking at everyone that's on the platform. They're watching to see if our entire teams are sincere and focused. If you're able to, record video of your service, and see what the worship team looks like. Are they full of life and passionate about what they're doing? Or do they look like they'd rather be doing something else? Regularly remind them of the importance of their function.

Another tip is that anytime you want the congregation to sing, have the worship team sing. During times when you want to hear the congregation, just have the vocalists pull their microphones down. When the congregation sees mouths moving, it's an indication that theirs should be, too. This is especially important for the start of songs, to avoid the impression that it's a solo.

6. Check your connections.

Your connection as a leader with the congregation will either produce a spectator or a participator mindset. You don't have to preach a sermon, but you always want to incorporate connecting points with the congregation. Saying things like "Good morning," "Let's sing this together…" and giving a few clear verbal cues throughout a song will go a long way. When people feel connected to you, they'll begin to trust you, and as such, they'll follow you more readily. Without the connection, you become a performer on a stage. Pray about things you can say and ways you can cue them that it's their time to worship, too.

7. Start strong and end clearly.

Make sure that there is clear definition in the starting and ending of songs. This doesn't mean that you have to put the awkward music break between every song. However, people should be able to tell when you're moving from one song to the next. Make sure that the band knows when they're coming in and how they're ending songs. Adding a ritard to the final phrase is generally enough to give that signal that a song is ending. This will help you stay connected to the congregation, once you've built the bridge. When people get confused, they stop singing. Light the way ahead, and they'll stay on the journey with you!

This is not an exhaustive list, nor is it an instant cure. As you begin to address these and other issues one by one, the wall of silence will begin to crack. Don't give up and don't be discouraged! There will come a day when that wall will come tumbling down, and you will look out to see a congregation that is joyfully singing God's praises!

Worship is to the Christian life what the mainspring is to a watch, what the engine is to a car. It is the very core, the most essential element.

—*John MacArthur*

Top 10 Church Sound Problems

Leon Sievers

Sound problems can be caused by anything from architectural defects to misguided equipment operators. Here are some of the most troublesome sound problems that churches struggle with and what can be done about them:

1. Echo or excessive reverberation.

This can be the result of poor architectural design or timing variations between speakers. Timing problems occur in large rooms in which speakers face each other from different sides of a room. If a church has a long, narrow sanctuary and puts a speaker on the back wall, that speaker should have a slight sound delay. Otherwise, the sound waves from the front speaker will arrive at the back of the sanctuary after the rear speaker releases its waves. It's easier to place all of the speakers at the front of a room and adjust their volume and position to reach the back row.

Some buildings have flat, reflective surfaces that make sound waves act like bumper cars. For example, if a church holds a potluck dinner in a gymnasium or multipurpose facility with hard surfaces, table conversation will become a muddy hum that gradually increases in volume. A speaker's voice will bounce around the room. This problem can be remedied by hanging fabric panels, banners, or baffles on the walls or from the ceiling. Check what's offered at Acoustical Solutions, AcousticalSolution.com, or Acoustics First Corporation, AcousticsFirst.com, for off-the-shelf solutions and consultation.

2. Feedback.

This sound problem occurs when amplified sound from a speaker or monitor circulates through a microphone and is amplified again, giving off an obnoxious squeal. This kind of sound loop is due to monitor placement as well as microphone technique. If a singer points a microphone directly into a monitor or if there isn't sufficient distance between the microphone and the monitor, feedback is inevitable. Feedback also happens when a speaker moves around on a platform, pointing the microphone in various directions. For churches with such speakers, several manufacturers offer a feedback controller that eliminates feedback by constantly shifting audio frequency.

3. Inadequate training.

Sound equipment, no matter how costly, won't perform well if technicians don't know how to use it. After determining that a person has a solid interest in serving as a sound technician, work with the person until that person is qualified to serve. Invest in training materials such as books, videos, and trade publications.

The best sound system can be compromised by a performer. A singer who holds a microphone far from his mouth, for example, forces a technician to turn up the volume on a channel, which could result in feedback. Singers should adjust their microphones according to the volume of their voices. On a high, strong note, the microphone should be moved away from the mouth; on a low, soft note, in closer.

4. Poor communication.

Technicians must explain what they're doing to performers. For example, a performer might want more reverb in her monitor, but the sound technician knows that singers maintain better pitch quality without hearing reverb in the monitors. The sound technician could mix some reverb into the system and eliminate it in the monitor, but if the singer doesn't understand what the technician is doing, she will perform with less confidence. The moral for technicians is to be diplomatic. The moral for performers is to trust the technician.

5. Muddy sound.

Inexperienced technicians are often plagued by muddy sound, which is quite often the result of monitor wash. For example, if the worship leader has a monitor on the platform, it is usually pointed at the back wall and away from the congregation. If the monitor is turned up too loud or includes too varied a mix, the sound will bounce off the back wall and collide with other sounds on the way to the congregation. The solution could be as simple as adjusting the volume of the monitor. If a worship team is large enough, it might need multiple monitors. Monitor mixing is an art that requires much practice, however.

6. Hot or dead spots.

Hot spots are places in a room where sound energy is densely concentrated, and dead spots are where there is no sound. Both are usually caused by misplaced speakers. The laws of physics are the same in the house of the Lord as they are in Carnegie Hall. It doesn't matter how expensive speakers are; if they're situated incorrectly, they won't work properly. Speakers should almost always be placed by a professional or someone who understands room acoustics.

7. Noise.

One of the secrets to maintaining high sound quality is isolating sound. Air ducts sometimes transport unwanted mechanical noise throughout a building. Exterior noise of cars, trains, or sirens can be intrusive if a church isn't well insulated. Noise problems can be averted most effectively when a church is being built, but there are ways to filter it out in existing buildings.

8. Poor installation.

Churches should consult with professional sound technicians on the purchase, installation, and operation of sound equipment. A good sound company should have a list of recently completed projects and be willing to show them to you.

9. Misconceptions.

It is critical for a church to define its need for a microphone before purchasing it. Microphones are like lenses on a camera. You choose them based on the effect you want. Frequency response, sensitivity, and impedance are key factors. High-impedance microphones produce noise (crackling, thuds) when moved or bumped. Mikes with lower-impedance—somewhere between 300 and 600 ohms—are better for churches.

Soprano vocalists often have high-frequency response in their voices and do not want a microphone with built-in boosts in the upper register. Male vocalists can get by with most microphones, but they'll do better with a boost in high-frequency response. For a good all-purpose microphone, consider a dynamic cardioid, which should cost from $100 to $150. Microphones designed to amplify a grand piano or an orchestra will cost more.

10. Budget miscues.

A budget is not an accurate measure of what sound system a church should buy. Churches have been going to vendors for years, saying, "We have a $3,500 sound budget," and vendors have been giving them $3,500 sound systems. What church leaders don't understand is that a sound system can be purchased in increments over several years. Also, function is more important than price. Sound systems should be designed around usage factors, such as what kind of music a church performs, how loud the music is played, and how large the church is.

Dying of Inspiration Overload

Charles Lee

All of us need inspiration.

It reminds us of our hopes, dreams, and the kind of lives we hope to live. It sparks, fuels, and keeps our creativity alive.

Nevertheless, inspiration can also become an addictive drug that causes delusion, distraction, and ultimately great harm. It has the power to lure us into unreal expectations and give us a false sense of accomplishment and productivity.

Let's admit it…most of us are inspiration junkies. We often need the latest information, networking opportunity, and conference to give us an extra-added push or edge over our "competition." Some will disguise this need as professional and/or personal development.

Ouch…yes, it hurts.

The reality is that there's plenty of inspiration to go around, especially in our digital age. I don't think we lack information that can inspire. As mentioned earlier, we all need inspiration. The problem arises when inspiration becomes the "thing" we aspire for (i.e., the end of our pursuit).

Inspiration is a great additive to our work, but it should never become our end goal. In other words, it's a means to an end and not the end itself. Inspiration often tricks our minds into thinking that we are moving forward toward accomplishing our goals. Mental advancement in thought must have some corresponding movement in the physical world.

Could it be that many of us are dying of inspiration overload?

Here are some suggestions on curbing our addictive relationship with inspiration:

Limit Meetings.

You don't need to meet everyone that asks for a meeting. Don't let your insecurity of letting others down get in the way of living a healthy and productive life. Each meeting is actually precious time away from doing what you're designed to do. How many times after a day of meetings have you thought, "Why does it feel like I haven't accomplished much today?" Unnecessary meetings can kill your productivity.

Limit Online Information Intake.

Determine how much time you will spend each day/week on taking in information online. A "short" excursion online in following a trail of information can turn minutes into hours. Ask yourself, especially during work hours, "Is this necessary or a fun option?" Use something like Evernote to bookmark interesting information for leisure. Remember, you still have work to do.

Limit New Ventures.

As a serial entrepreneur, I have to constantly remind myself that "new" work must be meaningful and add to my current direction. This means that a good opportunity is not the same as the right one. Although you may not always be able to discern the difference, it is still valuable to have these kinds of conversations. Work toward refining your direction into a few areas as the year goes by (unless you have millions of dollars to play with and don't mind blowing some of it). This is not to say you shouldn't risk. There's always risk involved. All I'm saying is that you should risk in the right areas.

The "Worship" Elephant in the Room

Brenton Brown

I'm sure it hasn't escaped your notice that there's definitely an awkward incongruity with the genre of music we call "worship." My job as a worship leader, my primary purpose—really the only purpose—is to lift the name of Jesus above every other name and to help others do the same, to lift His name above all the other names and words and tasks and things and people that clamor for our attention in this world. As worship leaders, we are to simply lead others, and indeed, even our own souls, in the worship of God.

But as musicians who aspire to—and, in fact, do occasionally—make a living playing this kind of music, one of our important goals is to make our own names known. Obscurity does not feed a family. As working musicians, our job is to sell records. And to do that, we have to let people know about us. In a very real and practical way, we have to lift our names above all the other names—even the other names in "worship"—so that people will recognize, acknowledge, and hopefully buy what we make!

I think everyone who bumps into the worship genre, even unbelievers, quickly becomes aware of its tricky combination of priorities. We're people who promote our names, and then go on to say that Jesus' name is above every other name...hmmm.

I suppose it's worth saying that the awkwardness is not quite as severe for CCM musicians. There, it seems, the goal is to make art that also makes known our God. But the language is clearer. They are artists. They make art. They sell art. No problems. The categories seem easier to see and recognize. But worship leaders, on the other hand—a title, by the way, that does not exist in either the Old or New Testaments—are afflicted with the reminder of our purpose every time we're mentioned, interviewed, advertised, played on radio, pasted on a poster, or tagged on a web page. Whenever our name is being lifted up, we're reminded that it's Jesus' name who should be lifted higher still.

It's definitely awkward! And for those of you who know me or maybe track what I do, I just needed to mention the elephant shuffling his feet quietly in the room. Jude tells me I should probably relax, that unless I "speak up," the message won't be heard, I guess in the same way that John the Baptist spoke up to announce and make way for the (humble) King of Glory. But if you ever see me enlarging my name in a way that doesn't make His name higher or honor Him, please let me know.

This is a pretty narrow road—no doubt the same kind of road that all of us walk. But like any path walked in faith, it can be done much more easily within the safety of the community of believers.

Maybe another answer to the awkwardness lies in that little comment I made about "worship leading" not being a named category in Scripture. We all know what we mean by the words "worship leader." They're shorthand for describing the person who leads the singing we do when we get together to meet with each other and worship God. Put this way, as a song leader, the role becomes significantly less elevated or bloated. Who's Brenton Brown or Matt Redman or Paul Baloche or Kathryn Scott, etc.? They're just people in our community of believers who happen to write songs, songs that the church sometimes makes use of to worship God.

But God's mission, God's church, and God's kingdom will certainly continue to grow with or without these songs! The increase of His government will know no end, whether a few musicians in the 20th century throw their tunes into the mix or not. In the light of God's sovereign plan for His people and the Earth, it's laughable to think that a few song leaders would make a difference either way in His purposes. In the end, we're just musicians— maybe we're "artists," who knows—who go about their work in this time of history and hope that it helps the cause of God's mission and God's people. We are no more sacred or secular than carpenters or firemen or painters or artists. We are just people who have been welcomed into the wide, wide world of God's love and grace. And as working musicians, this is what we bring when we meet.

My Two Pet Peeves in Worship

Steven Furtick

Recently, I tweeted the following about a problem that exists in a lot of churches:

Two pet peeves: 1) Pastors who don't engage in worship; 2) Worship musicians who don't engage with the Word.

I think these are two big roadblocks for taking your church to a whole new level in worship.

1. Pastors who don't engage in worship.

Pastors, you're the primary worship leaders at your churches. And that's even if you don't have a lick of musical talent and your voice would offend people if they heard it.

Your church is never going to go further in worship than you're going to lead it. And what you need to understand is that you set the tone not only with the Word but also by your example. Your worship before God is preaching a sermon on the greatness of God long before you ever open up your mouth to speak about God. And it's a sermon people listen to and apply to their own worship. Immediately.

But this goes beyond your leadership. You will never graduate past your need to worship God. You've been *called* to preach, but you were *created* to worship. There isn't an advanced level of Christianity where you no longer have to engage with God in passionate praise.

So don't let your mind become so occupied with what you're called to do—preach—that you lose sight of what you have been created to do—worship.

2. Worship musicians who don't engage with the Word.

This is ultimately an honor issue. Yes, honoring your pastor is part of it. He's been preparing for this all week, and one of the best ways you can support him is by actively responding to the Word.

But really, this is about honoring the Word of God. Just like your pastor, before you're a musician, you're a worshipper. And there is no such thing as true worship divorced from God's Word.

The Word gives us a God worth worshipping. A God worth leading others to worship. And the intensity of your own personal worship and your effectiveness in leading others in theirs is directly related to your engagement with it.

So whether you're preaching or playing music this weekend, choose to fully engage. Pastors, put your notes down and worship the God you've been studying about all week. Worship musicians, catch your breath for a minute, and then pick up your Bible, a pen, and press into the God who is the source of your creativity and talent.

And then watch as the worship in your church is taken to a whole new level.

6

OUTREACH
& EVANGELISM

The authority by which the Christian leader leads is not power but love, not force but example, not coercion but reasoned persuasion. Leaders have power, but power is safe only in the hands of those who humble themselves to serve.

—John Stott

PART
6
OUTREACH
& EVANGELISM

A New Way to Be Christian

Gabe Lyons

Over the past eight years, I've dedicated much of my work to understanding how a new generation is applying the Gospel in post-Christian societies. That work has informed and been illuminated in my book, *The Next Christians: The Good News About the End of Christian America,* where I hope to cultivate a rooted optimism that the future for the church in American culture is bright.

Just looking across the pond to Europe, it's easy to surmise what society can look like when the church loses its vibrancy. In Europe's case, the potent edge that once catalyzed the Renaissance and much of her values became rubbish within only a few generations. It should be a stark reminder that just one generation stands between ultimate collapse toward the falling edge or a resurrection of what could be—or better said—what *ought* to be. So it is with the American church and our opportunity in this generation. If we have the eyes to see (and I can tell you from my experience that a new generation does), the greatest days for the church just might lie ahead.

But to understand the opportunity, we need to remember where we've come from.

The church of the 20th century had two dominant ways of teaching and modeling the Christian's role in society. The first was to separate. The *Separatist* view urged Christians to spend time and money among their own—venturing out too far from the fold could have dire consequences. The goal was to protect oneself from the corrupted nature of the world. Culture was sinful, and our job was to man the fort, fight those who opposed it, and in the pursuit of being faithful, win over as many converts as possible.

The second approach I call the *Cultural* view. Cultural Christians saw the label "Christian" as an important part of their cultural identity. They were generally good people who identified with a form of religious Christianity. In some cases, their connection to faith was no more than a genealogical hand-me-down, something they were born into. For others, their understanding of being Christian meant being good citizens—volunteering their time in schools, hospitals, and neighborhood community groups. They attended church on holidays and for special occasions, but never quite personalized the work of Jesus as the main motivator for the life and work they did. In both cases, the intentions have been good, but missed the holistic mark to which the Gospel calls us forth. Which leads to the larger development at hand.

I've observed, and many of our churches are experiencing, a new, yet historic, way of seeing the faithful approach 21st century culture. Some aren't quite sure what to do with it. Is this just a warmed-over social Gospel, or is something deeper underway? For the Next Christians I describe, taking the Gospel seriously means living within the tension of the two previously stated approaches to the world. They aren't "throwing the baby out with the bathwater." Instead, they are bringing a much-needed gravity to what the Gospel demands from a follower of Christ in the West.

Restorers, as I've come to call them, hold tightly to Jesus' redemptive work on the cross and his resurrection as the main motivator for why they give their lives to bring God's transforming love and renewal into every area of the world. These *restorers* exhibit the mindset, humility, and commitment that seem destined to rejuvenate the momentum of the faith. They have a peculiar way of thinking, being, and doing that is radically different from previous generations. I call them restorers because they envision the world as it was meant to be, and motivated by the Good News, they work toward that vision. They are purposeful about their careers and generous with their time and possessions.

PART

OUTREACH
& EVANGELISM

They don't separate from the world or blend in; rather, they thoughtfully *engage*. Fully aware of the sea change underway, they are optimistic that God is on the move—doing something unique in our time.

The Next Christians sit in your churches. Or maybe left a long time ago because they felt the church didn't "get" them. But rest assured, they haven't left God's church and possess some of the greatest hope for how a new generation's confidence in the Christian faith will be restored.

Sit down with them. Take them to coffee. Listen to their heart. Don't judge their work without understanding their motive. Mentor them, disciple them, and then get out of their way. A new way of being Christian is bursting forth. Their lives are filled with tensions that demand love, discernment, and engagement. When you get the chance, take them under your wing. And when they are ready to fly, unleash them to restore.

10 Things Every New Believer Should Know

Brian Mavis

Recently, a twenty-something friend became a Christian, and he asked me, "What are the top ten things for a new Christian to learn within the first year?" (Apparently, he is a David Letterman fan.)

This is a wise question, because if you are off by a few degrees at the start and you travel that path for a while, you will be off by miles later. I know that from experience. I have been a Christian for more than twenty-five years, and God has had to redirect me on multiple things because of what I mistakenly believed early on about being a Christian. And it is better to learn sooner than later.

So here are the ten things (not necessarily in any particular order) that I thought my new Christian friend should sink down deep into his heart, head, and hands as he travels his first year with Jesus:

1. The one thing that the Bible emphasizes more than us loving God and people is that God loves us.

He loves us first and most. God isn't in heaven plucking a daisy saying, "I love you" when you obey and "I love you not" when you sin. He cannot not love you (Rom. 5:8 and 1 Jn. 4:16).

2. Your motivation to and the purpose of learning, serving, worshipping, giving, reaching, reading, praying, etc. is to grow relationally more in love with God and people (Mt. 22:36–40).

3. You not only are saved by grace, but you grow by it, too.

A common trap for new and growing Christians is trying to clean up their lives without God's help. This is a false equation: The less you sin = the less you need God's grace. You can't sin less and love more without the strength of God's grace.

4. Don't trample all over the Great Commandment (love God, love people) trying to obey the Great Commission (go and make disciples).

New and enthusiastic Christians often do this. Instead, lead people to Jesus by loving people to Jesus (1 Cor. 13:1–3). If they ask why you live the way you do, humbly and simply share with them why you put your hope in Jesus.

5. Love your neighbors—your literal neighbors—the ones you have, not the ones you wish you had.

Do this because you are a Christian, not just because you want them to be Christians.

6. Focus on Jesus, His cross, His resurrection, and His kingdom.

When you confessed Jesus as the living Lord and Messiah, you never said—and will never say—anything more meaningful. Jesus is God with skin. No other "religious leader" (Moses, Buddha, Muhammad) is His equal. They were mere men; Jesus is God who became a man. He is the center and circumference—the hub and rim of all of life and creation. All of the world's greatest gifts—love, life, truth, grace, etc.—have a name. Jesus.

7. God cares about your whole life, not just your "spiritual life."

It is a mistake to think that God is only concerned about a section of your life called "your soul" or "your spirit." God cares about and is to be Lord of all of your life—personal, emotional, social, familial, financial, physical, vocational, sexual, intellectual, and so on.

8. Love other Christians who go to different churches (or no church at all) and who aren't like you.

Unfortunately, many Christians and churches view their "brand" of Christianity as the only true or most true type of Christianity. They may not think they are the only Christians, but they do think they are the best or most right ones. This is a prideful and sinful attitude that grieves Jesus and dismembers His body. Strive for unity in the body of Christ by praying humbly and thankfully for other Christians.

9. Pray with your Bible open.

There are many different spiritual exercises (fasting, solitude, serving, etc.), but the two most important ones are communicating and communing with God through prayer and listening to and learning about God through the Scriptures. Prayerfully read about Jesus (in Matthew, Mark, Luke, and John). Prayerfully read about the beginning of the church in a book called Acts. Prayerfully read some letters written by Christians for Christians—some good ones to start with are James, Philippians, and Ephesians.

10. Find a Christian mentor.

You will need help and encouragement in this journey with Jesus. Ask an older Christian (of the same gender as you) to mentor you. Look for someone who displays the attitudes and actions that were described above. Be a blessing to them in return.

   Christianity is not a list, but a life; it's not a chart, but a charter. But new Christians will learn new things. Some of those things will be true but not important. Some things will be off by degrees that can lead them astray. Other things will be just plain wrong. Help new Christians learn to follow Jesus by being their best at what matters most to Him.

Becoming a Reproducing Church

Dave Ferguson

There is no doubt that we are now seeing a movement of multi-site churches: one out of four megachurches are multi-site, seven of the ten fastest growing churches are multi-site, nine of the ten largest churches are multi-site, and 33 percent of all churches are currently considering the multi-site option. While the multi-site option is very important (and I'm a huge fan and advocate!), it is only a slice of what is happening in the church today. The better term to represent what is happening is the "REPRODUCING CHURCH." We are seeing a renewed desire and focus on reproducing leaders, reproducing small organic churches, reproducing and planting new churches, and efforts toward reproducing whole networks.

For the past eight years here at Community Christian Church, we have been aggressively pursuing this idea of becoming a reproducing church! And it has been the most amazing journey. Here are some of the positive shifts that we have experienced over those eight years:

POSITIVE SHIFT #1: Church Growth to Missional Movement

When you make the transition to being a reproducing church, one of the first things you begin to realize is that it is not about church growth at a single site! It's about accomplishing the Jesus mission: "But you will receive power when the Holy Spirit comes on you; and you will be my witnesses in Jerusalem, in Judea, all of Samaria, and to the ends of the Earth" (Acts 1:8). And to accomplish this mission, we must reproduce over and over and over again! You are a part of a missional movement!

POSITIVE SHIFT #2: Ministry Manager to Spiritual Entrepreneur

In a reproducing church, the job of the staff goes beyond managing ministries to challenge each staff person to think of themselves as a spiritual entrepreneur. John Ciesniewski, who was the campus pastor at our first and largest site in Naperville (2000+ people every weekend), comes to me and says, "Let me start the new site in Shorewood!" So we send him out with 100 people to start a new location, and two years later there are 500+ people attending that location! A ministry manager values programming and recruiting, while the spiritual entrepreneur values new things more than the established, the lost more than the found, and going more than staying.

POSITIVE SHIFT #3: Owning to Leasing, Renting, or Borrowing

Once you leave behind the idea of church growth at a single site and your staff begins to see themselves as spiritual entrepreneurs, you begin to rethink facilities. You realize that you just can't build buildings big enough or fast enough to keep up with what God wants to do! At Community Christian/ NewThing, we have sites and new churches meeting in public schools, Christian schools, colleges, community centers, and clubhouses, in addition to buildings that we own.

POSITIVE SHIFT #4: Reactive to Proactive

The church growth paradigm has your staff managing ministries and reacting to growth. If there are no more spaces in the parking lot, you react and expand the parking lot! If there are no more classrooms for Sunday school space, you react and add an addition to the facility! If the auditorium is 80 percent full, you react and add more seating! But the reproducing church is not reactive; it is proactive...it is all about leader readiness! When you have the right small group leader, you send that person out to start a new small group. When you have the right campus pastor, you send that person out with his/her team to start a new site. When you have the right church planter, you send out that church planter and team to start a brand new church. It's not about parking spaces, available classrooms, or the 80 percent rule; it's about leader readiness.

The Apostle Paul explains to young Timothy how to accomplish the Jesus mission: "And the things you have heard me say in the presence of many witnesses entrust to reliable men who will also be qualified to teach others" (II Timothy 2:2). Paul is describing four generations of reproduction: Paul to Timothy to "reliable men" to "others." That is the reproducing church!

10 Things You Need to Know About Unchurched People

Kem Meyer

1. People don't care about the church database.

Talk about what makes life better for the guest, not about behind-the-scenes software or systems. When you say, "Remember to check-in to F1" or "Sign-in to the database," it communicates that it's all about us and our processes, not about the guest—and they couldn't care less. Keep it simple and focused on the guest. Say, "Remember to check-in to get your name tag," or "door prize" or "food" ... whatever makes the check-in about them. Don't talk about the database or F1.

2. People aren't motivated by your need. They're motivated by theirs.

It's about great things that are good for the guest, not about what you or the church needs. When guests hear, "We really need small group leaders," or "We really need your help with this," they hear desperation and selfishness. Again, this communicates our need; it's all about us. We want to make it about the guest. Instead, say, "Here's a cool opportunity you'll want to hear about," or "You might want to check out this one-of-a-kind experience," or "Come find out the fun ways you can be part of the behind-the-scenes." This makes it about the guest, not us, and it motivates them to act.

PART

6

OUTREACH
& EVANGELISM

3. People don't care about their next step until they know they're valued where they are now.

Encourage next steps, but affirm what people are doing now. When someone hears, "You need to step it up," or "It's time to go deeper," it communicates that they aren't OK where they're at, and they're not as good as they should be. Of course, that's not your intent, but it is the filter many of our guests receive it through. Instead, we can encourage people to "take their next steps." Try "This might be your next step," or "What is your next step?" or "Here are some next step opportunities for you to consider." But remember, everyone's next step looks very different. One person's next step might be to invest more serving time or to volunteer at a higher-impact capacity, but for another, it may be to finish out the evening without leaving early. And each of these next steps is equally important.

4. People don't know who you are, no matter how long you've been around the church.

Introduce yourself—every time. If, by chance, there is just one person in the group that doesn't know you, and you just get up and start talking, it communicates two things: One, it communicates exclusivity (everyone's already in the club except for you), and two, it communicates that you are "all that" in assuming that people automatically know who you are. So take the time to introduce yourself and why you're the one standing in front of the group (if necessary).

5. People multi-task and can't remember squat.

Visually support your verbal announcement to make it attention getting and memorable. It's human nature to tune out the talking head in the front of the room as you look through your purse, write notes to your friend, or mentally run through your to-do list for the week. If you're lucky enough that people are listening to you when you're talking, there is no guarantee they will remember what you said when they walk out of the room and back into their life. Whenever possible, visually support your verbal announcement to grab and hold attention, clarify information, and raise the interest level of your audience. It doesn't have to be fancy or elaborate; you can reinforce your verbal announcement with a printed program, PowerPoint slide, table tent, postcard, basic signage, etc. But remember, don't read directly from your visual aids. They exist as a separate component that reinforces your announcement.

6. People are turned off by lack of preparation.

Prepare to cast vision for the opportunity by rehearsing it so your audience "catches it" within 90 seconds. If it's important enough to announce, then it's important enough to prepare for. Your vision casting should answer these questions: What's so special about this opportunity? Why should I spend my time on it? How is it going to make me and my life better? (In no more than 90 seconds.)

7. People relate when you talk about them or people like them.

Tailor your announcement to your audience. Whenever possible, taking the extra minute to customize a broad message to a specific audience makes a bigger impact. Even if the message doesn't change but you find a way to highlight a unique component for your specific audience, it makes all the difference. For example, if you're talking about the food drop to a group of moms, tell them about the opportunity to include their entire family. Help them see how they can specifically use the information you're sharing.

8. People feel left out and frustrated when you use insiders' language.

Avoid the use of acronyms or insiders' language. Don't assume everyone is in the know, because most people aren't. For example, instead of talking about MC3, talk about GCC's food pantry. Instead of talking about Oasis, talk about your gathering for middle-schoolers. Once people are on the inside, feel free to use the insiders' language. But it's never cool to use it in announcements for large groups, connection events, first-serve opportunities, etc. When you do, you can bet that you're alienating guests. (The specific ministry examples used here are for illustrative purposes only.)

9. People aren't impressed with your theological vocabulary and holy dialect.

Use normal, everyday language. When we use phrases traditionally associated with Christianity, guests either don't get it or will run from us so they don't "catch it." These phrases are weird and scary to guests (actually, to the majority of people): "demonic spirit," "binding the hands of Satan," "forces of evil," and the overuse of an entire list of "blessed" phrases. Keep it simple, keep it real, and avoid over-spiritualizing your conversation.

10. People love stories, not lectures.

Use stories and illustrations whenever possible. Don't just read the information; make it yours. Bring in the human interest. You'll draw people in, spark interest, and engage that personal connection. Then it's no longer a boring announcement but a conversation they don't want to miss.

6 Common Perceptions of Christians

Dan Kimball

Every now and then, we experience an epiphany of some sort that drastically changes our life's course. For me, it's an extremely vivid memory of what happened when I took the time to step outside the busyness of ministry and listen to some college students from what was known to be one of the more anti-Christian campuses in California. It was these "pagan" students who gave me such incredible hope for the Church.

I was leading a young adults' ministry we had recently started at the church I was on staff with at the time, and occasionally during worship gatherings, we showed man-on-the-street video interviews to set up the sermon. For an upcoming message series on evangelism, we decided to go to this college campus to interview students and hear firsthand their thoughts about Christianity. We asked two questions: *"What do you think of when you hear the name 'Jesus'?"* and *"What do you think of when you hear the word 'Christian'?"*

When they answered the first question, the students smiled and their eyes lit up. We heard comments of admiration such as, "Jesus is beautiful," "He is a wise man, like a shaman or a guru," "He came to liberate women." One girl even said, "He was enlightened. I'm on my way to becoming Christian."

What an incredible experience! These students on the very campus I kept hearing was so "pagan" talked about Jesus with great passion. However, when we asked the second question, the mood shifted. We heard things like, "Christians and the Church have messed things up," and "The Church took the teachings of Jesus and turned them into dogmatic rules." One guy said, "Christians don't apply the message of love that Jesus gave," then jokingly added, "They all should be taken out back and shot."

Now, I realize you could quickly dismiss these comments—"They may like some things about Jesus, but they obviously don't know about His judgment and teaching on sin and repentance." That may be true, but what's important, and so haunting, is that these students were so open to Jesus. Yet, they didn't at all like what they have equated and understood to be "Church" and "Christianity." They definitely liked Jesus, but they did not like the Church.

Inside the Church Office Bubble

After those interviews, I did a lot of thinking about the polarity of the responses to the two questions. Something important to note is that only two of the 16 students interviewed even knew any Christians personally. So most of those students had based their impressions of the Church on church leaders they saw in the media or on the more aggressive street evangelists passing out tracts and holding up signs. They hadn't been in a friendship or relationship with a Christian to know any different.

As I thought about it even more, I had another pretty horrifying revelation. I looked at my own life and schedule and realized I, too, wasn't building friendships with those outside the church. My schedule had become consumed with church meetings, and when I wasn't in a meeting, I was in my office or at home preparing for the Sunday sermon. Even my social time was spent only with Christians, usually key leaders in the church. Yes, I had casual acquaintances with non-Christians, like the auto mechanic I saw on occasion. And yes, I was involved in local compassion projects our church did when we went out and fed the homeless. But those weren't actual friendships. I wasn't hanging out with them on a regular basis. I wasn't having them over for dinner or going to movies with them like I did in my friendships with Christians.

And as I talked with numerous other pastors and our church staff, as well as Christians who worked outside the church, I realized that we were all doing the same thing. We were all immersed in this strange Christian Bubble.

No wonder 14 of the 16 students we'd interviewed didn't know any Christians. All the Christians were too busy going to the myriad of church activities, meetings, and Christian concerts that we as church leaders scheduled for them. We were so busy staying in Christian "community" that we had become isolated in our own subculture. It started making sense why those outside the Church got their impressions of Christians primarily from the media and aggressive street evangelists.

What They Think About the Church

When I realized that I had become part of this Christian Bubble and subculture, I knew I had to escape it. But to do so required me to make some significant decisions about my weekly schedule. I re-scheduled my various staff meetings for Mondays and Tuesdays in the church office. But on Wednesdays and Thursdays, I studied for sermons and held other meetings in a local coffeehouse (not Christian) instead of the church office.

Over time, as I built trust with the coffeehouse "regulars," and especially the baristas, I was able to engage in conversations with them and ask a lot of questions. Surprisingly, it wasn't difficult at all to discuss religion, Jesus, and Church. They were actually very willing to talk about their views and beliefs—but it required me to listen instead of doing all the talking (like many of us are used to doing).

Now when I travel, I try to find a local coffeehouse where I can listen, observe, and talk to people. Eventually, the conversation comes around to their thoughts on Jesus and the Church. I hear the same comments everywhere I go. No one ever says, "The Church is after your money," or "The sermons are irrelevant," as you might expect. Rather, the six most common perceptions of the Church among post-Christian 20- and 30-somethings include:

- The Church is an organized religion with a political agenda.
- The Church is judgmental and negative.
- The Church is dominated by males and oppresses females.
- The Church is homophobic.
- The Church arrogantly claims all other religions are wrong.
- The Church is full of fundamentalists who take the whole Bible literally.

While it's essential that we as church leaders thoroughly explore all six of these perceptions and listen to what these emerging voices identify as barriers to putting faith in Jesus and becoming part of a church community, I want to focus on three that seem to be especially prevalent in our current culture— and in my conversations with non-Christians.

Perception No. 1: The "Organized Religion" Barrier

I can't count how many times I've heard "organized religion" used to describe the Church. But there are specific reasons why people see the Church as organized religion and feel they don't need it: *I can relate to God without the structure.* I rarely talk to anyone who's not seeking "God." But emerging generations don't see "church" as the place to explore who He is. Instead, they understand and strongly believe that they can pray to a caring and personal God without being in a church. They also fear the church will try to control how they dress and act and organize their faith the way the leaders think it should be patterned.

The Church is about hierarchy, power, and control with a political agenda. Emerging generations have a strong sense that most churches are all right-winged fundamentalist and everyone in the church is expected to vote a certain way. While we may know that most churches don't have political agendas, the impression on the outside is that most do. *The Church is filled with leaders who function like CEOs and desire power and control.* Think about the titles of your staff—senior pastor, associate pastor, executive pastor, executive assistant—all throwbacks to the '80s when churches began applying business principles to their infrastructure and using some of the business world's language and metaphors. To baby boomers, this made sense. But in our emerging culture, language like this can come across as very unlike Jesus. Alicia, a 24-year-old that I talk with at the local coffeehouse, made this observation: *Church leaders seem to focus more on acting like businessmen, raising funds to build bigger buildings for their own organized religious corporations, than they do on taking the time to teach about social action for the poor and marginalized. I think Jesus would've cared more about raising money for the poor than building yet another mini-mall church.* I fully understand and believe in the need for building new, well-equipped church buildings. But put yourself in an outsider's shoes who doesn't know the hearts of the pastors and church leaders and only sees elaborate buildings on large campuses. So those are three main reasons why "organized religion" is often a barrier to this group. And while you may be inclined to dismiss their reasons because they aren't actually accurate, remember this is how we are being perceived to those on the outside. It's important to listen to and address their perceptions. I believe there are several things we can do to dispel the "organized religion" stereotype.

Communicate how your church is organized and why you practice
your faith in this way, its basis in Scripture, etc. Explain that a church is like
a family and all healthy families do need "organization." Communicating this
and not letting the "organization" strangle the life out of your church is key.

Be aware of your biases. I'm convinced that emerging generations are
open to hearing hard things that go against today's culture. We shouldn't be
afraid to share how Jesus said some strong things about what sin is and the
need for repentance. However, be careful how much your personal biases and
opinions slip into your preaching. Avoid saying, "Jesus thinks this..." when
you really don't know what He thinks, subtly using God and Jesus to back your
opinions about various social or political issues that aren't clear in Scripture.

Evaluate your titles for church leaders and the number of hoops
people have to jump through to meet with them. If you're using titles such
as senior or executive pastor, have you ever paused to ask why and what that
communicates?

Listen to the younger voices. We need to not only make it easier for young
people to be involved in our churches, we also need to show them that they're
needed in all areas—not just isolated in youth and young adult ministries.
They need to know that we respect their opinions on the direction of the entire
church. Make sure your board has one or two younger elders, and set up a
leadership training structure to include people of all ages.

Perception No. 2: Judgmental and Negative

Recently, I was in the airport when I spotted a young man in his 20s wearing
a black T-shirt with the word "INTOLERANT" in large white letters across the
front. Below the word, the shirt read, "Jesus says..." My first thought was *Uh-
oh.* Written across the back of the shirt in big, bold letters was: "Islam is a lie!
Homosexuality is sin! Abortion is murder!" You could see people rolling their
eyes, thinking, *Those Christians...they're pretty messed up and angry.*

The whole experience reminded me of how essential it is to understand that
even if we are expressing truth, *how* we express it is extremely critical. In my
interviews and conversations with post-Christian 20- and 30-somethings, this
kind of negative impression of the Church surfaced repeatedly. Besides T-shirts
like the one I just described, this unflattering perception stems from a gamut
of observations and experiences: Christians protesting with large signs telling
people they're going to hell, seeing Christians on television crediting God for

natural disasters to punish sinners, and being approached by Christians who put people on the defensive and invade their privacy.

Why is it that we in the Church focus on the negatives? Why do people on the outside know us only for what we stand against? Perhaps the main question we should be asking ourselves is how do we address this misperception that's keeping thousands of people from the Church and from Christ?

Teach how and when to talk about sin. I'm convinced that people in emerging generations actually want to be informed about Jesus and His teachings, even the ones that require repentance and change. But our approach makes all the difference. If we go around pointing out people's sins, the reaction will usually be negative. But if we share how we can become more loving and more like Jesus by changing in certain ways, then it's often accepted as a positive thing.

Focus more on what we stand *for*. Those who like Jesus but not the Church see Him as one who stood up for the poor and oppressed. Scripture mandates that His churches follow Christ's instruction to care for "the least of these." By doing so, we also earn the respect of those outside the Church. They are also looking for a church that expresses love and "does not judge" as Jesus taught.

I am part of a team that planted Vintage Faith Church in Santa Cruz, California, and over the past three years, I've noticed a pattern in people when they come to our church for the first few times. More often than not, they aren't asking about the specifics of our doctrinal statement or denominational distinction. Instead, they ask: *What is your church doing for the poor? How are you responding to the AIDS pandemic? How is caring for each other and those in the community a real part of the life of your church? What's the attitude of the church leaders toward those who don't believe everything they do?* Post-Christian emerging generations are watching to see if Jesus' Church is taking the care of the marginalized and being a loving versus negative community as seriously as Jesus did.

Teach your church to break out of the Christian Bubble. As leaders, we can use preaching and the example of our own lives to teach people in our churches that their attitudes impact those outside the Church. Unless we're creating cultures in our church in which people see themselves as missionaries in their day-to-day worlds, unless we're challenging Christians to break out of the Christian Bubble and start listening to the hearts and cries of people around them, only the loudest, often-negative voices in the Church will be heard.

Perception No. 5: "All Other Religions Are Wrong!"

It may sound hard to believe, but I've found that most people of different faiths and those who believe all paths lead to God are actually willing to open the Bible and engage in positive conversations about exclusive passages claiming Jesus is the only way to God. Yet before we can have those conversations, we have to build relationships and understand other faiths well enough to talk about them intelligently and compassionately. So to be effective missionaries in our emerging culture, what do we need to understand about where people are coming from?

Our culture is post-Christian. About a year ago, I watched an episode of a popular TV sitcom in which the family was arguing over which religion a new baby would be dedicated in. The father wanted the baby baptized, the mother wanted a Hindu ceremony, and the grandparents wanted a Jewish bris. In the end, they compromised and did all three.

That episode represents where we are today. In my experience talking to people of other faiths, most aren't steadfastly committed to any one specific religion. Instead, they appreciate all faiths and hold to a more mixed personal belief system. So I don't think emerging generations are all becoming hard-core Buddhists or Wiccans. Most don't study any one specific religion too deeply, but they still have an overall pluralistic belief in God. They are aware of global faiths, and most think everyone should believe what they want to.

We need to develop a basic understanding of world faiths. While we don't have to become experts, as leaders we should acquire at least a basic understanding, so that when we teach in our churches and meet people of other faiths or those who hold a pluralistic view, we can talk intelligently about other religions. A basic knowledge shows people of other faiths that we respect and are interested in their beliefs enough to do some homework. It also helps counter the impression that all Christians are dogmatic and close-minded.

Train your church to understand world faiths. I know of one church that devoted five weeks in its main worship gathering to learning about world religions, even inviting individuals from various faiths to come and be interviewed. Whatever you do, whether it's a weeknight class or a focus in the worship gatherings, the important thing is to train and prepare your people to live with the right heart and attitudes in our pluralistic culture. More than just offering information about other faiths, how we respond to and talk about them in our churches is absolutely critical.

Can your congregation explain why not all paths lead to God? People in emerging generations are open to discussing this truth. But they're looking for conversation, not a lecture, and facts, not rhetoric. Simply quoting a Bible verse and smugly saying, "Case closed," will only alienate them. Despite what you read and hear about our relativistic world, when you logically and gently lay out the facts before someone who's interested in your opinion, there is actually great response. Most people have never really thought about the implications of what it means when they say, "All paths lead to God."

Changing the Perceptions

The more I listen to those outside the Church, the more I realize that we in the Church need to be prepared to respond to these perceptions. Now more than ever before, we should be thinking—and equipping others to think—deeper theologically because people outside the Church are asking questions that require it.

While the comments of the "pagan" students I mentioned at the beginning could be depressing, I think they're actually hopeful. These students are open to Jesus. Perhaps we live in times when we need to refocus our discussion with people on Jesus. But that requires us to break out of the cozy Christian Bubble—or church office—and be in relationship with them. It also requires us to create new understandings of the Church, so that we'll no longer be seen as a negative, judgmental, homophobic, organized religion that oppresses women and thinks all other religions are wrong. Instead, we'll be perceived as a loving and welcoming family that's a positive agent of change, holds women in the highest respect, and has a regard for other beliefs.

PART
6
OUTREACH
& EVANGELISM

I firmly believe that as leaders responsible for teaching our congregants, we can begin to change these perceptions and show post-Christian 20- and 30-somethings that church is vital to their lives. What I think most people mean when they say, "I like Jesus but not the Church," is that they like Jesus, but they don't like what people have turned the Church into. We need to explain that if they truly like Jesus, then they cannot help but also like the Church because it's His Church and His bride. They need the Church because it's the expression of Jesus as His body.

May those who like Jesus but not the Church understand the Jesus of the Bible and the full, wonderful life that His life, death, and resurrection bring. And may they move from liking Jesus to loving Him, and from not liking the Church to loving it.

This article originally appeared in the Mar/Apr 2007 issue of Outreach *magazine. For more outreach features, tips, and fresh ideas, visit Outreachmagazine.com.*

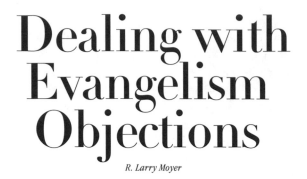

Dealing with Evangelism Objections

R. Larry Moyer

One of the biggest reasons people don't evangelize is their fear of being unable to answer objections. No passage in the entire Bible gives us more help than 2 Timothy 2:23–25.

But avoid foolish and ignorant disputes, knowing that they generate strife. And a servant of the Lord must not quarrel but be gentle to all, able to teach, patient, in humility correcting those who are in opposition, if God perhaps will grant them repentance, so that they may know the truth.

Paul's primary focus was not how to answer objections but how to respond to the one who objects to the message. We can be tempted to be prideful, contentious, and conceited when confronting error. Such an attitude can permeate evangelism and have a negative impact on our relationships with unbelievers. Focusing on the argument rather than the person breeds more of the same thing—more arguments.

In contrast, Paul lists three attributes in verse 24 (NKJV) that we should display when confronted with these arguments. We should be:

- Gentle to all—be approachable in our demeanor.
- Able to teach—sincerely desire to lead people to the truth.
- Patient—restraint in the face of opposition.

Lost people need our patience, not our pride. Those who do not have the Lord need our integrity, not our intellect. They need our maturity, not our immaturity. Lost people do not need to know how much we know. They need to know how much we care.

Verse 25 states we should correct those who oppose us in humility. Why? The answer is so simple we miss it. When someone objects to the gospel message, the problem is ultimately spiritual, not intellectual. They will only come to the truth when God brings them. This is clarified in verse 25 (NKJV):

"If God perhaps will grant them repentance." The word *repentance* means that God might "change their minds."

So Paul's advice to Timothy could be summarized in one sentence. In responding to those who object to the gospel message, use a gentle attitude, not a hostile argument.

Tony Evans: Why God Isn't Blessing the American Church

Brian Orme

Recently, I had the chance to chat with Dr. Tony Evans about his new book, Oneness Embraced. *In this interview, we talk about why God is holding back his blessing on the church, getting rid of our inner racist, and moving toward a deeper unity in the church today.*

ChurchLeaders: In your book *Oneness Embraced***, you say that the church has missed the kingdom. Can you describe what you mean by that statement?**

Tony Evans: Because the church exists for the church, and the church is not supposed to exist for the church. The church is supposed to exist for the kingdom. The kingdom is the comprehensive rule of God over every area of life, but what we have done is we have politics to the world, entertainment to the world, and so we're watching the world take over things that God's kingdom should be over, and the church should be managing and manifesting His kingdom.

CL: You've been in ministry for many years—what made right now the best time to write this book on unity?

TE: Well, when I saw all the chaos in the culture and began to study the importance of unity in the Scripture, it became clear to me that this racial division, cultural division, political division that we're experiencing within the church is blocking God from doing what He wants to do because He's predicated the manifestation of His glory on whether His church is functioning as one or not.

CL: Do you really believe that God's going to postpone His blessing and work in the church because of our lack of unity?

TE: Absolutely. That's a fundamental principle. He does this in a number of places in Scripture: Ephesians 2, Ephesians 3:10. So the oneness issue is not a sideline issue. It's not even a sideline issue in the family. God says that when the husband and wife are divided, tell the husband, "Don't bother to pray." God's not listening (1 Peter 3:7).

So the issue of unity has everything to do with God's absence or presence. God first checks with the church house before He does anything with the White House. We want things to be better in the country, and God can't even get them better on Sunday morning. And one of the major divisions is racial, so in light of all this, I think that this was the time to make a big call for unity.

CL: In *Oneness Embraced,* **you discuss the different agenda between the white church and the African-American church. What do those agendas look like?**

TE: The white church has different priorities, and that's why the white church votes Republican and the black church votes Democrat, because the priorities are different, and pastors don't understand Biblical unity. We're asking God to choose sides when every Christian ought to be Republican lite, Democrat lite, or Independent lite. You ought to be "lite" because the alternate allegiance is to another kingdom. The illustration I use in the book is a football game—there are three teams that are on the field on Sunday: home team, visiting team, and team of officials. The team of officials doesn't belong to either team on the field. They're on the field, but they're not of the field. They belong to the league office. Their job is to represent the interests of the league on the field of play. Sometimes, they're going to be for the home team. Sometimes, they're going to be for the visiting team, but they never take sides, because if they do, they lose credibility with the league office, and the commissioner is no longer on their side.

PART
6
OUTREACH
& EVANGELISM

We've lost the commissioner, the Lord Jesus Christ, because we've taken black sides, white sides, Democratic sides, Republican sides, and He's saying, "You've left the league office," which is the kingdom of God. So what we're saying is that those priorities should be brought under the umbrella of the kingdom. So if the white church is concerned about abortion, they ought to be, because life in the womb is critical, but if the black church is concerned about justice, they ought to be. We ought to be concerned about whole life, not term. We ought to be concerned about life from womb to term, cradle to grave. That's all one item, one issue, but each segment of the church may prioritize a certain element of that issue, thus reducing unity.

CL: Is the popular saying true—that Sunday morning is the most segregated day of the week? What's your reaction to that statement?

TE: Well, there has been progress, but it's still a true statement. You know, people play sports together, they do drugs together, they party together, but when it comes to church, they go different directions. But there's a historical reason for that. The black church was not allowed to participate in mainline Christianity, so it developed its own style and own approach, and that has led in two different directions in terms of the issue of unity.

CL: Do you think all of us have some sense of inner racism?

TE: Oh, I think to some degree, and it may not be black or white. It could be classes. It could be showing up in classism. It could be showing up in culturalism where you reject certain cultures because of how they speak or their background, and you stereotype. So it can be on different levels, of course, and we may not even recognize until we're faced with it. So we may not think we have it.

CL: What are some things that we could do to break through our personal racism?

TE: Well, I think individually, you have to be intentional. You have to say individually, "I am going to get to know some people who are different than me. I want to find out how they think and how they live, and I want to learn. I want to be a learner." And so it's an intentional thing. The same thing with your family. You want to expose differences to your family and your kids. When everybody left the public schools, for example, they went into the private schools, and they basically said, "I just want this one way," and so you must be intentional about that, but be responsible. Obviously, you can't relate to everybody.

CL: Do you think big events are helpful to create racial unity in the church?

TE: Well, I think it's okay to be catalytic, to launch you, but if there's nothing to follow through that keeps you in touch with each other ongoing...I was with Billy Graham in his home, and he was decrying to me that his one regret is that churches would come together across racial lines for his crusade event, but they wouldn't talk to each other after the crusade was over. There needs to be something ongoing. We've got the school initiative; it gives you the ability to keep going because you always have schools, you always have new kids. That means new families in the same community—so you're reaching your community, and if all the churches are doing it, you're reaching your whole neighborhood or city.

CL: Our demographics are fallen—the places we live are already segregated. In some places, churches are trying to work through that separation, but there may be a black church that doesn't have white people in their community or a white church that is surrounded by white people. How should we handle this segregation and work toward unity?

TE: Oh, that's easy. Churches go across the city. They go to mission fields across the city, across the railroad tracks—so you join forces with the minority church, if you're an Anglo church, that's ministering to the downtrodden because it's a poor neighborhood. Now you get to minister to the poor, you get to know your black brothers and sisters in Christ, you get to meet a social need, and you don't have to get on an airplane. You just have to get in the car.

CL: How important do you think it is to actually worship together with each other?

TE: As an event, it's nice. It's just not enough.

CL: Not enough?

TE: It's not enough. It's not near enough. To have an annual reconciliation rally—OK, you'll get some individuals who get to know each other, maybe you'll get a few families who get to know each other—but there will be no real effect long term because there's no real ministry together.

CL: Do you think it's harder for a white church to embrace a black church or a black to embrace a white?

TE: Oh, I think it's much harder for whites to embrace black churches because the issue of interracial dating and marriage is a huge issue, and that issue alone will cause whites not to come and stay, especially when the kids become teenagers.

CL: Well, what's your personal thought on interracial marriage?

TE: It's not an issue in the Bible. In the Bible, the issue is spiritual, you see. You're not to wed a non-believer. The issue is spiritual. Moses married an African woman, and they caused a little chaos, but God straightened everybody out.

CL: Some people might say that racial reconciliation can easily become an agenda that sidetracks the mission of the church. What's your reaction to that thinking?

TE: Biblical reconciliation is the mission of the church because Jesus died to make the two one. So that is the mission of the church; the problem is it hasn't been defined properly. It can become a distraction when it becomes an end in itself, but Biblical reconciliation is not for the purpose of reconciling. It is for the purpose of impact. So you're reconciling for a bigger goal. When that becomes your definition, now you're not sidetracked.

PART

6

OUTREACH
& EVANGELISM

Top 3 Mistakes Churches Make with New Believers

Bob Franquiz

I started Calvary Fellowship in Miami, FL 10 years ago. My goal was to reach people far from God and disciple them to maturity. Here was my problem: after 18 months of ministry, we hadn't seen one person come to know Christ at Calvary. This realization led to serious changes that took place in our church. Let me fast forward eight years to the past 18 months at Calvary. In the past year and a half we've seen more than 1,000 people make first time decisions to follow Jesus. If you count the recommitments to the Lord, that number is closer to 3,000. Whenever I tell that story people ask me, what happened? What changed?

First, let me say that this was not an overnight change. Much like losing weight physically, it was a process that happened as a result of some key decisions we made. What we learned is that just because you reach people, that doesn't mean you have the infrastructure in place to keep people. So while our initial challenge was that we weren't reaching anyone, our next challenge was our lack of being able to keep those we reach. Today, 85 percent of those we reach decide to call Calvary home.

Unfortunately, there's no magic wand to fix this problem. This changes as a result of identifying the reasons new believers fall through the cracks and fixing the problem areas.

So what are the reasons that prevent new believers from "sticking" in your church? I have found that there are several, but three major mistakes that churches make in particular. If you fix these areas, you'll be well on your way to doing what you and I are called to do: reach people and disciple them to maturity in Christ.

Mistake #1: New Believers Aren't Asked to Indicate Their Decision

You cannot follow up with anyone if you aren't aware of the decision they made. The only way to ensure that you can follow with a new believer is to give them the opportunity to indicate their decision. This can be done in several ways. The "Come Forward" invitation became popular because when people came forward they were clearly identifying their decision to follow Jesus. While I cut my teeth in "the come forward" style of evangelism, this is not the method we use. We use a connection card for several reasons. The most important reason being the opportunity for them to put their contact information on the front of the card. This contact information now gives us the ability to implement our follow up system so these new believers can take their first steps of faith.

Mistake #2: New Believers Aren't Given a Clear Next-Step

Many churches get the contact information of new believers yet still find most of them falling though the cracks. The reason they disappear seemingly is because the church has not given the new believer a clear next step. I have found that churches tend to go in one of two directions here:

1. They give too many next steps. They tell the new believer of every opportunity available to them and the new believer is overwhelmed by the options. It's like taking someone to the Cheesecake Factory for the first time. There's so many options, that without a friend to help you decide, you'd probably eat the free bread and go home. New believers have just made the biggest decision of their lives. Quite honestly, many wouldn't be able to even completely explain the decision they just made. That's why the church needs to give them a clear next step.

2. The step is too big. Imagine going to a church for the first time and sitting in an auditorium with 500 other people. You enjoy the message and when the Pastor gives the invitation for people to pray and receive Christ you respond to the call to salvation. A few days later, you get a letter in the mail from the Pastor inviting you to a small group because "that's where the real life change happens." The majority of people won't make the jump. It's not because they're against small groups (they probably don't know what small groups are). The issue is, the jump is too big. An auditorium gives

a person a level of anonymity and freedom. A small group of 12 has
zero anonymity and little freedom to "kick the tires" and investigate their
new found faith.

Mistake #3: New Believers Aren't Valued in the Church's Culture

"It's next to impossible to reach new believers and help them grow to
maturity if your culture says that new believers don't matter. Reaching
new believers and retaining them only happens when your entire church
in alignment with the vision of reaching people and discipling them. I have
learned that while the pulpit steers the ship, the church's culture can lean
the ship in a certain direction. A church culture that doesn't value new
believers cannot help them take steps of faith. The reason is, new believers
don't know the basics, much less the "inside baseball" needed to function
in many churches. So, they move on. Even worse, many times they just stay
home.

Your staff, leaders, volunteers and congregation need to value evangelism
and those who respond. Simply put, you can't help new believers grow without
the help of the congregation. If people aren't inviting their friends, there
won't be much evangelism needed. If those who do invite their friends won't
engage them after the service and help them take next steps, few are "Type A"
enough to seek discipleship without the encouragement of someone else.

If churches are going to be experts at anything, we should be experts in
reaching people and seeing them grow to maturity. I believe that your church
can be the kind of church where people can stay a lifetime because they never
stop growing. But for that happen, we need to be great at following up with
the most precious gifts a church can be given... new converts to Jesus. The
greatest stewardship given to us by God is the stewardship of people. I pray
we gain the skills necessary to overcoming these mistakes and get about the
business of making disciples.

8 Reasons Why People Aren't Coming Back

Greg Atkinson

Today, I'm flying back from San Diego, CA, after doing a secret shopper visit for the Rock Church. As a secret shopper or mystery worshiper of churches around the country, I've found there are some reasons that I will tell a church I would not return for a second visit, and some may be news to you. Whether I'm working with a church plant of 60 people or a mega-church of more than 15,000, some things are universal and should be present regardless of church size. Throughout this article, we'll look at actions and areas every church needs to address.

The Front Door

Before a guest ever steps foot on your church's physical campus, he or she has probably already checked out your church website. What every church should have clearly visible on their homepage is a section or button for first-time guests. Once clicked on, this should take you to a page that addresses FAQs, service times, directions, parking instructions (Is there a side of the building that is better to park on if one has kids?), what to expect (upbeat music and relevant, practical, Biblical preaching in a come as you are atmosphere, etc.), what to wear (Are jeans okay? Are shorts okay?), and encouragement for them to be sure to stop by Guest Central or your church's information booth to pick up a first-time guest packet.

What Stinks?

It's important that no church ever underestimates the sense of smell. While sight is the strongest sense for short-term memory, the sense of smell is the strongest and most vivid for long-term memories. If you've ever smelled something and had memories you hadn't thought of in years come flooding back, that's your sense of smell in action. Every church has the potential for positive or negative smells. Mold is a bad smell. Coffee is a good smell. Bleach is a bad smell. Citrus is a good smell. Many churches have restrooms that are disgusting and smell bad. This lack of attention to detail can be costly and discourage many from ever returning. As best you can, try to walk into the lobby or entrance of your church with a new nose.

Park Here

One of Tim Stevens' three "growth lids" that he thinks every growing church should have is someone who is constantly watching the parking. Tim says, "This is why Visitor Parking is so crucial. If it's difficult for newcomers to go to your church, they won't go." Some would argue that guests want to remain anonymous and don't want special parking. Of course, some want to go unnoticed and will choose to park in regular parking (a minority), but for the rest of newcomers, they are appreciative of a close parking space; it's a kind gesture in an already intimidating and nerve-racking experience of attending a church for the first time, especially a large one with a huge campus.

This Way, Parents

One way to assure guests will not return is to have a confusing, long, or hard to find process for getting their kids registered and in the right classroom. Wise churches have signs for first-time guest kids' check-in and make the process quick and painless. Regular attendees may know to go up to the check-in kiosk and enter their phone number or swipe their card, but guests will be clueless and need a manned station that is clearly marked for guests and have a volunteer walk them through the registration. Then have that person or another helper walk you to your kid's class, explaining what will be going on and how to go about picking their kids back up. If they must have a sticker with corresponding numbers on it to get their kids, this needs to be explained to them. Signage for the kids check-in should start in the entryway of the guest parking. Do not assume people know where to go once they enter the building.

Give It Away

Something subtle but powerful is a church that has a generous spirit. Chris Hodges at Church of the Highlands in Birmingham, AL, is big on this. They have a coffee shop, but they also have a designated area where people can get free coffee and not pay anything. They also give away their message CDs. Too many churches charge for everything and wonder why no one buys CDs of the message. If you want to bless people and create a generous spirit throughout your church, give away free coffee and message CDs (and other surprises throughout the year). Chris Hodges will have ice cream trucks pull up outside the church doors and give away free ice cream to congregants leaving on a hot, summer day.

Security Counts

One issue that is huge to a secret shopper and visiting families is security. If a parent is worried about their child's safety, they will not enjoy the service and will likely not return. A children's classroom must be clean, safe, and secure. Security also includes the check-out process. If anyone can walk into a classroom and pick up a kid, you're asking for trouble and will turn off potential newcomers. It's important that your kids' volunteers are trained well and know to ask for the parent's sticker when picking up their kids. This is vital and goes a long way to ensuring a tragedy doesn't occur and a parent has peace of mind.

The Visible Pastor

Accessibility of the senior pastor is another subtle and powerful statement of a church. Even pastors of the largest churches in America make an intentional and strategic effort to be seen, greeted, and hugged after a service. They may have a bodyguard present for security reasons, but they are available and willing to pray with people that need to speak to their pastor. Some churches have a designated "Guest Central," like Steve Stroope at Lake Pointe in Rockwall, TX, or Brady Boyd at New Life in Colorado Springs. Some have a "Meet and Greet" like Charles Hill in Utah. Some pastors stand down at the altar and meet and pray with people like Kevin Myers at 12Stone in Atlanta. Some walk around the campus shaking hands like Don Wilson at Christ's Church of the Valley in Phoenix. Erwin McManus at Mosaic LA has an "After Party," at which the pastor is present and available to meet with newcomers. This, especially in a large church, goes a long way toward countering the rock star or unavailable pastor stigma that so many guests walk into the church expecting.

Finish Strong

It's simply not enough for greeters and parking lot attendants to say "Hello" or "Welcome" when one walks into their church. To go to another level, have your first impressions team stationed at their posts when the service ends to say, "Goodbye" or "Have a nice week." This goes a long way to wrapping a bow around the entire morning experience and will send them off with a lasting positive impression.

Do these eight things and you'll see a greater return and higher percentage of second- and third-time guests.

When Are People Most Willing to Hear About Your Church?

LifeWay Research finds people are most willing to hear about a local congregation through a family member (63 percent) and through a friend or neighbor from the church (56 percent). Less than half are open to receive information about a church any other way. Yet, 48 percent of Americans are willing to receive information about a local congregation through an informative ad in the newspaper, 46 percent through an outdoor sign or billboard, and 45 percent through letters mailed to the home. As is commonly thought, Americans are most likely to be open to consider matters of faith during the Christmas (47 percent) and Easter seasons (38 percent) as well as after a major national crisis such as 9/11 (38 percent). They are most likely to be open to invitations from non-denominational churches and least open to invitations from Mormons. Thirty-three percent would read a Bible as their likely first response if they wanted more information about God. Only 19 percent would attend a church service, and 10 percent would talk to a Christian friend.

Christian Post 3/26/09

5 Reasons Why You Should Twitter in Church

Scott Williams

Thou shall not Twitter in church...says who?

I haven't seen that anywhere in the Bible. I have seen Twitter in the Bible: "Like a swallow, like a crane, so I twitter..." Isaiah 38:14 NASB

In all seriousness, there are many people that believe you shouldn't Twitter in church. As a pastor, I personally say, "Get your tweet on!" As a matter of fact, I say, "Tweet and tweet often!"

Many times, "church people" can look at particular methodology and technology as a negative thing. Technology is basically neutral; it's what you do with it that allows it to have positive or negative implications. I know there are some varying opinions about texting and utilizing social media during church. Personally, I use the YouVersion Bible app on my iPhone during church, and it has this great option of sharing Scripture instantly with the Twitter world. Not only can you share Scripture with YouVersion, but also any person sitting in any church service around the globe can share thoughts, points, and notes from sermons as they are happening.

Today, we live in a more shared world than ever as information access and people connectedness just happens. The beauty of this world is that people can engage with God, engage with their past, and share pieces of that engagement with the world, all at the same time. There are entire real, living, breathing online church services where online congregants share information throughout their service. These services are just as real and God encountering as a physical building. Again, I say, "Tweet and tweet often!"

Here are five reasons to Twitter during church:

1. You have the opportunity to be a real-time extension of your pastor's voice while he/she is communicating God's word. You and your pastor

PART

6

OUTREACH
& EVANGELISM

can do some tag-team teaching while you are being fed all at the same time.

2. If the pastor shares something that moves you, inspires you, or changes your life, there is a good chance it will have the same impact on the lives of some of your Twitter followers as well. Here is a tweet awhile back from Pastor Steven Furtick: "Preaching recently, I noticed the crowd was too busy tweeting to verbally respond. Click-clack is the new amen."

3. When Jesus said, "Go into all the world and preach the Gospel..." *all the world* applies to the Internet world as well as the Twitter world. Do your part by going into all the Twitter world, tweeting the Good News.

4. You will have a stored database of your compelling thoughts and notes from your favorite sermons. Use a #hashtag to keep up with the information that you share.

5. Many times, people suffer from (SADD) Sermon Attention Deficit Disorder. So instead of just wandering off into space, simply wander off into the space of the World Wide Web. It's better use of your time Twittering great thoughts, instead of drawing on the back of offering envelops.

Some people, including pastors, get upset and complain about these new age people being a distraction when they are using their mobile phone Bible and Twittering in church. I think doodling on the offering envelopes is more distracting...Hmm, I have not seen a big push to remove those offering envelopes from the church.

Thou shall Twitter in church. Remember, God's omnipresence applies to Twitter as well. Get your tweet on!

*If those who
prepare for leadership
are looking for the safe place, who
will lead the church into
the dangerous places?*

—Erwin McManus

7 Outreach Suggestions for Churches Meeting in Schools

Ron Edmondson

I get lots of e-mails asking how we do certain things as a church. I usually figure that when several people are asking the same question, it represents a larger audience wanting to know the same answers. This article is an example of that thought.

   Recently, I was asked what suggestions I have for a church planning to start meeting in a school facility. Grace Community Church has met in our high school for three years now, and it has been a blessing to us and the school, from feedback I have received. Here are seven suggestions for churches meeting in a school. Most of these are more philosophy than actions, but with them as our paradigm, it helps direct our actions.

Grow volunteers.

Being in a borrowed facility forces the church to rely on lots of volunteer labor to set up and tear down each week. This can be stressful on people, but it also creates an opportunity to raise up new volunteer leadership. Our church would never happen without the countless hours of donated time, but in the process, volunteers have sharpened their leadership skills and realized the joy of investing in God's Kingdom and seeing the results it brings.

Love the school.

We support the school we are in more than just on Sunday morning. We support their activities, we attend their ballgames, and we try to meet needs the school has as we are made aware of them.

Realize it's not a rental situation.

You may be paying rent, but more than renting a space, you are borrowing a facility that has another intended purpose. We realize that the school building's primary purpose is to educate children during the week. We know we are an added burden to the facility. We see it as a win/win for our school, but we don't take it for granted that we are secondary in importance at the school.

Be a blessing.

At the end of our time in the school, whenever that may come, our goal is that we will actually be missed by the school…and not just for the money we bring to the table. We have as a goal to be a blessing to the school. With that as a goal and mindset, it forces us to find ways to help the school outside of the money we pay for usage.

Don't interrupt school.

We respect the facility as a place for education, and we never try to use our influence at the school to trump a school activity. We know we are a secondary use so we gladly bow out if a school situation arises. Our school doesn't do much on Sundays, and if it did, that may create problems, but the few times there has been a Sunday conflict, we have tried to be accommodating to the school's needs more than our own. We would rather be inconvenienced than for them to be because of us.

View your money as a contribution.

It changes the perspective of our staff and key leaders when we see our money going to make the education process better, not just as a rental line item on our income statement. Schools are always struggling to fund adequate resources, and we think our money helps. That makes writing checks so much more pleasant!

Acknowledge critical players.

The relationships you have with school officials are critical to making any agreement work. There are some people who make meeting in a school a positive or negative experience. That may include school district officials, the school administration, teachers, and custodians. We especially are sensitive to the teachers who teach in areas where we meet in the school because we realize we are sharing space with them. Our experience is that the custodians play a large role in our success in the school, so we try to respect and show appreciation to them.

PART

6

OUTREACH
& EVANGELISM

Are Mass Evangelism Efforts Effective?

R. Larry Moyer

Some people question the value of mass evangelism efforts and even wonder if they don't do more harm than good. There are several answers to that question but the bottom line is "It depends how they're done."

Mass evangelism efforts that are most effective are those that are bathed in prayer, the gospel is made crystal clear, and someone begins to disciple new converts once a week for eight weeks, one-on-one. When those things are done, I could testify to many mass evangelism efforts that have been very effective. Unfortunately though, many times they are not characterized by the above three that I just mentioned. For example, often the gospel is not presented clearly, and a person can become a Pharisee instead of a Christian. In other words, he's gone through all kinds of emotions but hasn't actually come to Christ, and that makes him harder to reach. Good follow-up for mass evangelism not only involves following up with those who have come to Christ but also following up with those that did not trust Christ during the event.

Mass evangelism efforts that are the most effective are based on relationships with people that have already been introduced to spiritual things and then someone says to them, "Would you come hear the speaker—I think you'll enjoy him." In other words, personal evangelism done right aids mass evangelism, and mass evangelism done right aids personal evangelism. I mentioned the latter because sometimes even if people don't come to Christ, the gospel is introduced, and that allows for a one-on-one discussion later.

None of that changes the fact though that a variety of factors has to be examined. Cost can be one of them. It's important that mass evangelism is done well and carefully thought through. Then the dollars spent are worth it, not only in terms of people coming to Christ but also seed that is sown that generates discussions later.

With all that said, it continues to be realized that most people come to Christ through one-to-one encounters. That's why we need to train people how to build relationships with non-Christians, turn conversations into spiritual things, and introduce people to Christ. There are even some areas where mass evangelism efforts are not allowed or possible. The more people we have trained to share Christ one to one, the more people we will see come to the Savior.

We should not throw out either mass evangelism or personal evangelism. Instead, we should seek to do both well in a way that honors both God and the teachings in Scripture. When done right, they support one another.

PART

6

OUTREACH
& EVANGELISM

4 Keys to Creating an Irresistible Church

Greg Atkinson

Let me preface what I'm about to write by saying that basic and foundational things like prayer, discipleship, and evangelism (having an externally-focused church as I've stated before) are all a given. Each church should take the Great Commission seriously and have an emphasis on the "Go" and on the "make disciples." I start everything with prayer, and so please know that what I'm about to discuss is with the above stated things as must-haves and what I consider foundational to a healthy church.

With that being said, let me share with you the big four that I look for when I visit a church, secret shop a church, or consult with a church. As the title says and Scriptures encourage us—we should compel them to come in. The big four that I look for when I do a secret shopper are First Impressions, Children's, Security, and Worship. Yes, worship is last, and I have listed them in the order that I weigh them.

As many studies have shown us, people make up their mind whether or not they will return long before the worship service and especially the sermon. Most visitors will know in the first 10 minutes if they will return to your church.

First Impressions

Let's start with what I consider to be the most crucial of all ministries at a church. Whether you call it First Impressions, Hospitality, or Guest Relations—it matters and is paramount to breaking down walls and making guests feel welcome at your church.

"You've got 10 minutes. Somewhere between the parking lot and the children's center, the ten minutes pass…They should know they matter to us before they hear how much they matter to God," said Mark Waltz, Granger.

Something I tell all the churches I work with is: "You must be strategic and intentional about breaking down any barriers of intimidation. You must be strategic and intentional about creating warm, welcoming environments."

Now, I could spend an entire series on just first impressions. This is everything from your online presence (social media like Twitter, Facebook—as well as your website). For example, I did a secret shopper this past weekend, and I had created 13 pages in my report on just online presence before I ever left to attend their physical campus.

Once one comes to your physical campus, the real fun begins. First impressions then includes the parking lot, greeters, ushers, and people that greet you at your church's Welcome or Information Booth. First impressions also includes things like smell (your church may stink), signage (your church may be intimidating and confusing for new people), and how your facility is kept up and maintained. All these things play subtle parts in a guest's first impression of your church and their subconscious.

Children's Ministry

Maybe I'm biased because I'm 35 and have three elementary school-aged kids, but I believe in having a strong and attractive children's ministry. A lot of churches target parents in their mid-twenties to mid-forties, and the best way to compel them is to offer a children's ministry so dynamic that kids drag their parents to church.

Let me suggest that you make children's ministry a priority. I've seen churches that spent millions on their worship center and have dumpy children's facilities. I'd never return with my family to churches like that. Show me—show your community that kids are important and that you care about partnering with parents to be a help in their spiritual growth. We all know the statistics on the likelihood of people accepting Christ after age 18. Student ministries (children's through youth) are vital to fulfilling the Great Commission.

Security

This is probably the most overlooked part of most churches I visit. Most church leaders have never sat down and intentionally and strategically thought through how and why they do security. I wish this wasn't important and that you didn't have to have some kind of security presence, but unfortunately, that's not the case. If there had only been one church shooting, that would be enough. I'm sad to say that several churches have experienced the tragedy of shootings—not to mention molestation and kidnapping.

Bottom line: If I'm worried about my kids' safety, I'm not going to enjoy the worship service, and I will miss what God wants to do in my heart through the experience of corporate worship.

Security includes everything from people's cars in the parking lot, to the safety of infants in the nursery, to children's facilities, check-in and check-out procedures, mentally ill people acting out in the middle of a service, and protecting the senior pastor. Every great church with a well-known senior pastor that I've worked with had a bodyguard standing next to the pastor for his protection. This is not for show or something for rock stars—this is something real and needed to protect that man of God from people that mean to do him harm. When you stand for truth and speak against sin, you become a target for many that live in darkness. If you haven't already, think through every aspect of security in your organization. I just returned from a church in California that had security people covering every single entrance and exit to their children's ministry. It was a beautiful thing to see and made me feel safe as a parent.

Attractional Worship

I know there's a lot of discussion and debate about whether a church should be attractional or missional. I've talked extensively about it all over the country. I'm a both-and person and like for a church to seek to be both, but when it comes to the corporate worship service—I look for an attractional model. Again: COMPEL them to come in. Blow away your people and your community with excellence and an environment that allows the Holy Spirit of God to move.

I never got over Sally Morgenthaler's book *Worship Evangelism*. I think lost people can be moved by witnessing genuine and authentic worship happening. I also know God moves through the preaching of His Word. Please know I'm not talking to just large churches. I work with large churches, but my home church in Georgia is a church of 350 people. They do things with excellence, and for a small church, blow me away each week that I'm home.

Regardless of what size church you are, you should think through worship flow, song selection, authenticity, communication/preaching, and every aspect of what you want people to experience each week when you gather. Are sound, video, and lights important? I think so, but you don't have to have the best of the best to see God move. One of the most special and memorable services we did at Bent Tree when I was there was have a stripped down music set with no technology.

Whether you're in a school, movie theater, gym, or worship center—you can seek to create an environment where people encounter the Living God.

Please know these are not Biblical laws or Scriptural requirements. These are just four keys that I look for when I visit a church, and I've found over the years that the churches that do these four things well see God bless their church in amazing ways. Think through each as a team and prayerfully consider how you can do each to the best of your ability.

PART

7

YOUTH
& FAMILY

We don't need to make Jesus amazing; He already is.

—*Doug Fields*

PART

1

PERSONAL
GROWTH &
LEADERSHIP

PART

2

CHURCH
LEADERSHIP

PART

3

PREACHING
& TEACHING

PART

4

CHURCH
GROWTH

PART

5

WORSHIP
& CREATIVE

PART

6

OUTREACH
& EVANGELISM

PART

7

YOUTH
& FAMILY

PART

8

SMALL GROUP
& DISCIPLE

PART

9

PERSONAL
GROWTH
& LEADERSHIP

Teen Evangelism: Motivate Your Students to Share Their Faith

Greg Stier

When the teens in your youth ministry begin to share their faith, they will pray harder and worship louder. Many of them will read the Bible more diligently and walk in dependence on God more willingly. Why? Because the social stigma associated with evangelism helps teenagers to heighten their spiritual senses and deepen their spiritual thirst. There's something about the threat of losing friendships, popularity, and reputation that can help to trigger spiritual growth like nothing else. The act of evangelism is a visible, visceral way for Christian teenagers to pick up their cross, die to themselves, and follow Jesus.

If evangelism can help to spur spiritual growth in our teens, then how do we get them doing more of it? Here are three practical ways:

1. Make prayer for the lost a genuine priority.

If you want to see evangelism heat up in the lives of your teenagers, then their prayers for the lost must come to a boil. You can help facilitate this level of soul supplication in a variety of ways. You can include prayer for your teenagers' unreached friends as a key part of your weekly youth group meetings. Perhaps you can do a prayer retreat with your teens where you teach on prayer and then pray together as a youth group. During the prayer times, you can show them how to intercede to God on behalf of the lost souls of their friends with intensity and passion.

Just like Jesus taught his disciples to pray, you can teach yours. Remember that deep, soul-wrenching prayer can stoke the fire of evangelism in your heart and in theirs in unparalleled ways.

2. Inspire them to share their faith.

There are many powerful motivations for teens to share their faith with their friends. Among these motivations is the reality that when their friends put their faith in Christ, their sins will be forgiven, their purpose will become clear, and their eternal destination will become sure.

Remind your teens of all the good that will happen when their friends put their faith in Jesus. Also, remind them of what is at stake if they don't hear and respond to the gospel message. These twin realities will motivate your teens to share the gospel sooner rather than later.

3. Set yourself on fire.

If we dare to deploy teens to risk everything dear to them by reaching their friends at school, then we must be willing to risk as well. Getting our teens on fire for evangelism starts with setting ourselves ablaze. As John Wesley used to say, "When I preach, I set myself on fire, and people come to watch me burn." May your teens witness such an inferno in your heart and life that it can't help but ignite that same passion in them. May the fire that consumes you begin to consume them.

Practical Ways to Make Your Ministry Family-Oriented

Chris Folmsbee

Below are nine considerations youth workers might employ to provide a more family-oriented approach to youth ministry.

1. See the bigger picture and start younger.

A more family-oriented ministry cannot happen unless we work hard to start when our youth are children. This requires youth workers to have a broader perspective and definition of youth ministry and to be intentional about creating harmony with the church's work with children.

2. Develop and commit to a theology of formation.

A youth ministry that does not have a theology of formation often lacks the ability to see how others in the church might help them guide students into spiritual formation for the mission of God. I'm not referring to a programming structure as much as I am a pathway for developing teens and families toward becoming more like Jesus. Your *programs* can help this, but they can't *do* this. You need a theology of formation to guide your efforts.

3. Understand family systems.

Not every youth worker needs a degree in sociology or psychology. However, every youth worker does need to seek out and develop a working knowledge of how healthy families function and then help other families embrace those traits.

4. Lead by listening.

Listen well. How aware are you of the various needs your families have? There will be many, and they will be unique, and you may need to ask.

5. Resource families with tools and practices.

One of the easiest yet most helpful things you can do is provide tools and practices for families to use to engage spiritual formation. For example, my family has a prayer cube that we use before each meal. It was given to me by my youth pastor years ago.

6. Schedule fewer events/services and encourage the families in your faith community to use the extra time for family gatherings.

You may want to offer suggestions for families of ways to use their time. My experience has been that families want to do this but don't know what to do to engage all their children, who may be at various age levels.

7. Develop a team of parents who represent various families from various backgrounds.

Let families speak into your ministry. This will help ensure that you are engaging families right where they are. This is hard to do for many reasons, one of which is age. If you are a younger, less experienced youth worker, you may want to delegate the leadership and coordination of this team to a more mature staff person or volunteer while you sit back and learn.

8. Create opportunities for the youth and families to experience the youth ministry together.

This does not have to be elaborate or even often. However, your effort and willingness to do this will most likely be viewed by parents as helpful. Most will be grateful.

9. If you have a family yourself, lead your own family well, and others will learn from you.

I know too many youth workers whose families come after the youth ministry. That sucks. Lead your family well and model family formation, and you will help others do the same.

*If you're in anything
and never wanted to quit it,
you're not in much.*

—*T. D. Jakes*

3 Rules for Youth Leaders and Facebook

Josh Griffin

We love that our volunteers are on Twitter and Facebook! It seems like everyone is enjoying the benefits of social networking these days—so it shouldn't come as a surprise that your volunteers are interested or already involved for sure. Most use the technology to their groups' benefit, though from time to time, we've had to have conversations and consider removing volunteers for what they put online. At our training this week, I'm going to ask our leaders to apply these three simple guidelines when updating social networks:

Remember, what you post is public.

Here's the big deal—a joke that is funny between a few friends might not be funny at all out of context or in the harsh light of public view. Remember that everything you post—picture, status update, or essay—becomes completely public the second you click Share. You can never really take it back once it's out there, so be wise and use discernment with everything you post.

Remember, what you post influences students.

Your students are checking out your profile. They look up to you. They are eager to make a connection with you, and since they're always on Facebook, they'll almost always see what you post. But it is so much more than just seeing; what you say, what you value, what you show yourself doing...it all influences students—the good, bad, and ugly. When you give an inch, they may take it a mile. Of course, it works the other way as well. When you use social media positively, it can have a significant encouraging influence on them, too.

235

Remember, what you post is a reflection on your student ministry/church.

Your character and faith is reflected in every post that you make, so if you are doubtful about something, here's a simple rule to follow: DON'T POST IT. Just like behavior on a youth ministry trip is a reflection on the church and student ministry, know that what you post adds to or detracts from the reputation of the church and ministry...and ultimately Christ.

9 Mistakes Made by Youth Pastors

Jeremy Zach

Here are the nine most common mistakes made by both veteran and rookie youth pastors:

1. Bad budgeting with youth events

Youth pastors aren't typically known for their extreme wisdom in handling money. We find it hard to turn a profit on our events. If you're a youth pastor who is great at accounting, please contact me. For the rest of us, we need to work diligently on our money-management skills.

2. Not taking their critics seriously

Nine out of ten times, if someone does not like us or our youth ministry strategy, we write them off. We get very angry at them and tend to say a lot of un-Christian words about their lazy student and their bad parenting. Instead, we should give them a call and ask them "why" they don't like us. This doesn't always work but it's important to engage your critics.

3. Become a friend, not a leader

Students don't need anymore "friends." They don't want your friendship. They need more adults passionately following Jesus. Sometimes, youth pastors reverse the greatest commandment: Love People, Love God.

4. Falling in love with their mission statement

Students don't really care about your fancy mission statement. So, don't marry your mission statement—minister to your students.

5. Neglecting the value of church

Many youth pastors alienate their youth ministry from church. It is really hard working in the bigger church. It is so much easier doing things by ourselves. Things get done quicker and more efficiently. However, Scripture clearly commands the youth ministry department to get along with big church.

6. Underestimating adult leader recruitment

Youth pastors like to fly solo. Why waste so much energy developing leaders? Besides, it's difficult hearing "no" from someone we know will be a great youth leader. My advice: keep asking and praying God brings you more leaders.

7. Not pursuing a relationship with the senior pastor

Our assumption: Senior pastors do not have time for youth pastors, so why should youth pastors pursue a relationship? We are the children, so why should we seek a relationship with our parents? Well... because it will drastically help at a personal-connection level with your boss and establish a synergy within the staff.

8. Neglecting the school and the community

Youth ministries enjoy staying in-house. A youth ministry can become a lot more complacent when it is inward focused. Give a call up to your local school and ask them what their needs are. Your students spend more time on the school campus than they do on your church campus. If your students are spending more time on your church campus, you have bigger problems to worry about.

9. Failing to grow and mature

Many youth pastors are not feeding their soul. Some youth pastors jump from job to job wondering why they have the same problems with church. Honestly, youth pastors typically come with a lot of personal baggage. Constantly refining and developing your character is the best investment as a youth pastor. We need to take our sanctification process seriously.

5 Ways to Avoid Becoming Irrelevant to Teens

Terrace Crawford

Do you feel like your ministry is becoming irrelevant to teenagers? Are you looking for creative ways to get out of "that rut?" Maybe this will help.

Get Connected to Teens.

I speak to a number of youth pastors each and every week. I'm always asking them questions about their ministry and how they do what they do. I'm very surprised by the number of them that seem to be disconnected from teens throughout the week. I believe one of the things that could cause you to become irrelevant to teens is by being disconnected from them. If you only talk to them on Sunday, you need to make a change. I encourage you to get in their world. Show up on their turf!

Action item: Meet with a couple of students each week. Be intentional about getting connected to your students. Grab a cup of coffee, meet them for ice cream, or have lunch with them at school.

Reinvent Your Events.

Another thing I've noticed in my conversations with youth ministers is how they seem to duplicate the same things every year in their ministry. The same camp, the same missions project, and the same events. Why is this? I understand we want some things to become a tradition or we feel that certain events will create momentum ... but there are too many things available to us as leaders for us to be repeating everything we did last year. Just because it worked last year doesn't mean it will work next year.

Action item: Spend a day (or even a half a day) evaluating what events you are passionate about. Then determine which ones you could scrap and allow for new adventures or projects.

Ask Questions!

When I'm around students, I am always asking questions. Often, getting a response from them is like pulling teeth...but I don't give up. I ask questions like "What music do you enjoy?" "What do you and your friends like to do?" "What do you really like about what we do?" Sometimes, their responses give me great insight into determining how we should shape our ministry. Don't be afraid to ask questions...and prepare yourself for their honesty!

Action item: Come up with some excellent ice-breaker questions and keep them handy.

Think Outside the Box.

Making some changes or tweaking things just a bit can make things really interesting. For example: we have a number of students who love to longboard. They will often bring them to church and ride before and after our services. One day, I decided to tell our Student Leadership Team to promote a "Bring Your Longboard to Church Day." We had a lot of guests show up with longboard in hand that day! Things like this have helped us think outside the box about what we are doing in order to be more effective...and yes, more relevant to teens.

Action item: Try anything once. Don't be afraid to tweak something just for test purposes. Then debrief it with your leadership team and determine if you should try it again.

Let Teens Take Over.

We have students leading in a lot of different areas in our ministry, but last fall when I felt the Lord leading me to step away from the mic and allow teens to completely takeover, I was skeptical. I took a few days and prayed over this idea. Then, in January, we began a series called "STORY" and let students, who were already greeting and leading games and worship, take the mic, too! Teenagers were encouraged to tell their stories of how God had worked in their lives. God used this in many ways: It became our longest running series ever (three months!), students invited their friends, and God used it to create a safe community where teens are comfortable sharing.

Action item: Evaluate your ministry and question what areas you might give up control to youth. Then provide coaching to students who take you up on the offer and want to lead.

Why Teenagers Are Not the Church of Tomorrow

Greg Stier

Did you ever notice that throughout Scripture God seems somewhat determined when it comes to using young people to accomplish some of his most significant purposes? He used a teenaged Jewish girl named Esther to save a nation from certain destruction. He used Josiah, the boy king, to launch a national revival. He used a shepherd boy named David to defeat a giant and trigger a significant military victory. He used Jeremiah, the young prophet, to bring down his wrath on a disobedient nation.

In Jeremiah 1:6–7 NKJV, the young prophet wrote about his own inhibitions about God using him in such a significant way at such a young age, *"'Ah, Lord GOD! Behold, I cannot speak, for I am a youth.' But the Lord said to me: 'Do not say, "I am a youth." For you shall go to all to whom I send you, and whatever I command you, you shall speak.'"*

But it's not just in the Bible where we see this divine propensity toward using the "way too young;" we also see it in church history.

During the first Great Awakening in the United States, Jonathan Edwards wrote, *"The Revival has been chiefly amongst the young."* In 1859 during the Great Welch Revival, one witness reported, *"One of the most striking characteristics of the movement was its effect on young people and even on children. The youth of our congregations are nearly all the subjects of deep religious impressions. Very young people...children from 10 to 14 years of age, gather together to hold prayer meetings, and pray very fervently. In many places, the young people hold a prayer meeting of their own, and these sometimes proved instrumental in bringing the powerful influences of the revival to that particular locality. The majority of all converts of the revival...were young people."*

Why has God always seemed to use the really young or the really old or the really poor or the really unlikely? The answer seems to be hidden away in 1

Corinthians 1:26–29 NIV, *"Brothers and sisters, think of what you were when you were called. Not many of you were wise by human standards; not many were influential; not many were of noble birth. But God chose the foolish things of the world to shame the wise; God chose the weak things of the world to shame the strong. God chose the lowly things of this world and the despised things—and the things that are not—to nullify the things that are, so that no one may boast before him."*

What does all of this have to do with the teenagers in your world and your church? Simply this: If God has a propensity to choose to use the young to advance his message and mission, then we should, too!

We all know that the vast majority of people who come to Christ do so before the age of 18, so why aren't we investing more to reach that demographic? Not only are they more open, but they are more able to spread the gospel. Teenagers can take the gospel further faster than adults. The average teenager has *at least* 100 online and face-to-face friends and has hundreds of times more influence on those friends than a stranger has!

If teenagers can be inspired, equipped, and unleashed to share the gospel in a clear and compelling way, our communities can be reached for Christ. But you must be willing to call them and coach them. You must be willing to pray for and push them.

Teenagers are NOT the church of tomorrow, but the church of today. As soon as they believe in Christ, they are baptized by the Holy Spirit into the body of Christ and are given a gift to use and a message to preach. They don't become members of the church when they can tithe big and serve on a committee, but when they believe in Jesus. The future is not when these teenagers *grow up*. The future is when these teenagers *show up*.

The future is now!

What All Youth Pastors Wish Their Senior Pastor Knew

Perry Noble

I did some reflecting this past weekend of the time I spent in youth ministry...and the success and failures that I experienced. I have come up with the following list of things that I believe all youth pastors wish they could tell their senior pastor—here we go...

1. Pray for Me...And Tell Me That You Are Doing So!

There is something about a senior pastor that will pray over the area of youth ministry in the church that he serves. And there is something INCREDIBLE when a youth pastor is told by the pastor that he is being prayed for. I admit that I do not do this nearly enough...but that is changing after this week... Alden, Sandy: I GOT YOU!

2. Ask Me How Things Are Going!

I fear that all too often the senior pastor hires someone to do youth ministry...and then views that as the monkey off his back—when in fact I have rarely ever seen a **successful** youth ministry that didn't have the support of the senior pastor. I try my best to make it around to Alden and Sandy every week to ask them how things are going—and NOT because I feel like I have to—but because I CARE. The pastor I served under before coming here, Bill Rigsby, modeled this for me in an incredible way!

3. Support the Ministry (and Me) from the Pulpit!

The pastor is the lead communicator and vision caster in the church... and if he is not speaking about youth ministry and modeling a desire to reach teenagers, then the church will think it is not important. I told our church this morning that our 2,500-seat sanctuary will one day be our youth building because these teens are so fired up that they are going to turn this entire county upside down for Jesus Christ. You should have seen the expression of the people–they were FIRED UP…along with our teens!

And let me say this—support the actual youth pastor from the pulpit—in many churches, this dude simply serves as "announcement boy" and various other activities…and is rarely recognized—this, once again, was modeled by my former pastor beautifully.

One more thing—I understand well that MANY youth pastors seem to be gifted with stupidity. They do really dumb things at times…I KNOW I DID! It seems like I was ALWAYS in trouble. But Bill always supported me…he never EVER lectured me from the pulpit and never talked bad about me when I messed up. He WOULD talk to me in private, behind closed doors—but NEVER did he EVER tear me down in order to appease a ticked off parent. He had my back!

4. Don't Make Me Do Fundraisers!

I have NEVER EVER met a youth pastor that ENJOYS raising money—EVER! I have done it all: car washes, bake sales, T-shirt sales, youth auctions…you name it! And we would go out and work our tails off for $300—when there were several people in our church that could have written that check…had the senior pastor simply asked.

I know, I know, I hear the senior pastor's argument, "Well, if they work for it, they appreciate it more." Can I just say that if that is your attitude, then you are full of crap! They appreciate it more when a church believes in them enough to invest in them—period!

And my question is this—why is it that the senior pastor will make the youth group do fundraisers…but won't ask the senior adults to do the same when they desire to go to the mountains and pick apples? And please don't hand me, "Well, they pay the bills around here" crap—if they pay the bills and have a heart for missions, then they should realize that this world is not about them and that the largest mission field in America is teenagers!

So what do we do when a kid can't afford to go? Simple—the church covers the cost—period. And don't think that we can do that because we are a big church—I remember when we had 200 people coming, and I stood in front of our church and asked people to step up and write a check so that the kids could go to camp. As long as I am pastor, we WILL invest in kids and WILL NOT make them do fundraisers.

5. Pay Me Well!

I think I just heard a youth pastor shout, "**Amen**!"

Let's be honest—you don't go into youth ministry to make money—BUT youth ministers should NOT have to take a vow of poverty.

My first full-time job in youth ministry, I made $16,000 a year...it's hard to live on that. However, as I look at the national averages youth pastors, just aren't making enough money—and it needs to be kept in mind that they need to be able to do things...such as eat and have a place to live.

Pastors—a good youth minister is worth the money! He, through an awesome ministry, will attract more than enough tithing families who will give enough to pay his salary and support the ministry he is called to do. Paying youth pastors well is the job of the senior pastor—step up and make sure these people are being taken care of...because if you don't have an effective youth ministry—then you do not have an effective church.

To our parents and church members, let me say this—our entire youth staff is paid well—they are taken care of...and will always be—the leadership of this church will always make sure of that.

PART

7

YOUTH
& FAMILY

It is vitally important that our children be led to a personal relationship with Christ and instructed in His Word when they are young. If I could relive my life, I would devote my entire ministry to reaching children for God.

—D. L. Moody

Children's Volunteers Who Don't Quit

Jim Wideman

On any given Sunday, it can be heard from thousands of pulpits in churches of every size, "We need workers, we need workers, we need workers, we need workers, WE NEED WORKERS!" Wouldn't it be nice if recruiting workers were like a game of Red Rover? You remember, "Red rover, red rover, send workers right over!" It would be nice if it were that easy. I have had the privilege of working at some wonderful churches of different sizes, and the one thing they have all had in common was that I was always on the lookout for more workers. The truth is, the bigger the vision, the more people serving and helping it takes to make that vision reality.

Three Dog Night taught me something valuable years ago: "One is the loneliest number that you'll ever do!" The ministry was never designed to be done by only a select few. Our mission found in Matthew 28:19 says, "Therefore go and make disciples of all nations, baptizing them in the name of the Father and of the Son and of the Holy Spirit." That's a big job that calls for a great team. The Bible says Jesus had the Spirit of God without measure, yet the first thing He did when He started His earthly ministry was to recruit help. If Jesus needed help, you and I need truckloads of it.

Paul wrote to Timothy in 2 Timothy 2:2, "And the things you have heard me say in the presence of many witnesses entrust to reliable men who will also be qualified to teach others." In this verse, we see four groups of people taking the message of the gospel to others. Paul taught Timothy, Timothy taught reliable men, who were to teach others also. In thirty years of building teams of volunteers, this is what I've realized: "People need to be needed more than you and I need the help." Raising up volunteers that stick is a win-win for the local church and for the individual!

Encourage your team to recruit others. Jesus allowed His team to recruit two of the twelve. I shouldn't have to say this to people in the ministry, but be touchable, available, and friendly. I'm on the lookout for potential workers at church, special meetings, Starbucks, Sam's Club—in fact, I'm on the lookout for workers everywhere I go.

Identify giftings you are looking for, and be watchful for people who display them. Look for people who vocationally manage people. Look within your organization for people to promote; your answer to your need for workers isn't always someone from the outside. Pray team members in. Philippians 4:6 says, "Do not be anxious about anything, but in everything, by prayer and petition, with thanksgiving, present your requests to God." Be specific—make a list of what you need and want. If people were no problem, where could you use a worker? Make sure you qualify all candidates. I require potential volunteers to complete an application, submit references, allow us to do a criminal background check if they are working with minors, and conduct an interview.

Once you've located them and qualified each candidate, here are twenty things I believe you need to do to cultivate volunteers that stick in your ministry.

1. Start volunteers slowly.

Don't dump them in a class with a Sunday school for a quarter and say, "Tag, you're it." If you're a dumper, the word is out on you! Start new recruits out watching, and add responsibility slowly. This is also the time to teach them your church's way of doing things. Train them in your policies and procedures; these should answer the questions: "What do you want me to do?" and "How do you want me to do it?"

2. Immerse them in your vision.

Use every method available to you: spoken, written—whether on blogs, websites, or brochures—and visual. Let pictures and video tell your story. Vision is contagious. Over the years, I realized my vision is what kept me going. If that vision wouldn't allow me to quit, neither would it allow others to quit.

3. Give them a model or example.

People do what they see. "Show" is a much better way to train than "tell." When you model ministry on an ongoing basis, it keeps everyone moving forward on the same page.

4. Build trust.

If you want your volunteers to trust you, be a person of integrity and do what you say. Prove yourself; don't lead by position only. Show people you are worthy to be followed.

5. Be real and transparent.

People like a leader who puts their pants on one leg at a time. Be normal; admit your struggles and shortcomings. Be approachable. Put yourself in the volunteer's place, and look for ways to make their load lighter.

6. Invest your time in others.

The time you spend in others is never wasted. You cannot develop leaders without investing your time in them. Discipleship is taking someone who is Christ-like in an area and letting their Christ-likeness rub off on others.

7. Believe in them.

Give them a chance to do ministry. Let them learn by doing. "But Jim, they're not as good as me!" There was a day you were not as good as you, but you learned by doing. Now it's time to return the favor.

8 Encourage others.

Everyone I know could use a little encouragement. They not only respond well to it, but they flourish. Here's a great habit to develop: Catch people doing things right! In fact, have your key staff write three thank-you notes each week—this practice will change your ministry.

9. Be a coach.

Coaches motivate, teach, make corrections, maintain team spirit, and point their team to the next level, both corporately and individually. Even the greatest athletes in the world have a coach.

10. Ask for commitment.

The greater the commitment, the sweeter the victory. Every time I've asked volunteers for a greater commitment, those who rallied and said yes were the best volunteers I ever had. Rotating workers might be a quick fix, but it doesn't produce long time volunteers.

11. Set goals for growth.

Don't allow people or ministries to stay stagnant or stuck. Help volunteers come up with goals to improve and grow. If you aim at nothing, you'll hit it every time. Goals are a good thing, but you'll never know where you are toward reaching them without constant evaluation. Evaluation is usually the missing link and should go hand in hand with goal setting.

12. Communicate on a regular basis.

No relationship can exist without communication. Communicate with more than meetings. Use every method possible. Let your workers know what they need to know to excel, and they will.

13. Give your volunteers the tools they need.

It's easier to do quality work with the right tools. Make sure you give all who serve what they need to minister effectively. What do they need? Start with creative environments; mix in exciting curriculum and teaching supplies plus audiovisual gadgets and gizmos. If we want folks to reach the sight-and-sound generation, then give them sights and sounds to work with.

14. Check on volunteers systematically.

People only do what's *inspected*, not just expected. I found out years ago I couldn't spend all my time teaching the children. I was more valuable as a problem-solver and leader of leaders than just a teacher of kids. See for yourself what's going on. Observe your workers in action.

15. Conduct regular equipping meetings.

If you give your workers knowledge and wisdom, then you should also give them the power to do the ministry with excellence. Teach them what to do and show them how you want them to do it. These kinds of meetings are more about developing skill-sets than information.

16. Care enough to confront.

As a parent, I confront my kids because I love them, so if I love my volunteers, I'll confront them when their actions need to change or improve. Confront in kindness always.

17. Ask for ideas and opinions when appropriate.

You can give out solutions all by yourself or involve others in the solution process. It's still your decision, but volunteers stay put when they are listened to.

18. Promote and entrust.

Turn over more to those with ability. People stay put when you recognize their abilities.

19. Say thanks and show them you value and esteem them.

Everyone likes to hear the magic words "please" and "thank you." When it comes from your heart, "thank you" is always welcomed.

20. Give them someone else to develop and disciple.

Make them accountable to impart what they have learned to someone else. Ministries excel when you develop depth at all key positions. Teams with depth at all key positions win consistently.

This is a lifetime commitment. This process won't happen overnight. It can only happen after you commit yourself to be a leader of leaders. To pull this off, you must have a goal. You have to have a plan. Each day, you must strive to be a better leader than you were the day before. Concentrate on what you can do for others rather than what others can do for you. Remember you gain those you serve.

Each of these steps is easy to do—the hard part is doing them all at the same time. Commit to make these a part of your leadership lifestyle.

6 Tips to Guide Your Ministry with Parents

Dan Scott

How do we engage parents, who act more like agents and personal assistants, to be the primary influence in their child's spiritual formation?

First of all, let me say this. This generation of kids is very family oriented. When asked, the majority of these kids will say Mom or Dad is their hero. This is a fact that can offer all of us hope for this generation. We all have to engage parents to parent.

Also, if you talk with most parents, they will all tell you with sincerity that they care. They wonder if they are really raising their kids well. I don't know any parent who wants their kids to end up spoiled, misguided, or confused. But parenting is hard work.

Just Friday, I was having a conversation with a fellow staff member at the church. He said point blank, "I never thought parenting would be as difficult as it has been."

And he's right. We want our kids to be safe. We want them to love Jesus. We hope they do well in school, have friends, behave in public, and have great manners at the dinner table. We work really hard at doing all of this, then one morning we hear something from the basement.

"When did they learn that word?"

Somewhere between the school bus, some show on TV, and my own road rage, of course, they learned that word.

As parents, it's too easy to coast. I think we're all roller coasters of involvement. It's no wonder our kids are confused whether to call us friends or parents. But I've said it before, and I'll say it again: Parents are called to parent.

Parents have exponentially more time with their kids than we do at the church. How can we spend some of our resources helping parents be the best caregivers they can be?

Here are some principles to guide your ministry with parents:

1. Invite them along for the ride.

We often think that if parents want to know something, they'll just ask us. Or if they don't like something, they'll just tell us. The truth is more like they'll ask or tell someone else before they talk with us.

How are we inviting parents into the right conversations? We need to seek out their advice on their kids. We need to have their input. We don't necessarily need to implement everything they suggest; we can't. We can ask good questions and listen. Remember we partner with them, not the other way around. The more we help parents understand that we're here to help them, the more likely they will come to us with a need.

2. Regularly communicate vision.

Take every opportunity to share your ministry goals with parents. Do this in ways parents receive information. Most likely, your church bulletin is not that place. How could you use social media with parents? Maybe a weekly newsletter will work? How many face-to-face conversations are you having with parents? How about focus groups?

Whatever you choose, keep in mind that you'll need multiple avenues to communicate the same information. We are living in an information-saturated world; most people need to see or hear something at least seven times before they actually hear it.

3. Harness the power of influence.

You will always have at least one set of parents who are on board with your plan. Inspire them to influence other parents with whom they travel this journey. Many of us can't know every single parent in our ministries, but we can know several with whom we can partner to help other parents.

Even this week, think of three sets of parents that can be part of a focus group. Share a meal with them, and let them help you in this difficult task.

4. Treat parents with respect.

This sounds obvious, but I'm pretty sure we can come across as arrogant sometimes. We may have the plan and the "expertise," but do we have the grace to deliver it in a way that doesn't make a parent feel stupid? Truth be told, we don't have all the answers. Many of us who work in children's and student ministry don't have kids in those age groups. We have theory, but we don't always have hard evidence that what we say will work in the lives of these kids. Collectively, the parents in your ministry have more intelligence than we do; let's all approach them with humility.

5. Hold training initiatives.

Many parents just don't know where to start. Hold training events that help your parents with practical information they can use immediately. They can include content: media, pop culture awareness, Internet awareness, etc. You must also offer opportunities for parents to discuss solutions to the issues they face and give them strategies to help them transform their family for the better.

Before you can create these events, you should know what your families need. Talk to five or ten families and have them list the top five issues or questions they face as parents. Create events that answer specific needs for the families in your church and community.

6. Don't give up.

Change doesn't happen overnight. Don't get discouraged. Keep investing the time into parents. It's easy to invest into kids. They (usually) respond positively and will love you no matter what. For parents, it's just gonna take time. Remember, we're only responsible to be true to our calling and share vision with parents. It's their choice whether or not they take you up on it. And while you're not giving up, pray, pray, and pray some more. This is about the Spirit of God working in their lives. Pray that he moves in their hearts and transforms their families.

10 Keys to an Excellent Nursery

Dale Hudson

We are finishing up the remodeling of our church nursery. It has been such a fun project for me. I love the nursery. There is nothing more precious to me than walking through our nursery on the weekends.

What are some of the keys to an excellent nursery? Here are my top ten tips for creating a loving and nurturing environment for the little ones.

1. Sanitary.

- It should look, smell, and sparkle with cleanliness.
- This means weekly cleaning, disinfecting toys after every service, washing sheets, etc.

2. Sane.

- This starts with your nursery director. This person will set the tone for your nursery. The director should be someone with a pleasant personality. Someone who stays calm and collected even when children are crying at their highest decibels. Someone who connects well with parents and has experience as the parent of small children.
- There will be crying. There will be times when a child is not having a good day. There will be days when a child is having separation anxiety. But sanity can still be attained. Bubble blowers, an aquarium, and other techniques can be used to keep things sane.
- Have proper adult to child ratios. This is vital. We strive for one adult for every child. It's a lot easier for a volunteer to keep things sane when they are placed in a proper ratio.

3. Secure.

- Create an environment where parents feel comfortable leaving their most precious possession.

- Security tags. Children are only released to the person who checked them in and has the matching security tag.
- Only people who have been through an interview and background check process are allowed to serve.
- Only females are allowed to change diapers.
- Have security cameras in every room.
- Never allow a volunteer to be alone with a child. No exceptions. If you don't have two volunteers, then don't open the room.
- We have a police officer stationed in the nursery hallway. You can never be too secure. Parents will notice and appreciate it.

4. Sick-free.

- Have a child wellness policy posted at each room and hold to it.

5. Soggy-free. (Just made that word up, I think)

- Make 1 Corinthians 15:51 your theme verse. It says, *"We will not all sleep...but we will all be changed."*
- Put a sticker on the fresh diaper that says, "I was changed."

6. Scheduled.

- Seeds of faith can be planted in children's hearts and minds even in their early months.
- Have a scheduled time during the hour to sing to the children, tell them a Bible story, pray over them, and tell them, "Jesus loves you."
- We have a key Bible verse promise on the wall in each room. Our volunteers pray these Bible promises over the children. We partner with parents as they pray the verse over their child during the week as well.

7. Servant Filled.

- The people serving in the nursery should be people who want to be there. I'm not a proponent of "requiring" parents to serve in the nursery. Some will want to, but for others, the best thing for them is to be worshiping and serving in another area.
- Look for people who have the heart of a servant. People who are willing to change diapers, get down on the floor, hold a crying child, and rock a baby to sleep.

8. Soothing.

- Families should walk into a soothing environment.
- Play soft lullabies in your hallways.
- Use relaxing colors.
- Pick people to be your greeters who are full of smiles and a gentle spirit.

9. Safe.

- Wall outlets and cabinets should be childproof.
- Know the allergies and special dietary needs of children.
- Regularly check toys and equipment for safety.

10. Supplied.

- Sunday morning is not the time to run out of wet wipes. Keep inventory of your supplies.
- Use the church's diapers instead of parent's diapers. Parents will appreciate it, and you never know...you may bless a family that is in financial hardship. Diapers are expensive for a family on a limited budget.
- The nursery is one of the most important areas of a church. It is where the earliest foundations are laid for a lifetime of following Christ. A growing nursery also means you are reaching young families, which reflects a healthy church.

Our ability to reach seekers is directly related to how well we care for their children.

—Bill Hybels

Why We Wrote Our Own Curriculum

Sam Luce

I want to start this article by saying I do not know everything there is to know about curriculum production, and I am in no way thinking of one curriculum company as I write this. My goal is to get us as children's pastors to ask hard questions of ourselves and of the curriculum we give our teams to teach our kids each week.

I personally believe that there are some problems that are systemic in the children's ministry curriculum arena. I have been a kids' pastor full time for nearly 14 years and have used every curriculum under the sun. Here are some of the problems that led to a few of my fellow kids' pastors and me writing our own curriculum.

1. Kids' Curriculum Typically Falls Into Two Camps: Fun or Biblically Accurate

Rarely does a curriculum do both well. This to me is very sad, because it says that the things we are using to teach our kids this precious hour we are given each week are not engaging nor are they transformational. The end result is a watered-down, weak, uninspiring introduction to the most engaging transformational person in human history.

2. Too Safe

I sadly get the feeling that most curriculum is made way too safe so it appeals to every type of church in America. The problem I have with this is not that people are trying to make money selling curriculum; it's that they are leaving out some really important stuff to broaden their appeal. For example, there is rarely a mention of the Holy Spirit in any kids' curriculum out there. I know there are some abuses in people's theology when it comes to the Holy Spirit, but He is the third person of the Godhead. There are definitely some things we can teach kids about the Holy Spirit without delving into strangeness. Other topics I think need to be addressed more to our kids and they aren't: Jesus in the Old Testament, what is the gospel, communion, baptism are a just a few. **My opinion is that if the things you are writing or teaching don't offend anyone, they probably are not Biblically accurate.** Jesus offended others with the truth all the time.

3. Scalability

It seems that most people who write curriculum are not from a local church. Even though people on staff used to be kids' pastors, time makes you forget. There is something about understanding what activities would work best in a class setting in a small church and a large church. Great super creative activities play out differently in a brainstorming session than they do in a room full of two-year-olds.

4. Lack of a Pastoral Perspective

I am not a professional educator. I have crazy amounts of respect for people who are and routinely ask for their wisdom. I would be crazy not to. There is, however, something to be said for the perspective of someone whose gift is the pastoring of people. This is one of the main reasons people write their own curriculum, and quite honestly, the very people who recognize this problem are typically not the most gifted at writing curriculum. There needs to be better dialog between pastors and writers. They need each other's perspective to be better at what they individually do best.

5. Lack of Christ-centeredness

I think most curriculum tries to be everything to everyone. The end result is the gospel message is not clearly communicated. As much as curriculums out there talk about Jesus, I am not sure if they communicate the message of Christ clearly enough. If kids know all about the Bible but don't understand the Gospel, we have lost a huge opportunity.

6. Moralism

In our quest to teach kids concrete ideas about faith with application, we have to be very careful not to make the point of the story about us and not about Jesus. I don't want my kids to be kind. I want my kids to understand that, because of what Christ did for me, I am empowered to love beyond my capacity. I want every kid who leaves Uptown to understand the gospel, because in my opinion, we are seeing kids leave the faith because they never understand what the gospel is. The gospel is compelling. The last thing any of us want to produce is "good kids" because good kids don't make a difference in this world—Christ-centered, gospel-empowered kids do.

In closing, I just want to say that I in no way mean to offend anyone, but if you are offended, my beef is not with you per se. My goal is to ask hard questions so our kids can benefit and Christ can be magnified. I am not selling anything or pushing a particular product.

Lastly, don't just complain—do something about it. Be part of the solution not just a part of the problem. Whatever you use, make it better, and push the people who make what you use to make it better, because it's not about you and me. It's about the kids who listen every week to the greatest story ever.

5 Ways to Help Kids Pray

Tina Houser

As a child, I remember that every day closed with one of my parents sitting on the side of my bed, the covers pulled up under my chin, and me muttering...

Now I lay me down to sleep.
I pray the Lord my soul to keep.
IF I SHOULD DIE BEFORE I WAKE,
I pray the Lord my soul to take.

Night after night after night after night, that third line sent chills through me. Most certainly, some frightened adult had written that prayer poem out of a desire of his heart, but it lived on to torture children all over the world, right before they went down for a restful night's sleep. After a while, I just let the words tumble out of my mouth and tried not to think about what any of it actually meant. And this is one of the prominent ways we teach children to pray—a rhyme that is said over and over without real meaning to the child.

Another way we teach children to pray is nothing short of a Santa's wish list. We ask children to share their requests, which is another way of saying, "Let's tell God what you want Him to do for you." They quickly rattle off a long "to-do" list of relatives and friends who are sick and pets that are missing. Then we acknowledge that God answers prayer only if God does it the way we've suggested. This may come as a surprise, but God really answers every prayer. His answers are of such a wide variety that we can't even imagine the possibilities. It's an every day occurrence, though, to hear someone say, "God still answers prayer," when what they mean is, "God answered in the way I wanted Him to."

Is this how we should teach our children to pray? Scary prayers? Prayers that fall from their tongues without thought? Prayers that find themselves alongside nursery rhymes? Prayers that instruct God exactly what He's supposed to do for us? What would your best friend think if every time you spoke with him, you just said the same rhyme? And she most certainly wouldn't stick around as your friend if all you ever talked to her about was what you wanted her to do for you. Something needs to change in the way we teach our children to pray.

We're just downright good at getting ourselves into messes and then praying that God will get us out of them somehow. Instead of praying for deliverance from the mess, what if we started teaching our children to pray in the middle of the mess, not with their minds set on deliverance, but simply asking God to help them see how they can grow in His wisdom by going through it? How about praying for the strength to make it through to the other side?

If you look back on your life and identify the times when you grew spiritually—those times when spiritual growth seemed to come in leaps and bounds—I venture to say that it was in times of struggle. It was during those times when there were more questions about life than there were answers that you felt God moving in your life in a tremendous way. That's when you saw miracles happen. That's when you found yourself resting in His presence. Through those times, spiritual truth became clearer. So why do we shy away from that? Why do we pray that we never have to experience it? Why do we teach our children to pray safe prayers that if answered in the way they are prayed would only keep them from searching for God's truth and His plan for their lives?

As a newlywed, 34 years ago, I woke my husband up in the middle of the night to ask him a question, "Why do we need to pray if God already knows everything?" I was content to ask the question then roll over and go back to sleep. My husband, on the other hand, wrestled with the question the rest of the night. Over the years, we've come back to that conversation, and it's been a growing time. So why do we pray? It's about coming into His presence. It's about being part of a relationship that is alive and full of meaning. I've talked to a lot of children's workers, and they all hang their heads in unison when I talk about those times when we look up and see parents at the door. We put our words in high speed and quickly tell the kids to bow their heads and close their eyes so we can pray. While you have your head bowed, the kids are putting their jackets on and not at all thinking about spending time in the presence of God. That sure doesn't feel like leading the children to a relationship that is alive and full. The Lord deserves an apology.

One of the first things you can do to elevate the importance of prayer is change where it falls in your time with the kids. We open with a ceremonial prayer and then close haphazardly. The children know what to expect so their brains experience something similar to the sound that depicts the off-screen teacher on the Charlie Brown cartoons…blah-blah-blah-blah-blah. Think about the ways you experience a friend. You share a meal together. You go to a game with rowdy fans together. You sit with him in silence as he grieves the loss of a loved one. You sing karaoke with her. You sit quietly on a dock waiting for a fish to bite. We need to teach our kids that there are an endless number of ways they can experience the presence of God through prayer.

Prayer is a spiritual discipline, and like other disciplines, it needs to be practiced and experienced on a regular basis in order to become something that we can't imagine living without. So our challenge is to give children an opportunity to experience the presence of God in different ways. They need to be shown how each time they engage in a conversation with God, it can be new and fresh. Prayer should be a time of evaluation, when each person makes a conscious effort to identify their spiritual condition and expose that before the Lord.

The best way to teach kids to pray is to help them understand that there is no set place or position or time of day. Since God is omnipresent and prayer is experiencing the presence of God, then anywhere, any time, any position is in fair territory. Let me just get your creative juices flowing with these prompting ideas.

Let John the Baptist help you pray. When John was in the wilderness, he told the people that: (1) they needed to confess their sins, (2) they needed to exchange their old lives for a new one, (3) they needed to be baptized, (4) they needed to stay on track, and (5) they needed to live authentic lives. Help the kids identify where they are in these five points. If they need to confess their sins (point #1), then tell them to put one finger of one hand in the palm of the other hand. If they have asked the Lord to forgive them of their sins, but need help staying on track so they don't slide back into those old habits (point #4), then tell them to put four fingers of one hand in the palm of the other hand. Each point gives them a way to talk to the Lord about where they are spiritually.

Pray like Daniel. Daniel's disobedience to King Nebuchadnezzar's law was obvious because he prayed three times a day at his window. When Daniel prayed, he was unashamed. He didn't care what other people thought of him. He only knew that he was devoted to God. You probably have a window in your worship room and most kids have a window in their bedroom. Use a

Crayola window marker to write on the window. You can simply write, "Pray Today" on the window, or the kids can actually write out their prayer in its entirety on the window. Then kneel down at that window and look to the sky. Concentrating on the sky will act as a focal point and help kids clear their minds of other thoughts.

Pray like Moses. When Moses heard of Koreh's plans of rebellion, the Bible tells us that Moses' first reaction was to drop to the ground and pray. So instruct the kids to kneel all the way and bend over with their faces to the floor. Teach the children that when they are threatened by anything, they can pray like Moses and lay themselves before God.

Pray with the unseen paper clip. Lay a paper clip on the table; the paper clip will represent the child. That paper clip is you! Cover the paper clip with your hand so you can feel it under your knuckles. Then place a bar magnet over your knuckles. Slowly lift your hand with the bar magnet still against the knuckles. The paper clip will hang from the palm of your hand as long as the magnet stays in place. You can't see the paper clip hanging there, but you can feel the power of the magnet. Pray that even though we can't see where God is leading, we will always feel God's presence. Seeing this object lesson will give the kids a way to associate with God leading them in ways they can't see.

Pray a color. This is especially good with younger children. Pull one crayon from a full box. Thank God for everything you can think of that is that color. Smother God with thankfulness prayers of a particular color. That seems like a much better way to say goodnight than "IF I SHOULD DIE BEFORE I WAKE."

Let's raise this generation of kids to feel at ease with prayer and know it as a real conversation, not just a rhyme or a give-me list. Let's raise them to not be afraid of going through any life situation, because God will be with them and teach them great spiritual truth on the journey.

5 Strategies for Small-Church Children's Ministry

Greg Baird

Small Church, BIG Challenge

What do you do when only two kids show up on Sunday, and they're four and twelve?

Start by thinking S.M.A.L.L.

Janice hurried through the building checking each of the three classrooms. She'd invested several hours already that week ensuring everything would be ready for the kids. Janice loved the kids of First Church of the Valley; she'd overseen the children's ministry there for almost two years now and thoroughly enjoyed her part-time position. She had to admit, though, that sometimes she was frustrated, not knowing how many kids might show up or if they'd be preschoolers or preteens. She was often preoccupied by questions about her small children's ministry: How do I prepare for the unknown? How do I make ministry relevant for just a few kids with such varied ages? And even more important: Is our ministry really effective with this unique group of kids?

Thousands of children's ministry leaders face these same questions every week. They work incredibly hard to minister effectively to the kids who arrive at their doors. They face the challenging prospect of not knowing how many kids might show up (two or 25?), along with the even bigger challenge of meeting kids' needs—when the kids are all over the age spectrum. So how do you keep a small church ministry effective and relevant?

You think S.M.A.L.L!

S: Start with a Plan

To create impact in any size children's ministry, you must begin with a plan. Plan how you'll effectively reach kids in your children's ministry. Recruit for the classes you'll offer—even if those classes are occasionally empty—based on your average weekly attendance (track attendance for three months to get a close average). Do the necessary volunteer screening and training to prepare volunteers. Prepare teaching materials, including curriculum and supplies. Prepare your space and be ready.

Note: Being ready doesn't mean having a healthy stack of word puzzles and coloring pages ready for kids. It means being prepared with a full lesson plan that maximizes every moment your volunteers have with kids.

It's easier to lower your preparedness standards when you think there might be just a few kids. It's easy to slip into the mindset of "winging it." But remind yourself of this: Reality is just the opposite. With only a handful of kids, you have greater opportunity than ever to make a deep and lasting impact. Prepare for it! Regardless of who or how many might show up, start with a plan.

M: Move to Plan B

Your Plan A is in place: You're prepared for your average attendance and ready to go. But if drastically fewer kids show up, or if kids' age ranges are awkward (for instance, you have a four-year-old and a twelve-year-old sitting at the table staring blankly at you), then move to Plan B.

Plan B is your plan for what you'll do if your number or ages vary dramatically from what you'd normally expect. Determine beforehand how you'll handle such variances. Who'll lead? How will you organize your volunteers? Will you dismiss some volunteers, or use them in other ways? How will you mix age groups so older kids interact with and mentor younger kids? Is your curriculum geared to engage all ages? Where will kids go? Think through all the troublesome scenarios you've experience in the past year: Too many kids, not enough kids, major age gaps, group imbalances (10 preschoolers and one teen, for instance). If it's a possibility, plan for it. That doesn't mean you need to create a new plan every week, but have a plan prepared for the major scenarios you face. Typically, you can simply adjust Plan A, but you need Plan B for the big obstacles.

Note: Plan B isn't winging it. Making up Plan B as you go isn't acceptable; have it ready and your volunteers trained to adapt in advance.

A: Always Focus on Relationships

Ministry happens best through relationships. This is true in mega churches, medium churches, and small churches. The difference (and your advantage) is when you have a very small number of kids, you have an exponentially larger opportunity to invest in relationships with them.

Whether you're in Plan A mode or resorting to Plan B, relationships must be at the center of your efforts. Curriculum and resources are important. Facilities and programs are important. But it's relationships—and almost nothing else—that greatly impact the life of a child for Jesus. Jesus Himself invested deeply in a small group aside from His wider ministry. Why? Because there's greater impact in small numbers. There's greater opportunity to teach, engage, guide, understand, befriend, and demonstrate your faith up close. So rather than bemoaning the fact that so few kids came, celebrate the fact that you have more time and energy to pour yourself into the lives of a few—just as Jesus did.

L: Let Kids Engage

One of the wonderful (and many would say most important) ways kids learn is by becoming fully engaged in what you're teaching.

When you have 100 kids in children's church, engaged participation isn't always possible. Personal discovery isn't always easy. Guiding children in life-changing experiences may be watered down because there may be too many kids and too few adults. But with a small group of kids? What a blessing! There are so many ways to let kids participate. Think about these for starters:

- Teaching—Let kids "co-teach" the lesson. Engage them in reading the Scripture or retelling or acting out the biblical events.
- Mentoring—Allow older kids to help younger kids engage in all aspects of the lesson. Younger kids are thrilled by an older child's attention, and older kids love to take on leadership roles. You have the perfect opportunity to invest in kids in a way that trains them to be leaders in children's ministry—today!
- Clarification—You can engage kids deeply in what you're teaching with dialogue that gauges their understanding of the lesson and the principles you're teaching. As you talk with kids and listen to their feedback, address their misunderstandings or clarify how what they're leaning applies to

their lives. In a smaller setting, you have the ability to answer questions as kids think through what they're learning.

- Mobility—With a small group of kids, you're blessed with flexibility. A spur-of-the-moment jaunt outside with five kids to enjoy the warm sunshine during a lesson on creation is totally doable. Not always so with a class of 25. Smaller groups offer mobility and open the door to creative ideas. Move to new locations—other rooms, outside, or in the pastor's office (or not!)— to stimulate kids' interest and engagement.
- Service—Service is a win-win for your kids and your church. Work with other departments such as adult classes or small groups to pinpoint ways your kids can serve them. Maybe it's taking offerings, passing out brochures, cleaning up, or any number of seemingly small ways to serve. Engage kids in service projects for the community, too, and use these as a teaching tool. At a church I served at, we had children help create care packages for summer short-term missions groups to deliver to low-income neighborhoods. These packages opened doors to share the gospel. The kids who created the packages didn't deliver them, but they were just as much a part of sharing their faith as those who actually made deliveries—and we made sure the kids knew it.

Note: "Engaged kids" isn't equivalent to kids working busily on a worksheet for the duration of class. Think of engaged as "involved, interested, and engrossed." Not exactly what you get with a worksheet.

L: Laugh!

One of the key characteristics of any children's ministry is fun. When kids and adults have fun together, everyone's engaged. And if what kids are engaged in is meaningful and purposeful, then they're learning in a way that impacts their lives for the better.

But fun can be threatened. Don't allow your attitude to sour when you don't have many kids show up. I remember feeling frustrated when the number I expected didn't materialize. Instead of focusing on the kids who were there, I'd focus on the kids who weren't. That attitude took the fun out of the experience for everyone. Have fun with the kids who are there. Don't minimize their attendance by thinking of those who didn't show.

You may only have a few kids show up, but S.M.A.L.L. thinking will lead to flexibility, relationships, engaged kids, and laughter that strengthens your ministry—on every scale!

Big Things About "Small"

First, let's explore what it means to be "small." Church culture today tends to attach a negative stigma to the idea of being small. After all, if you're "small," you must not be doing something right...you must not be as effective...you must not be as attractive. If you're small—well, you must not be as good...right?

WRONG!

Nothing could be further from the truth. Small is good. In fact, small is great. More precisely, "small" is the norm in churches across the country and around the globe. And "small" in children's ministry can be a wonderful thing. In his book, *Energizing Children's Ministry in the Smaller Church*, Rick Chromey points out these positives when it comes to children's ministry in smaller churches:

- Significant Impact—Smaller churches have the opportunity to make significant impact on a child's faith because they can often offer greater focus on each child.
- Parent Ministry—Small churches have great potential for effective parent ministry by more involved ministry to parents and getting parents involved in ministry.
- Family Ties—Small churches offer a close community of Christians, allowing children more opportunities to get to know other adults and kids in a much more personal way—and letting them see other Christians live their faith.
- Service Avenues—Small churches typically offer kids more opportunities to serve and lead in the church.
- Exploration—Small churches offer the flexibility to test and try new, creative, and innovative ideas with children that allow them to experientially develop their faith.

In short, your small church is uniquely positioned to have a big impact on the children in your ministry. You have flexibility and face-time with kids that are not afforded to bigger churches. Your small church is a force to be reckoned with on the front lines for God!

PART

8

SMALL GROUP
LEADERSHIP

You can be committed to church but not committed to Christ, but you cannot be committed to Christ and not committed to church.

—Joel Osteen

7 Elements of a Successful Group

Craig Groeschel

Over the years, Amy and I have participated in several different small groups. Some were much more successful than others.

Here are the elements we've found essential for a great group:

1. **A great group needs a leader.** When everyone is always voting on what we do next, we never do much. A good leader makes for a good group.

2. **A great group is built around God's word.** Too often, small groups become all about fellowship. While fellowship is always essential, doing life around God's word is what truly makes the difference.

3. **A great group is a safe group.** If people can't discuss openly without fear of judgment, rejection, or gossip, the group is doomed to fail.

4. **A great group looks outward.** Serving together is life changing.

5. **A great group births new groups.** If a group stays together for too long, they usually grow stale. Healthy groups produce new groups.

6. **A great group takes breaks.** We often take the summer off from consistent meetings. We're all busy. The break makes us long to be together more.

7. **A great group hurts together.** I just got off the phone after talking to a young woman with four children who just lost her 39-year-old husband. Even though she is devastated, she told me confidently that her Life Group would be there for her. God is glorified through such a group.

Habits of a Healthy Group Leader

Joel Comiskey

"How could this man multiply his cell group six times? He lacks the enthusiasm and bubbly excitement so necessary for small group multiplication." Then in my interview, Carl Everett, the man they call "Mr. Multiplication," confirmed my suspicion and told me that he was a very shy person. "How did you multiply your group so many times?" I inquired.

"Prayer, prayer, and prayer," he asserted.

Carl and his wife, Gaynel, lead a cell at Bethany World Prayer Center in Louisiana. Their cell preparation includes fasting and prayer the day of the cell meeting. Before the meeting, they anoint the food, the sidewalks, the yard, every room in the house, even each seat to be used that night. They wait until after the meeting (during the refreshment time) to eat. The Everetts' example is not unusual at Bethany.

Is a day of fasting and prayer the only reason why some cell leaders succeed at evangelizing and giving birth to new groups while others stagnate? I visited eight prominent cell churches in search of the answer. More than 700 cell leaders completed my 29-question survey that explored such areas as the cell leader's training, social status, devotions, education, preparation of material, age, spiritual gifts, and gender. This statistical analysis helped me discover common patterns across eight diverse cultures.

For example, I discovered that healthy cell leaders come in all shapes and sizes, and the anointing for successful cell leadership doesn't reside with a mysterious few. Some believe that healthy cell leaders are specially gifted, more educated, and own more vibrant personalities than other leaders. Not so. The educated and uneducated, married and single, shy and outgoing, those gifted as teachers and those gifted as evangelists equally multiply their small groups.

However, several characteristics do distinguish successful cell leaders. These differentiating factors relate to what a person does as a part of his or her typical weekly lifestyle. It has nothing to do with personality, background, or how long one has been a Christian. Instead, healthy cell leaders have incorporated certain habits into their lives. You can join them.

Consistent Devotional Life

"I couldn't believe that the President of the United States wanted to meet with me! You better believe that I prepared for that special meeting. I wanted to honor him. I arrived at the White House hours early just to be ready. How awesome to be in the presence of the President!"

This scenario illustrates the excitement and anticipation of an important meeting. I've never met with the President, but someone far greater desires to meet and talk with you and me every day—Jesus Christ. He's the King of kings and the Lord of lords.

The life of a healthy cell leader begins and ends with God. Only God can give success. My survey of cell leaders clearly showed that time spent with God is the single most important principle behind successful cell leadership. A cell leader filled with the power and love of Jesus Christ knows how to minister to a hurting member of the group, how to deal with the constant talker, or how to wait for a reply to a question.

Why, then, don't cell leaders properly prioritize this time? There are at least three hindrances. First and foremost is drowsiness. We've all battled sleepiness during personal devotions. I'll never forget David Cho's advice about early morning devotions: "Get out of bed!" In bed, deep prayer can too easily become deep sleep. Instead, get up, wash your face, drink some coffee, or go for a jog if necessary. Get the blood flowing.

Another impediment is our mind. How often I have approached the throne of God only to battle my thoughts—what that person thought of my comments last night or when I should wash my car. "Your thoughts, Lord, not mine" is the battle of devotions. Ask Him to take over your thoughts in the "listening room."

Lack of time is another problem. Leave the fast-food mentality at McDonald's. In order to drink deeply from the Divine, you must spend time in deep meditation. As the Psalmist says, deep calls to deep (Psalm 42:7). Don't leave your devotional time without touching God, feeling the glow of His glory. This demands extended periods before God's throne. One or two short visits won't suffice.

Balanced Family Life

Everything smelled of success. The cells were multiplying. The church was growing and experiencing salvation and healing. But as staff members talked, it became evident that many cell leaders were suffering in their personal lives. They were busy every night of the week. One pastor asked, "Isn't it a contradiction to succeed in cell ministry but fail with our families?" Of course it is! In the life of a healthy cell leader, family is paramount. God desires to maximize our effectiveness as cell leaders, but not at the expense of our family life.

Cell ministry is a family affair and is meant to draw your family closer together. It's best to place your family inside your cell ministry. For example, your teenager can direct the children's cell or lead worship. Your child can lead the icebreaker. My wife, Celyce, and I minister together as a team in our cell. She plans the icebreaker and prepares the refreshments. I prepare the worship and the lesson. When she's leading the group, I care for our two-year-old. Likewise, she covers for me when I'm ministering.

After cell meetings, we analyze together what happened. Once Celyce told me, "Joel, you should have been more gracious with Inez. I know she talked too much, but you could have handled it better." "That's not what I wanted to hear," I thought. But it's what I needed to hear. Our intimacy grows as we pastor our group together and openly discuss the details of each meeting, sharing our observations and learning together. This honest feedback also helps us mature as cell leaders.

Leadership Development

George Whitefield and John Wesley were contemporaries in seventeenth-century England. Both dedicated themselves to God's work in the same small group at Oxford University. Both were excellent in open-air preaching. Both witnessed thousands of conversions through their ministries. Yet John Wesley left behind a 100,000-member church, while George Whitefield could point to little tangible fruit toward the end of his ministry. Why? Wesley dedicated himself to training and releasing small-group leaders, while Whitefield was too busy preaching and doing the work of the ministry.

Yes, it's exciting to lead a cell group. But what will your group look like when you leave it in the hands of your current intern? Will it continue to meet or will it fold? Will you look back at your leadership with joy as you recall the cell groups that you left behind, or will you wonder how so much effort could result in so little?

We all know about the tyranny of the urgent. The cell lesson needs fine-tuning, someone must bring the refreshments, John needs a ride, and on and on the list goes. Cell leaders can be overwhelmed with worship choruses, icebreakers, calls, visits, etc. Everything demands immediate attention. Or does it? In the midst of a fast-paced life, are there priorities? Can a cell leader confidently say, "This one thing I do"?

Yes. Successful cell leaders look beyond the urgency of the present to the importance of future daughter cells. Because of that, they spend priority time training new leaders. This passion to raise up new leadership drives successful cell leaders to spend quality time with potential leadership. As a result, common cell members become visionary leaders.

Leadership success in the cell church is clear: how many leaders have been spotted, trained, and deployed? Raising up future leaders is a Biblical way of life. Moses tutored Joshua, and Elijah trained Elisha. The Apostles were recruited and trained by Jesus. Barnabas discipled Paul, who in turn developed Timothy. The Lord has brought future leaders to your group. Are you developing them?

Inviting New People

The way to add future leaders to your group is to invite people to your cell—and keep inviting. Most cell leaders have heard the well-intentioned promises of those who failed to follow through. "Steve promised to come." "I planned dessert for four people who didn't show." Have you heard these comments before? Have you made them yourself? Welcome to cell leadership!

Experienced group leaders understand that you have to personally invite 25 people for 15 to say they will attend. Of those 15, eight to ten actually will show up. Of those, only five to seven will attend regularly after a month or so. Don't let rejection discourage you. Successful cell leaders don't depend on one or two verbal commitments. They continually invite new people.

One group at Bethany World Prayer Center faithfully met each week but experienced little growth. One member previously attended a group that had multiplied. After analyzing both groups, he said, "In the other cell group, we received a constant flow of visitors."

Another cell was celebrating the birth of a new group. The cell leader testified that the group went through a dry, difficult period. With only six people, the group did all of the "right things" to win non-Christians and receive visitors, but few visited and fewer stayed. Yet they kept on trying, praying, and inviting until they broke through. Several visitors started attending and invited their friends. Because this cell resisted discouragement, the mix came together.

Cell leader, you personally must be vigilant about inviting new people. The right mix for your group is right around the corner. New blood in your cell will bring new life. Newcomers invigorate your group with their fresh insight. Keep inviting and don't give up.

Visitation

Luis Salas has a large, well-worn map hanging in the entryway of his Bogota apartment. This "war map" is overflowing with names of potential cell members. "I'm always dreaming and praying about new people to invite to my cell groups," he said. "All day long I think about them and eventually make personal contact with them."

In just 18 months, Luis multiplied his original cell to 250 cells because he goes after potential members. More importantly, he follows up with them after they visit. Some of them become cell members and then cell leaders.

If you want your cell to grow and multiply, one vital key to effective cell evangelism is immediate contact of visitors. When someone new attends your group, plan an immediate visit, send a card, and/or pick up the telephone and call. The saying is true: "People don't care how much you know until they know how much you care."

Natural Evangelism

New members sense a freedom to share deeply in the warm atmosphere of an accepting, loving group. The "cell atmosphere" is the most effective way to expose non-Christians to the truth of the Gospel.

During one cell meeting, leader René Naranjo of Ecuador began a lesson on how Jesus cleared out the temple (John 2). Discussion flowed from the Jewish temple, to our own bodies as God's temple, to home cells as God's temple today. René guided the discussion when necessary, but the conversation flowed naturally and orderly. One couple said little, but they were asked to share their thoughts. This couple lacked a personal relationship with Jesus Christ, yet no one pounced on them with the Good News. They felt liberty to express themselves. René closed the cell by asking those who wanted to receive Jesus Christ to pray a simple prayer with him and visit with him after the meeting concluded.

In the last six months, René Naranjo has planted three daughter cells. He personally supervises these new cells and disciples the leaders. In his cell group, non-Christians feel comfortable to express their opinions, as he graciously points them to the Savior.

Are you targeting non-Christians in your group and including them in the lesson? Cell evangelism is not a programmatic, canned approach. Rather, it's a personal process of sharing Good News about forgiveness of sin and new life in Jesus. Because of the intimate, caring atmosphere of small groups, evangelism happens naturally.

A Parable of Three Gardeners

A man had a beautiful garden that yielded rich and abundant food. His neighbor saw it and planted his own garden in the spring, but he did nothing to it: no watering, cultivating, or fertilizing. In the fall, his garden was devastated, overgrown with weeds and bearing no fruit. He initially concluded that gardening does not work. After more thought, he decided that the problem was bad soil or maybe that he lacked a "green thumb." Meanwhile, a third neighbor started a garden. Though his garden did not immediately yield as much as the first man's, he worked hard and continued learning. As he practiced new ideas year after year, his garden reaped an increasingly abundant harvest.

The truth of this parable is obvious. I traversed the globe to discover the secrets of small-group growth, and the same principles made the difference between cell growth and stagnation in every country, culture, and church. Prayer, hard work, and the steady application of proven principles set apart the successful cell group leaders. The insights outlined here will work for you if you are willing to pay the price. These habits require time and effort.

Successful cell leaders spend time seeking God's face and are dependent on Him for the direction of their group. They prepare themselves first and then turn their attention to the lesson. They pray diligently for their members as well as for non-Christian contacts. But successful cell leaders do not stop with prayer. They come down from the mountaintop and interact with real people, full of problems and pain. They pastor their cell members and visit them regularly. They invite new people, visit newcomers, and evangelize naturally in their small groups. By developing these habits, any cell leader can lead a group to grow and multiply. That is God's heart and His Great Commission. How are you doing?

Train the Group, Not Just the Leader

Alan Danielson

Training new small group leaders is a no-brainer, so we have training events, create online training courses, send leaders home with resources, and provide small group coaches. Yet with all of this training, it's not uncommon for those of us in church leadership to be frustrated by the fact that there's a disconnect between what we've trained group leaders to accomplish and what the groups are actually doing.

There are a few reasons this happens: First, leader training is like drinking from a fire hose. Leaders get tons of information and don't really have time to process it before they start meeting with their groups.

Second, leaders may take the training to heart, but are afraid to ask their groups to do what they are being asked to do. For example, if groups are being asked to use a particular curriculum for a campaign, some groups won't like it. They might be in the middle of a 22-week study of Revelation, and this new curriculum will mess up their calendar. Some leaders just don't have the guts to tell their group that they need to use an alternative curriculum for a few weeks.

Thirdly, some leaders simply have their own agendas. They may not like what you are asking them to do, so they just decide not to do it. After all, who in the group is going to know? They weren't at leader training. They don't know what leaders were asked to do.

For this reason, I'm a huge believer in adding a new layer to training: group training. It's possible to train not only the leader, but also the entire group. Group training should not replace leader training; rather it should be in addition to leader training. The great thing about group training is that it can be subliminal enough that groups don't realize they are being trained.

Here are a few ways to train entire small groups:

1. Teach your church's small group values/expectations through the weekend messages.

2. Teach your church's small group values/expectations through the curriculum.

3. Give away free group DVDs to everyone that shares an expanded vision of small group ministry at your church (people like free stuff).

4. Share stories that exemplify the values you want your groups to live out.

5. Put a short 90-second training clip on the front end of each week's video curriculum.

The point of group training is to create another level of accountability. The more people in a group who know what is expected of the group, the more likely the group will be to live out those expectations.

Top 10 Mistakes Small Group Leaders Make

Randall Neighbour

Let me begin with a confession. I am the most qualified person to write this article. I am guilty of every mistake covered here. If you don't believe me, ask my wife! She doesn't like to say bad things about me but will be brutally honest if necessary. The mistakes I have made through the years help me see gaps in my spiritual walk and skills as a leader. Instead of trampling my self-esteem with guilt, I use mistakes as learning experiences. If I don't repeat them, I have learned something more valuable than any training class can offer. I see my primary task as a leader to help my group reach the lost and raise up leaders, expanding the works of God's people. When this doesn't happen consistently, I know I'm making mistakes that will kill my group. This may sound overly dramatic to you, but it's painfully true. Small groups die all the time, and it's usually due to one or more of the reasons discussed below.

A few weeks ago, I asked five hundred small group leaders three questions. What's the biggest mistake you've made as a small group leader? How did you correct the problem or avoid making it a second time? What have you learned from the experience, or how has it changed your leadership style? Those who answered were very honest, and it took guts. Everyone likes to toot their own horn, but few will reveal their failures. Up front, I'd like to thank those leaders who made this article possible. You are a blessing to the body of Christ! As you read these common mistakes submitted by real small group leaders, you will probably see areas in which your ministry needs improvement. This list is by no means complete, but it touches on key issues that will make or break your ministry as a small group leader.

PART

8

SMALL GROUP
LEADERSHIP

"I operated passively without goals."

Leaders who "follow their nose" never gain any ground in reaching the lost or developing leaders. They wander aimlessly without a plan of action to storm the gates of Hell and set captives free. As I visit with successful small group leaders around the world, they all have common goals of reaching X number of people for Christ by a certain date and raising up enough leaders to pastor the new believers in new groups. This drives the leader to invest time with his members and unsaved friends and relatives attached to the group. The responsibility of meeting the goal is not completely shouldered by the leader, but he or she owns the goal and sets the example for the rest of the group.

These leaders are also accountable to their church leadership. Each week, they eagerly meet with their pastor or coach to find ways to meet or exceed the stated goal. If you want to succeed as a leader, set realistic growth goals. Submit your goals to your leadership so you can be held accountable. Then get to work meeting those goals, removing all obstacles that get in your way. Remember, run as to win the prize.

"I released an untrained apprentice."

Years ago, I watched a small group leader multiply his group and give half his members to his apprentice. As the weeks passed, I watched the new leader struggle as she lost member after member. They didn't feel loved by her, and she didn't know how to love them with servanthood. The leader's mistake stemmed from not giving the responsibility of the original group to the apprentice months before the multiplication date. Although she facilitated the meeting a dozen times, she had very little servanthood experience. What she lacked was the daily interaction between a leader and members that refines the leader and builds a new team. If you're not transferring an increasing amount of leadership responsibility to your apprentice, you're setting them up for defeat. You'll also wound group members you dearly love when they multiply off with this new leader. Give your apprentice the reigns of leadership a little at a time over the course of six months, and then back off and let them be the "senior leader." Your role then will be one of a consultant, and if you've trained them well, you will experience some rest as they lead the members.

The best way to view your apprentice is to see and treat them like a real small group leader. Challenge them to serve the group members between meetings. Help them set up ministry visits to pray for members in their homes and join them. Spend an hour a week or more on your knees in prayer with them for the needs of the group, and you will release strong leaders. Very little of leadership development has to do with facilitating meetings. It's all about developing a servant's heart for others.

"I was leading as if I was the senior pastor."

The role of the small group leader is often mistaken to be more than it should be. If you're making this mistake, the indicators are clear. You are worn out because you have mistakenly taken on the whole load of pastoral care for each member. Your pastoral staff doesn't know what's going on with your members because they only hear about problems when it's too late to be supportive. You're riddled with guilt because you work a full-time job or raise a house full of kids and you just can't be a full-time minister. Did that about cover how you feel right now? The best way to correct this mistake is to clearly understand your role. You are a faithful undershepherd, caring for someone else's sheep. If they get sick or are attacked by wolves in the field, you help them to the best of your ability and get help. The sheep entrusted to you do not belong to you, so you are obligated to find the senior shepherd (your pastor) or the ranch hand (your coach) who is there to help.

This news should set you free! Your role is to encourage, minister to, and love your members unconditionally. You're a vital part of the care-giving system of your church, but not the whole system!

If you've been acting like the senior pastor, the best way to correct the problem is to ask your group and your pastoral staff to forgive you. Ask them to hold you accountable for a balanced ministry and take some of the load you're leaving behind. Small group leadership should be a joy, not a burden.

"I pastored the wrong people."

There are four kinds of Christians with whom you will come into contact in your small group: 1) your group members, 2) somebody else's group members, 3) church friends who refuse to join your group, and 4) other church's members who show up at your meetings. The last three will not build your group and make it strong if you shepherd them. When a group member from another group approaches me with a complaint about their group or leader, I do not take ownership of the problem. Assisting a runaway is an offense punishable by law! I promptly see them home, and I don't let them wander off. If the issue can't be worked it out in the group in which they are a member, he or she should visit with the coach or pastor above the group, not with other group leaders in the church.

When my church friends want the benefits of group life—counseling, ministry, and support, just to name a few—but are unwilling to join a group, I am unable to give them much of my time either. If they want a deeper relationship with me, I invite them to join my group! This way, we can minister to one another, and they can catch the vision for living in community. While I don't come off as "high and mighty," I do tell them what they're missing by resisting the invitation to join a biblical community. It's the best place to be in my Book (Acts 2, to be specific).

The same thing applies for believers who want to join my small group and maintain a church membership elsewhere. If they want the benefits of biblical community my group offers, they should be giving my church (and my group members) 110 percent of their time and energy. This includes attending our weekend services, daily involvement in my group member's lives, reaching people for Christ the group has befriended, and discipling members or being discipled by a member of the group. The bottom line is that a person cannot have two simultaneous spiritual authorities. He or she will run back to the first church to evade conflict and will not easily accept a challenge when it's given.

"I made community the highest goal of my group."

This mistake is tough. It seems so right when you're doing it! When the group fizzles, no one understands why. Small groups that focus on community, fellowship, and intimacy as the ultimate goal rarely see new believers in the group. God gave us community for a reason that transcends the "little corner of heaven" created in group life. If your group does not harness the power of biblical community to build the kingdom with new believers and new leaders, it will slowly die. The best way to avoid this mistake is to pray for the lost in every small group meeting.

Also, schedule a time to meet and hang out with your members' lost friends and family. Make a personal goal to help your members help these loved ones find Christ and join your loving community. If you're stuck in the community phase of group life, you must show your members this is what the victorious Christian life is all about! When your members catch a fire for reaching the lost, they will finally understand why community is so important and why it was created.

"I took shortcuts with equipping, discipleship, and accountability."

Pairing up members for accountability or sponsorship is a pain. The members don't really understand it and resist the self-discipline it demands. You may have even said to yourself, "Our church's equipping pathway is comprehensive, but my members seem to be doing OK without it."

Has this kind of thinking entered your mind? This mistake will come back to bite you, and it has huge, gnarly teeth. One day you'll think, "Why is my ministry as a small group leader so strained and going nowhere all at the same time?" Please, learn from the failure of others here! If you don't pair up your people for accountability, guess who gets to meet each member to encourage them to grow spiritually before work each work morning? YOU. If your members don't get discipled through the use of your equipping track and a mentor or accountability partner, guess who will baby-sit a bunch of immature believers through the never-ending small group cycle? You guessed it! YOU. But the results are really more impactful than your personal state of exhaustion.

Jesus modeled discipleship for us as He developed and released His twelve. They left and did all kinds of cool miracles because of His work with them. No equipping books way back then, you say? Yes, you're right. It was much harder without printed materials. You have it easy in the age of information in which we live!

Get busy pairing people up to work through your church's discipleship process or set your alarm for 5:00 a.m. There are no short cuts in discipleship, and if you try to take them, your alarm clock and a death-warmed-over look in the mirror will remind you every morning.

"My sole focus was the weekly small group meetings."

If you fail to create a seven-day-a-week relationship with your group members, your group will not grow because people aren't interested in another meeting. They want deep friendships where there are impromptu meals, baseball games, prayer, ministry time, and relaxing. Watching TV, surfing the Net, or sitting at the kitchen table and watching a pot of coffee disappear will dynamically change group life. Your members will tell their friends how much fun group life is—as opposed to a good small group meeting—and your group will flourish.

If your group only sees each other at the weekly meeting and at the Sunday services, you're not doing it right, and it's not a genuine "small group."

If you're making this mistake, don't worry; it's easy to fix. For example, invite a single person from your group over for dinner, and tell them to bring over a load of laundry. When you fold laundry together, they'll know you are interested in true Christian intimacy, not an attendance roster.

What you must do is reserve time to be with your group members between meetings. If you don't have the time to do this, make the time. Let go of things that are non-essential. Your golf game can suffer, your kids may not be in as many after school activities, and your new "open-door policy" at home will make for less private time, but this is your ministry, and it deserves more than leftovers! Remember, group life must be a high priority in your life for it to work. God has called you to it, and He wants to use your group to win souls and raise up leaders. It takes a sizeable time investment, but it's worth it.

"I appointed myself as the Holy Man (or Holy Woman)."

Answering all the Bible questions and maintaining dominant spiritual authority will make you a very lonely person! No one will join you in leadership because they don't measure up. People won't get close to you because you can't just be that special friend in a time of need . . . you have to fix the problem. It's also stepping on God's toes. If you're making this mistake, ask your group members for forgiveness in your next meeting. Tell them you love them and that you need help with a pride issue. That's the root of this problem.

The way to avoid this mistake is to prayerfully ask yourself, "How can God be glorified through someone else right now?" He will be faithful to show you how the whole body builds itself up by every supporting ligament. Even baby Christians can minister to others very effectively. The Holy Spirit operates at full strength in all who believe and give it away freely.

"I operated out of a vocational paradigm."

If you see small group leadership as a job at the church, you'll hate the position. Your role is one of a calling. A hired hand quits when the going gets tough. A called man or woman just sees the obstacles as new ways God will reveal His power. See the difference?

The way to avoid or recover from this mistake is to simply read the last mistake below. Drink at the well often, and you will never be thirsty. Prayer is the key here, and this will birth a calling in you, empowering you to do great things for God.

"I had no prayer life."

The biggest mistake small group leaders make is to cut off the lifeline to God's power and wisdom. It comes from above, and it solves all the problems a leader faces. Jesus modeled a life of prayer for us. As I reflect on His integral part of the Trinity, I see why Jesus prayed so much while on Earth. He was recently separated from His Father and the Holy Spirit and missed His family!

God created us in His image, and our spiritual nature thirsts for community with Him through prayer. If you don't pray much, don't expect much power in your ministry! Pray alone, with group members, family, friends, children, neighbors, co-workers, your boss, and total strangers when you feel led by the Spirit to do so. Prayer is powerful, and the more you pray, the better your ministry will be!

There are only two kinds of mistakes...

Good mistakes are the ones you learn from; bad mistakes are the ones that you repeat or ignore. God has given you a unique opportunity to shake up Satan's kingdom with the power of community. Your group was designed by God to storm the gates of Hell and set captives free. Don't be afraid to make changes today in your ministry to see revival in your small group!

PART

8

SMALL GROUP
LEADERSHIP

Many leaders speak about groups as a way to build community. However, groups which are focused on fellowship, sharing, and community generally will have a hard time attracting more than a minority of believers, will lose vitality, and fade away. Groups must have an outward focus in order to stay healthy.

—Steve Cordle

Teaching Small Group Members to Pray Out Loud

Rick Howerton

Jesus taught the disciples to pray. We should do the same.

I've been in ministry for 36 years now. An unforgettable ministry conversation took place one afternoon after our Sunday gathering of Christ-followers. One of the small group leaders at our church was speaking with me about the growth he was seeing in his small group members. I was already on the edge of my seat, but when he told me about one of the members who had prayed aloud for the very first time the week prior, I was trounced on by a dancing heart. And as I was driving home that day, my tear ducts got into the game. You see, the "first time out-louder" the small group leader was telling me about has a fantastic wife and two incredible sons. During my drive home that afternoon, I realized that these young boys were going to grow up in a home where dad prayed for them at the dinner table, by their beds, on vacation, etc…The list could go on and on. And those kids will do with their own children what they have seen their dad do. Because a small group leader took the time and strategically was teaching his small group members to pray aloud, a mountain of believers for generations to come will know what it means to be prayed for by godly, caring parents, and as those children realize that God is real and alive, they will want to know about His Son Jesus and will most likely choose a relationship with Him.

It is vital that we small group leaders teach those in our groups how to pray…aloud.

Below you'll find a simple step-by-step process that will help you as you teach small group members how to pray aloud.

STEP ONE: The leader models "effortless" prayer.

I use the term "effortless" because prayer is effortless when the person praying simply speaks to God as he or she speaks to a greatly respected close friend. There are no old English terms, no "thee's" and "thou's," and there is no expectation to sound cool or theologically deep.

STEP TWO: The leader leads the group to do "Complete the Sentence" prayers.

This could be a sentence like, "God, this is _____, I want to thank you for_____, or God, would you help with _____." The leader lets everyone know that if you prefer to pray silently to God instead of out loud, just let the group know by squeezing the hand of the person next to you (if the group is that close) or say the word "Amen" to indicate you are going to pray silently. This is for those who still haven't gotten into voicing prayers aloud. This is a giant first step for some. But if someone continues for weeks to opt out, let them know that the group is on their team and is looking forward to celebrating his/her first voiced prayer.

STEP THREE: Each group member prays a one-sentence prayer for another group member.

The group leader gives each group member in attendance a 3 x 5 card. Each group member is to write down the one most important request they have that week. The group leader tells the group, "It's important that your friends hear someone pray out loud for their situation or need. People are encouraged when they hear others praying for them. I'm going to ask you to pray for the person's situation that is written on the card. If you're new at praying out loud, just say, "God, _____ has something he/she needs you involved in." The person praying then says what the need is followed by, "Thank you for what you're about to do."

STEP FOUR: The leader alerts and aids individuals learning to pray publicly.

The group leader contacts two people who are learning to pray aloud and let's them know he would like for them to pray at the group meeting next week. He helps them know what to do if necessary. When the group leader calls on these persons to pray, he should be certain the he prays first, giving them time to settle into what they are about to do. After the meeting, the group leader should be sure to call the persons who prayed, thanking them and encouraging them.

STEP FIVE: Over time, group members become comfortable with out-loud praying.

There are a few important guidelines the small group leader should keep in mind.

1. The group should make it part of their stated goal that every group member learn to and find the blessing of praying out loud.

2. The group leader should remind the group that praying out loud is important because it encourages the person being prayed for.

3. At each of the first four steps, the leader should go first, modeling prayer for everyone in the group.

4. The small group leader must keep in mind that people change and grow at different speeds.

5. The process outlined above is not a four-week process. The small group leader must take the pulse of the group and move at a pace that is right for the slowest responder in the group. This process may take months.

If a small group leader will be patient and wise as they teach group members to pray aloud, they just may change the world; for sure, they'll transform households and families.

10 Ways to Help Group Members Participate

Mike Mack

Nathan Tate was a cell leader in a quandary. He had great quiet time—sometimes during his cell meeting! Other weeks, the talkative folks in the room would dominate the discussion. Some people would appear distracted and unable to focus during the sharing time. Nate was frustrated, and the group's gatherings would end on a hollow note. How could Nate facilitate the group so all the members would participate and get their needs met?

1. Plan.

Nate realized that he needed to take a step back and make long-range plans and goals for the group. His facilitation strategy, like that of many small-group leaders, was "ready, shoot, aim." But people need to know the target before they can effectively work toward it. They need a reason for being together and a sense that their group is striving for something, not just existing. People come to a group with different expectations. Without stated goals from the beginning, conflicts invariably arise. Those conflicts can eventually lead to the group's disintegration. A group with no plan is like Jesus' story about a blind man leading another blind man—into a pit (Matt. 15:14)!

To avoid the pits, pray for God's guidance in determining your goals. Observe the people in your group. Ask them questions about their expectations, interests, and needs. Formulate some specific goals, and then suggest them during a meeting. Encourage the group to discuss the goals and share any others they feel are important. Give them the opportunity to take "ownership" of the group's goals.

2. Keep an eye (and ear, nose, mouth, and skin) on the details.

Nate started paying attention to the physical environment of the meeting after reading this quote by poet Stephen Spender: "There is always a tendency of the body to sabotage the attention of the mind by providing some distraction." Some of Nate's cell group members could not focus on spiritual matters because of an uncomfortable atmosphere.

Keep these in mind when setting up your meeting space:

Circle up, so everyone can see the face of every other person in the group. A circle helps everyone participate equally.

Check the thermostat. Just a few people in a room increase the temperature. One expert advises that 67 degrees is an ideal temperature for groups.

Sniff around. We get accustomed to the smells in our homes, but visitors sense them immediately. Pets, things children spill in odd places, heavy perfumes, the evening dinner, even room deodorizers can irritate noses. Try lighting a few candles or simmering potpourri in the house. Research shows, for instance, that peppermint helps keep people alert.

Make your meeting tasteful. Straight-from-the-oven brownies, fresh popcorn, or a beautifully arranged tray of fruit encourage group interaction. They also signal people that you planned ahead and want them there. Be creative and remember to provide for weight-watchers, diabetics, and others with medical or personal needs.

Find the right room size. A cell meeting may feel intimidating in a huge room, but a group of 12 adults may feel claustrophobic in a tiny room.

Let your light shine, but not too brightly. Low lamplights are better than bright florescent or overhead lighting. The room should be bright enough for everyone to read, but low enough to feel cozy.

Don't allow couples to share materials or Bibles. One of them will be less involved in the discussion.

Guard against distractions. Turn off telephone ringers and mute the volume on answering machines. Put pets in another room or outside. Turn off TV sets, radios, and computers during a meeting.

3. Don't leave out the Holy Spirit!

The Spirit is the real teacher and leader. Nate began to notice how Jesus stayed open to His Father's moving. In John 5:17, Jesus said, "My Father is always at his work to this very day, and I, too, am working." Later He said, "I tell you the truth, the Son can do nothing by himself; he can do only what he sees his Father doing, because whatever the Father does the Son also does" (v. 19). If Jesus admitted that He could do nothing Himself, why should we think we can?

4. Build relationships outside the meeting.

People participate more when they feel like "one of the gang." A cell isn't just a once-a-week meeting. It's a lifestyle! The early church met together "every day" (Acts 2:46), encouraging each other, caring for each other, instructing one another, etc. Nate looked for creative ways for members to "meet together": using the phone and the Internet, doing everyday things (like shopping) together, playing or watching sports, whatever worked.

5. Listen.

The best facilitator actively listens more than speaks. The more Nate followed the tips below to improve his listening skills, the better he was able to facilitate the group.

Be quiet. This should be obvious, but it often is the biggest obstruction to listening. The leader should be part of a discussion without monopolizing it.

Try to understand. The goal of listening is to understand what the person is really saying.

Empathize. Interject short statements to show you are listening, understand, and accept what the person is saying. "That sounds exciting!" or "That must have been a hard decision to make" are examples of how to show empathy. Also, pay attention to your facial expressions.

Don't judge. Especially when someone is already hurting, a judgmental attitude can do more harm than good. Don't condone sin, of course, but recognize the difference between accepting the person and what is being said and showing approval of the sin.

Avoid advising. People usually do not want nor need you to solve their problem. They just need someone to listen.

Verify and clarify. If you're not sure that you understand what someone is saying, speak up. "Here's what I hear you saying. Am I right?" is one clarifier.

Listen for what is not said. Try to hear the meaning behind the words. Watch body language and listen to tone of voice. Sometimes what a person is saying is lost behind a clutter of words.

Affirm. "Thanks for sharing that. I'm sure it isn't easy to talk about right now." This builds acceptance for talking about difficult things and makes it easier for someone else to share.

6. Be real!

The leader must take the lead (amazing insight, isn't it?). Little by little, Nate opened up and became increasingly transparent. He prayed for discernment, discussed it with his intern, and prayed that the group would be ready to go to the next level of transparency.

The leader who models vulnerability and openness with the group draws out the members. Nate found that people start wanting intimacy when they need it, when they have a deep hurt or serious need in their own lives. If trust has been built, intimacy happens naturally.

7. Love 'em.

Unconditional love for participants (and even "nonparticipants") goes a long way. It's easy to love lovable people, but our high calling is to love the people who are tough to love, too. Nate learned the truth about this: that we can do this only as we accept and live in the love God has for us. "We love because he first loved us" (1 John 4:19). The most important thing a cell leader can do is intentionally walk with God every day, experiencing the fullness of God's love so that it might be poured out to those we lead.

8. Laugh!

Have fun as a group before, during, and after the meeting, and your cell will open up like you never imagined.

"A cheerful heart is good medicine" for your group (Proverbs 17:22). When people laugh together, they usually share more openly together, too.

Laughter breaks down the walls we build around ourselves. It helps people burdened with life's demands to release pent-up emotions in a positive way. A good belly laugh just feels good, especially when you can forget about yourself and your troubles for a while.

Nate used history-sharing icebreakers to get the group laughing together. He asked everyone to bring a photo of himself or herself in elementary or high school. Out-of-date clothing and hairstyles were enough to get them laughing, and stories about their childhood or teen years kept them chuckling. He asked members to share the funniest thing that had ever happened to them. Other times, he asked couples what humorous things happened when they were dating. He also could have used a video or audio clip from a recording of a Christian comedian on the subject of the study.

9. Facilitate the group; disciple individuals.

Don't get these confused. Jesus taught the crowds, but He discipled Peter, John, James, and others individually, often taking one or two or three away separately to talk with them. Spend time with individuals from the group, and not just the intern. Nate found that writing notes of encouragement to members or making a phone call when he noticed a member needing ministry helped during the group's time together.

Lovingly discipline as necessary.

10. Discover and use one another's gifts.

Everyone has a gift, a passion, a personality, and a role in the group. The group's thumbprint is dependent on each person's unique gift. A spiritual gift inventory may work for some groups. Nate got the group involved in ministry with one another—all kinds of ministry, both inside and outside the group. During meetings, he asked the group to share with one another what gifts they saw in others. These were some of the best cell meetings in which Nate had ever been involved. This discussion took place:

Rob: "You know, Cindy, you have the gift of mercy."

Cindy: "Me? You've got to be kidding."

Rob: "Yeah, you! When I went through my job loss, you were the one who came to me and hugged me and cared for me and my family."

Kate: "That's right, Cindy. When I was sick you came to visit me and brought me chicken noodle soup and prayed with me."

Craig: "And when I went through my divorce, you accepted me and loved me and listened to me."

Cindy: "Really? I didn't think of that as a gift. That's just a part of who I am!"

As each person discovered his or her gift, passion, and personality, and how he or she could play an important role in the group, Nate's job of facilitating became easier and more effective. As he modeled these Top 10 ways to help the group participate, each member recognized that he or she is an integral member of the Body of Christ and began behaving accordingly, inside and outside the meeting. You can follow Nate's lead and turn the "quiet times" of your cell meetings into an experience of life and mutual love. Watch out! People will begin to minister, and you won't be able to stop them.

Do Senior Pastors Murder Their Small Group Ministries?

Alan Danielson

Every church that has a small group ministry must have one indispensable staff person. No, I'm not talking about a small group pastor. I'm not talking about a small group administrator. The position every successful small group church must have is this: *Senior Pastor of Small Groups*. What do I mean? I believe I can say with absolute certainty that no church can have a truly successful small group ministry unless the senior pastor is the front person and number one supporter of the ministry.

I've consulted with countless small group pastors who have the same question: "How do I get my senior pastor to support my ministry?" What a tragedy!! What an indictment!! Today, I'm writing to you, senior and lead pastors, so listen up.

Don't you dare hire a small group pastor or launch a small group ministry in your church if you aren't going to be the loudest voice and biggest supporter of that ministry! Rick Warren sets a fantastic example for us all when he says, "I'm the small group pastor of Saddleback Church." As a senior pastor myself, that philosophy has become my own.

Senior pastors who are not the *Senior Pastor of Small Groups* in their churches find themselves quickly frustrated with the results of their small group ministries. They blame the staff who are in charge of that ministry by saying, "I made a bad hire. I need a major league leader next time." They blame the members of the church saying, "My people just aren't interested in groups." They blame the culture at-large by saying, "Small Groups just aren't relevant anymore." My response to all of those is simple: HOG WASH!!

First, no small group pastor, no matter how gifted a leader, will be successful without the senior pastor's partnership (which goes way beyond support, by the way). Second, the people in a church will value what their senior pastor values. When they see a token commitment to groups on the senior pastor's part, their own commitment will be token as well. Third, people in our culture are desperate to belong. They are naturally "grouping" with people who love them, accept them, challenge them, and care for them all the time. Why do you think the TV show *Friends* was such a success for so long? The same "group" formula from that TV show is seen in countless shows like *Seinfeld*, *Big Bang Theory*, and *Entourage*. With coffee shops on every corner, you can't tell me that small groups are not culturally relevant.

So how can a senior pastor become the *Senior Pastor of Small Groups*? Here are a few thoughts:

- **Repent.** Turn away from your neglect of this necessary ministry.
- **Live It!** Be in a small group and be committed to it.
- **Educate Yourself.** Read books like *Creating Community* by Andy Stanley, *7 Deadly Sins of Small Group Ministry* by Donahue and Robinson, *Simple Small Groups* by Bill Search, and the brand new *Small Groups Big Impact* by Egli and Marable.
- **Stage Presence.** Champion small group announcements from the stage and on video.
- **Weekly Mentions.** Mention small groups at least once in every sermon. This naturally makes small groups a part of your church DNA. Tell a story about your own group or say something simple like, "Maybe you need to bring up today's message in your small group this week."
- **High Expectations.** Make small group participation mandatory for staff members and for church membership.
- **Small Group Questions.** Write a few small group discussion questions and tack them on at the end of your weekly sermon notes in the bulletin.
- **Small Group Real Estate**. Make sure small groups have great representation in the lobby, on your website, and in your bulletin.
- **Relevant Approach.** Maybe you think groups aren't relevant because your church's *approach* to groups is not relevant. Consider promoting groups in coffee shops, book clubs, and online video chat rooms. Limiting groups to classrooms in your facility or to homes is a mistake.
- **No Small Group A.D.D.** Don't just let groups have your attention when something is out of place or broken. Pay attention to groups all the time. Demonstrate your care for the ministry by being interested in it all the time.

Okay, I've railed on senior pastors enough. I recognize that senior pastors are stretched thin and that the demands on their time are huge. I also realize that expecting small group ministry success without making many (if not all) of the above commitments is an exercise in futility. Your time is valuable so don't waste it by only being partially committed to small groups.

The Reason Your Discipleship Process Is Frustrating

Heather Zempel

I've talked a lot recently about making disciples. I'm struck by the fact that Jesus told his followers to go "make" disciples, not "find" disciples.

Once upon a time, someone stumbled upon my blog because they did a Google search for "how to shorten the discipleship process." This prompted me to immediately write a blog post on how the discipleship process cannot be shortened. And if that's what you are looking for, then you are in the wrong business. This isn't FedEx. It's not even the Pony Express. It's discipleship: the life-long pursuit of God and invitation to others to follow you in that process.

In the Great Commission, Jesus instructed us to go into all the world and make disciples. As leaders, we think we are accepting that challenge, but in reality, we are trying to find disciples. Jesus said go make disciples, not go find disciples.

If the people in our groups are not growing, it's our fault. If we get discouraged after one month or one year or even three, we haven't yet grasped that discipleship takes time. Twelve Galilean guys spent three focused years with Jesus himself and still didn't show up for the prayer meeting on the most important night in history.

We often look for disciples. We look for a potential leader. We hope to find someone with maturity and gifts that we can raise up. We forget that Jesus told us to go make them. Not find them. If you can't find a potential leader in your group, in your ministry, or on your team, it's not their fault. Don't blame them for being immature or needing to grow. It's your fault. It's my fault. We are supposed to make disciples. And making disciples is long, hard work.

The only way to measure success in discipleship is by looking at reproduction. At multiplication. Two verses continually serve as guideposts for me. 2 Timothy 2:2 NLT—*"You have heard me teach things that have been confirmed by many reliable witnesses. Now teach these truths to other trustworthy people who will be able to pass them on to others."*

Discipleship is about shared truths. It's passing on what God has taught us to another. This is the environment of face-to-face discipleship.
1 Thessalonians 2:8 NLT—*"We loved you so much that we shared with you not only God's Good News but our own lives, too."*

Discipleship is also about doing life together. It's about shared experiences. It's about inviting them into the opportunities and activities that you do and letting them be a part of them and learn with you and from you. It's the environment of shoulder-to-shoulder discipleship.

PART

8

SMALL GROUP
LEADERSHIP

PART

9

PERSONAL GROWTH
& LEADERSHIP
PART II

Past boldness is no assurance of future boldness. Boldness demands continual reliance on God's spirit.

—Andy Stanley

Grace Grows the Church

Judah Smith

It was the morning of October 27, 2007, and my prayer time had degenerated into a venting session. I was the youth pastor at The City Church in Seattle at the time, and in my opinion, the youth ministry wasn't growing big enough or fast enough. My team and I were all trying our hardest, but we had hit a plateau and couldn't seem to break through.

The book of Acts with its supernatural stories and explosive church growth wasn't blessing me so much as it was frustrating me. "Why, God? Why don't we see these things here in Seattle? How can we make our youth group and church grow?"

My prayer time ended, and I got in the shower, still frustrated, still complaining to God. He's used to that, I'm sure. David was a great complainer. The entire book of Psalms can pretty much be summed up by: "God, why do the wicked have all the gold, glory, and girls, and here I am running for my life, and you don't even care; please, please, PLEASE help me…actually, come to think of it, you are God, and you are good, and I trust you, and sooner or later, things will work out for your glory and my salvation, and I guess I've got a great life after all, and I love you. Selah."

When I stepped out of the shower, God spoke to me. Not audibly—if He ever does that, I'll probably hide under the kitchen table—but a phrase branded itself on my brain: Grace grows the church. Immediately, I remembered Acts 4:33 NKJV: "And great grace was upon them all."

I didn't think too much about it at the time, but looking back, that was a defining moment in my life and ministry. I began to see grace everywhere I looked: in the Bible, in my church, in God's dealings with me.

I didn't know that a year later I would become the preaching pastor of our church, or that two years later, I would take over from my dad as lead pastor. Leading a church with a weekly attendance of over six thousand, a staff of over a hundred, and a multimillion-dollar budget is more than intimidating, and without that revelation of grace, I wouldn't have survived.

While the transition has not always been easy—change never is—God's grace has been more than enough. Our attendance is up, dozens are getting saved each week, giving has increased even in the midst of recession, and lives are being changed.

Grace is the central theme of the Bible. Taking grace out of the Bible would be like taking speed away from a running back: you wouldn't have much left. Fourteen New Testament books begin with a reference to grace, and fifteen end with one. The message is clear: Start with grace and end with grace, and you'll get the job done.

Think back to the origins of the church in Acts 2: a group of uneducated and fear-struck nobodies were filled with the power of the Spirit, and in one afternoon, three thousand people were saved. Soon the number grew to five, ten, twenty, one hundred thousand. In the words of their enemies, they turned the world upside down. Two thousand years later, two billion people are called Christians.

Was that the ingenuity of a man? Were the disciples holed up in the upper room, plotting how to create a worldwide phenomenon that would span two millennia? Did they just get lucky? Or was great grace upon them all?

Forget the spreadsheet, calculator, and pencil—you won't figure out how the Early Church grew with logic alone. It's no coincidence that the first time we see church growth mentioned, we hear that "The Lord added to the church daily those who were being saved" (Acts 2:47 NKJV).

Please don't misunderstand me; I'm not dismissing the importance of strategy or hard work. But they must begin and end with grace, or they won't last. If I have to be smart enough and tough enough to do this all on my own for the next thirty years, please, just shoot me now! As I've told my church more than once, if you were thirty years old and had six thousand people showing up every week expecting to hear something new, profound, and biblical, you'd be preaching grace, too!

Our greatest efforts and best-laid plans won't accomplish in a lifetime what God's grace will do in a moment. His grace is the reason we are serving Him in the first place. It's why we care about the lost and why we minister to people—even the mean ones. It's grace that draws in hurting people who need to belong before they can believe or behave.

It's grace that grows the church.

Tips for Leading Strong-Willed People in Your Ministry

Ron Edmondson

Have you ever tried to lead someone who didn't want to be led? The same children that were labeled "strong-willed" by their parents often grow up to be strong-willed adults. Perhaps you know one…perhaps you are one. (I know one personally…me!)

I believe leadership should be individualized for the needs of the follower. With that in mind, here are five tips for leading strong-willed people.

1. **Give clear expectations**—People respond best when they know what is expected of them, especially those with strong opinions of their own.

2. **Be consistent**—Strong-willed people need boundaries. They will test them, but they want to know what the limits of their freedom.

3. **Give freedom within the boundaries**—Once the guidelines and expectations are established, allow followers to express themselves freely within them.

4. **Pick your battles**—Don't cross a strong-willed person for issues of little importance to the overall vision of the organization. If you back them into a corner…they may bite.

5. **Respect their opinions and individualities**—Strong-willed people ultimately want to be heard (as all people do), but they resist most when their voice is silenced. Learn what matters to them and give credence to their opinions.

10 High-Impact Planning Ideas for Leaders

Will Mancini

1. **Write down your top 12 leaders and an action-item bullet point for each one.** How can you invest in each this year? How will you spend time with them? What tools do they need? Do they require more support, direction, coaching, or delegation? Don't just look at your existing structure, look to who is emerging.

2. **Schedule a benchmarking trip to visit a church that's 40 percent larger in weekend attendance than yours.** Ask the church to invest team-on-team time and connect one-on-one in the designated staff areas.

3. **Take the Clarity Quiz (available here: ChurchUnique.com/downloadable-tools) in your next staff meeting.** Use the quiz to prioritize a single staff goal for the next 90 days. Make the goal big, measurable, and define how each person will contribute.

4. **Schedule an offsite leadership retreat, and make it a bigger event than in years past.** Draw a pie chart for how much time to spend on fun stuff vs. strategic work. Delegate agenda development for each side of the pie chart, or brainstorm the agenda with your key leaders in early January.

5. **Schedule an "hour of vision" in your monthly meeting pattern.** Creating space for teams to have dialogue and to shape and own the vision is a huge move for the senior leader. Ask them a simple questions like, "What was your favorite thing about last year, and how to we do more of it?" Or ask them creative questions like, "If someone wrote a $25,000 check to your ministry, how would you spend it and why?"

PART

9

PERSONAL GROWTH & LEADERSHIP
PART II

6. **Cast a leadership vision to pray for people far from God**. Ask each person on the leadership team to share 3-5 people in their sphere of influence who are far from God. Pray for these people by name as a group every week this year.

7. **Schedule values-based leadership gatherings.** Design several staff or leadership gatherings throughout the year based on your church values. For example, if you have six values, plan six special gatherings. During each experience, highlight the designated value in a concrete way. Celebrate and honor individuals who are modeling the value well.

8. **Increase your culture of collaboration.** Find a coach or friend in ministry who can provide some staff training. Re-engage that personality assessment that came and went too quickly.

9. **Create a "stop doing" list and execute.** Whether your church is growing, plateaued, or declining, you will greatly benefit from identifying and eliminating the 20 percent of church's activity that is the lowest return on the mission. As a team, ask the question ruthlessly, "Why do we do what we do?"

10. **Take some new steps to develop leaders at every level of involvement.** Many pastors hope to do this but never get to it. But it's not that hard if you take a little time to plan. Spend three months designing, three months building behind the scenes, and set a launch date.

How to Listen to God's Voice:

A ChurchLeaders.com Q & A with Bill Hybels

Does God still speak to His followers today? Bill Hybels, the lead pastor of Willow Creek Community Church in South Barrington, Illinois, says, "Yes." In this interview, we talk to one of the most influential church leaders in America about his book *The Power of a Whisper,* why he believes God still speaks today, and the four filters for discerning His voice.

ChurchLeaders: You've said that it took 35 years to write *The Power of a Whisper*. Explain a little bit about how the book was cultivated—when you originally had the idea and how it came to fruition.

Bill Hybels: The book is really about one of the central themes of the activity of God in my life since I was a young child. All of these major events in my life were the result of whispers. I've talked about this with the Willow congregation for decades, but I would do a single message here or part of a message there, and I realized as the 35th anniversary was approaching that I had never done a complete apologetic of the whole concept of "Does God still speak today?" I had never just built a case for it and developed the whole thought process from A to Z. How does it get abused? What are the filters you put promptings through? How does it affect leadership? How does it affect parenting? How does it affect social justice issues? So the book was my attempt to take 35 years of my life and then 35 years of ministry and to build an irrefutable case for the fact that God still speaks.

CL: Why do you think the fact that God still talks today is so controversial for churches and ministry leaders?

BH: Well, because it can be so easily abused. All you have to do in a Christian leadership meeting is say, "We're going to go this direction because God told me we should..." Well, how do you trump that? Those are conversation enders. There are some whole circles in evangelicalism where that's called a foul ball—like that's out of play. And then the other extreme is, you know, "God told me to wear this shirt," and "God told me to tell you that you shouldn't be on the team," and this thing covers the full spectrum from ignoring it to craziness about it. So because it is so easily misunderstood and easily abused, most pastors want to stay away from the conversation. If they fire up the conversation, they have to live with the consequences, and it's probably easier if you just keep that part of Christianity out of the equation. No one pulls the trump card out, and it just makes things a little tidier.

But I can't deny how often God has spoken to me. I can't deny how many times God has spoken to other Willow leaders in ways that, if they hadn't reported it to me, everything would have been different with the unfolding history of our church. So I just decided I'm going to talk about it intelligently. I'm going to talk about it with the right caveats and qualifiers, and I'll deal with some of the messiness that comes when people don't understand it and get a little carried away.

CL: There are numerous examples of God talking to people—audibly—in Scripture. Why do you think it's such a difficult concept to believe God still speaks to us today?

BH: Fear. Just fear. If you open up that Pandora's Box, all kinds of stuff is going to come flying out of it. Next thing you know, some Bible study group leader is going to say, "God told me to, you know, do this or that…" and then a staff member is going to say, "God told me this…" and then you're going to have people saying, "God told me to sell my house and turn the proceeds into lottery tickets…" When you're running an organization, the last thing you want is a whole bunch of people running around saying, "God told me this or that…" because it does get messy.

I should probably add that, just so that I'm not disingenuous here, some people actually believe theologically that God no longer speaks. You know, that once the Scriptures were completed—that's it. I believe that's a difficult position to hold theologically, but some people do believe it, and so they shut down this conversation based on their theology. But the greater number of people, I think, shut down the conversation because of fear.

CL: Often when God speaks to His followers in the Bible, there's a high cost involved. Does it often work the same way today?

BH: Yes. We should never convey to leaders or teammates that when God does speak to you, the direction He's urging you to go is going to be successful and low-cost.

I was talking to Chuck Colson some time ago about this subject matter. He mentioned that he likes the book, and he said, "I started Prison Fellowship from a prompting, from a whisper." It was after Watergate, and he wanted to go back into business. He was in debt. He wanted to generate some income. In the middle of the night, he gets an unmistakable sense from God that he's to start a ministry to prisoners. He didn't want to do it. He knew what that would entail, but it was unmistakable. And it's been costly for him, but he did it.

We have to be careful that we don't romanticize the idea of promptings, because many promptings are calls or challenges by God to do extremely difficult things—it leads you to sacrifice and hardship and invisibility, and the reward comes in the next reality, not in this one.

CL: Sometimes, I think we want to hear God's voice so badly that we can manufacture it. What are some of the filters that we can use to make sure we're hearing the voice of God?

BH: I go to considerable lengths to help people discern if something is from God. Is this prompting from God? 1) Does it align with His attributes? Is it consistent with His character? 2) Is it Scriptural? If you ever get an impression in your head to do something that controverts Scripture, it's not from God. Game, set, match: It's not from God. He doesn't speak with a double voice. His promptings match His revealed Word. Sometimes, we get impressions about things, saying things or doing things that are not specifically addressed in Scripture—starting a new ministry or shutting one down or moving from one locale to another, what school to put your kid in, or something like that. 3) Is it wise? Would Jesus support such a decision? Jesus said be wise as serpents, gentle as doves. Is what you're planning or thinking—this idea coming from God—is it wise? 4) Is it in tune with your own character and wiring pattern and giftedness? 5) Do other trusted people who love God and love you affirm it? Do they counsel caution? Do they say, "I think you're off your rocker?"

CL: Do you think most leaders are in tune with listening to God's promptings and God's whispers, or do you feel like something is lacking?

BH: You know, I think what's lacking is the language around the subject matter. What's lacking is a Biblical framework to think it through with. What's lacking are the filters.

I'm with pastors a lot. It's a major part of what I do, and often when I'm talking on the subject matter, I'll say to them, "Were any of you headed a different way in your life but wound up in ministry because of some sense that God wanted you to be a pastor?" Well, everybody goes, "Yeah, I wouldn't be a pastor unless I felt God wanted me to be." I say, "All right, well, let's go around the room and talk about your experiences. How did you know God wanted you to be a pastor?" When you start having that conversation, then people say, "Well, it was an impression, and then I talked to my friends about it, and then they affirmed, and it was consistent with my giftings and…" It winds up being the five filters. So when I lead them through this process, I say, "Now, gang, every single Christ-follower in your congregation has a vocation, has a gift, is making decisions about family and finances and their future every day. You have to arm your people with language to discuss this idea, the theological framework, and the filters, and as you do, you'll empower your congregation to be more confident in hearing from God. You'll empower them to have the guts to respond."

5 Prices a Leader Must Be Willing to Pay

Perry Noble

Jesus gave some INCREDIBLE advice in Luke 14:28–30! Today, we will dive into five areas where we need to be willing to pay the price as a leader.

1. There Is a Financial Cost.

Books cost money. Conferences cost money. Putting yourself in a position to be stretched and grown cost money. AND one of the qualities that I've always noticed in leaders who were "getting it done" is that they were personally willing to pay a financial price.

2. There Is an Emotional Cost.

Leading in the church is one of the most emotionally draining things you will EVER do. You will discover that you can go from the highest of highs to the lowest of lows with one e-mail or phone call. Your heart and motives will be called into question. Critics who don't know you (nor do they want to know you) will malign, misrepresent, and attack you. On most days, you will feel overwhelmed and unworthy of your calling…and all of this requires that we be willing to pay the price emotionally.

3. There Is a Physical Cost.

Laziness and leadership do NOT go hand in hand. It takes blood, sweat, and tears in order to be developed to your fullest leadership potential…which means you get your butt out of bed and go to work! And yes, REST is essential…but it isn't possible to burn out if you've never actually been on fire. There are seasons where lots of time, energy, and focus is demanded—period.

PART

9

PERSONAL
GROWTH
& LEADERSHIP
PART II

4. There Is a Spiritual Cost.

The more influential you become as a leader, the greater the intensity of spiritual attack on your life. (BTW...I've had shots taken at me for saying this, but it's true. I've experienced it personally...and in the Scriptures, we see in Acts 19 a demon literally having a conversation with seven guys...he tells them he knows Jesus and has heard about Paul, probably because he was causing such a disturbance, but then tells the guys he hadn't even heard about them!!! Like it or not...the enemy doesn't pursue everyone with the same intensity.)

You will experience spiritual warfare. You will encounter temptation on a level that is greater than anything you could imagine. You have to be willing to fight the fight and pay the price if you want to be a godly leader.

5. There Is a Personal Cost.

All of the things listed above come around to this...there IS a personal cost when it comes to leadership. It will NEVER cease to affect you. Jesus knew this when He was in the garden and yet still fully surrendered to the Father and went to the cross.

Galatians 6:9 is a promise we should take to heart as leaders. Do not give up... do not throw in the towel. At times, the price is incredibly high...but none of us has been asked to pay the price that the ONE we say we follow had to pay! His assignment was MUCH tougher than ours...and it brought Him joy to fulfill it.

So...let's keep our eyes on Jesus and keep doing exactly what He has called us to do, knowing that He is with us, has equipped us, empowered us, and that II Corinthians 4:7 is as true today as it was when Paul wrote it!

DON'T GIVE UP!!!

18 Ways Leaders Ruin Their Reputation on Facebook

Paul Steinbrueck

Facebook is a great way for you to build and maintain relationships with people both inside your church and in your community. But Facebook is not without its risks. Every time you post something, you risk hurting, offending, or distancing yourself from people. So here are 18 things you want to avoid doing on Facebook...

First, the ugly...

1. Post something out of frustration in the heat of the moment. We all get frustrated at times. And if you want to engage people authentically, you need to "keep it real." But Facebooking when angry, frustrated, or hurt is never a good idea. Take a few minutes (or a few hours) to cool down, and then think again if you really want to use Facebook to vent.

2. Criticize people. Even if you don't use a person's name, chances are you're Facebook friends with that person or someone close enough to the situation to know who you're really talking about.

3. Embarrass yourself. Expect everyone in your congregation and your community to see everything you post to Facebook. So don't post anything you wouldn't be comfortable saying or showing from the pulpit on a Sunday morning.

4. Embarrass your family. Our spouses and kids say and do funny things all the time. Most of those things can be posted to Facebook with no problem, and they help people to see you're a normal person with a normal family. But be sensitive, and when in doubt, ask your spouse and kids if it's OK to share a quote, happening, or pic online.

5. Criticize other churches in the community. Every church has a different mission, ministry philosophy, style of worship, and theology. But we all share one Lord, one faith, and one baptism. We should be known for our unity not our division.

The self-absorbed...

6. Only talk about your church. Pastors, when people become Facebook friends with you, it's because they want to engage with you—a real person—not a spokesperson for your church.

7. Share everything posted to the church FB page. Even if you post personal updates to your Facebook profile, don't repost every church update as well. Some—yes, all—no.

8. Just talk about yourself. When you go to a social event, do you like hanging around with people who only talk about themselves and never ask you about you? Don't be one of those people online either.

The disingenuous...

9. Act like your life is perfect. Nobody is perfect, and everyone knows it. If you act like everything is good all the time, you'll be perceived as inauthentic, wearing a mask.

10. Act like you're always "joyful in the Lord." Nobody is happy all the time either.

11. Act like you have all the answers. Nobody likes a know-it-all either. Share insight and advice when asked. Be confident but not arrogant.

The offender...

12. Act like the language/morality police. Your Facebook friends are not perfect. They are going to swear, post questionable pictures of themselves, and share things you don't agree with. If something is really bad, consider contacting the person privately about it, but don't call people out publicly for what is unfortunately common behavior in our culture.

13. Roll out the fire and brimstone. I don't know if preaching about sin and hell worked with past generations, but it's not going to put you in a position to influence people on Facebook. People on Facebook respond much more favorably to hope and love.

14. Be overly political. It's OK to take stands on key issues, but unless you want to irk half your church and close the door to half the people in your community (not to mention risk losing your non-profit status), don't tow a party line.

15. Engage people in debates. Online (and offline) debates rarely cause anyone to shift their position on an issue. Discussion is great, but if things get heated or personal, it's time to lighten up.

The disengaged...

16. Post a lot of theological stuff that's over the heads of your friends. It's great for pastors to engage their Facebook friends in spiritual conversations, but avoid posting your doctoral thesis. It's not going to engage anyone and will put people off.

17. Login once every week or two. Relationships require consistency. You can take breaks, go on vacation, and don't need to be on Facebook every day, but you've got to be regular if you're going to build relationships in Facebook.

18. Fail to respond. When people send you messages, post to your wall, or post comments to your status updates and links, it's important to respond. Answer people's questions. Thank people for their insight and stories.

Stretching someone out of their comfort zone should be a means of developing people in their sweet spot, not taking them out of it. There's such a thing as being uncomfortable because you're being stretched. And then there's being uncomfortable because you're doing something you weren't created for.

—Steven Furtick

Holy Embarrassment

Mark Batterson

My most recent embarrassing moment? Listen, it's no fun getting a phone call at one o'clock in the afternoon asking you why you aren't at the wedding you're supposed to be officiating that was supposed to start at noon. I flat out forgot. I was at the mall, in a dressing room, trying on clothes. I had to get home, shower, put on a suit, and drive forty-five minutes through a snowstorm to get there. I finally arrived at three o'clock. My ego never did show up.

Embarrassing moments are horrible, no doubt. But they are also wonderful. Few things are as freeing as a little embarrassment. It frees us from the burden of pretense, and it forces us to stop taking ourselves so seriously. In a sense, embarrassment is one way we die to self. And dying to self is one way we come to life.

The words humor, humiliation, and humility are all etymologically related. In fact, humor is a derivative of humiliation. One dimension of humility is the ability to laugh at ourselves, and I'm convinced that the happiest, healthiest, and holiest people on the planet are those who laugh at themselves the most.

Too many people live as if the purpose of life is to avoid embarrassment at all costs. They never put themselves in situations that might be awkward. So they forfeit joy. They never reveal who they really are. So they forfeit intimacy. They never take risks. So they forfeit opportunity. They try to avoid embarrassment at all cost, and the cost is their soul—or, should I say, their soulprint.

I'm not suggesting that you go out and embarrass yourself by doing something stupid. And I'm certainly not encouraging embarrassment that is the byproduct of social cluelessness. But too often, we allow the fear of embarrassment to get between God and us. We're too embarrassed to share our faith or confront a friend or walk away from a sinful situation. But if embarrassment is the result of doing something right, it's holy embarrassment. And there are certain situations where embarrassment is the only way you can remain true to God and to yourself. It's either embarrassment or hypocrisy, embarrassment or sin, embarrassment or obedience. In those situations, embarrassment isn't something to be avoided. In fact, if we follow the example set by David, it is something to be cultivated and celebrated.

I will become even more undignified than this, and I will be humiliated in my own eyes. II Samuel 6:22

Excerpted from Soulprint *by Mark Batterson Copyright (c) 2011 by Mark Batterson.*

Who's Really Qualified to Lead the Church?

Brady Boyd

What qualifies someone to be a leader in the church? Can someone just announce to the rest of us that "God called me" or "God spoke to me"? How can we evaluate maturity and health in a person who wants to influence others in the local fellowship? What about a Bible school degree? Isn't that enough? What if the degree has lots of letters and abbreviations after it? Surely, that's enough? Timothy had the same questions for the Apostle Paul, and here is his answer as recorded in 1 Timothy 3:2–7:

"Now the overseer must be above reproach, the husband of but one wife, temperate, self-controlled, respectable, hospitable, able to teach, not given to drunkenness, not violent, but gentle, not quarrelsome, not a lover of money. He must manage his own family well and see that his children obey him with proper respect. If anyone does not know how to manage his own family, how he can take care of God's church? He must not be a recent convert, or he may become conceited and fall under the same judgment as the devil. He must also have a good reputation with outsiders, so that he will not fall into disgrace and into the devil's trap."

Paul was clearly pointing out that the bar should be raised more for leaders of the church than for others in the fellowship. Paul was not giving a long list of impossible rules—that's what the Pharisees were known for doing. No, Paul was giving a short list of reasonable expectations for a significant leader such as an elder or what we would call a pastor.

Paul was also saying that other people should evaluate potential leaders before they could lead. So often, I hear people say, "God is the only one who can appoint me" or "God is the only one who can restore me." It's true that God is the only redeemer of our souls, the giver of all our gifts, and the only one who can forgive our sins, but God has always used delegated human authority to evaluate men and women who desire to lead a local church. Paul was writing to humans who were trying to choose human leaders. Paul did not say, "Take everyone at their word, and give leadership to whoever wants it."

This same list of requirements is meant for those who have disqualified themselves from pastoral leadership and want to be restored. The same requirements that originally qualified us for leadership are the same for those wanting to start over. It also means that once again delegated human authority will have to recognize the work of God in a person's life the same as in the beginning of their ministry.

Basically, the three areas mentioned in 1 Timothy 3 and again in Titus 1 involve faith, family, and finances. If a leader has a personal, mature relationship with God that is evidently growing, has a vigorous, vibrant family, and has healthy personal finances, then leadership in the local church should be considered. If any of these three areas are unhealthy, it is a sign of either immaturity or a lack of character.

Let's not substitute health and maturity for talent, charm, or charisma. The local church is the Bride of Christ, and she deserves and requires our best care, forever and always.

The Two Tensions a Leader Must Manage in Ministry

Perry Noble

1. I Must Be Available to Everyone

I've said it before, and I will say it again; the leader who is always available to everyone at all times is seldom available to God.

Too many pastors/church leaders have what is commonly known as "The Messiah complex." They feel like they are the only ones who can meet with people, pray with the sick, solve the problems, and do all of the counseling as well. (AND in most cases, I do NOT blame the people but rather the leader who has a need to be needed, who is more dependent on the people than he/she is the power and presence of God in their lives.)

I've heard it said before, and I will say it again; if you NEED people, you can't LEAD people.

We cannot be available to everyone at all times. JESUS WASN'T! Luke 5:16 (as well as numerous other verses) talk about the fact that Jesus OFTEN sought solitude so that He could simply pray, reflect, and focus on the Father. We've GOT to do the same if we are going to be leaders that IMPACT God's Kingdom.

2. I Can't Be Available to Anyone

The problem in many cases when we try to fight lie #1 is that the pendulum swings to the extreme opposite, and we actually believe that the leader could not and should not ever be available to anyone, at anytime, for any reason. Thus, the pastor/church leader becomes more of a king than a servant and completely loses touch with the people he is called to lead.

Jesus was the PERFECT model for this. If ANYONE had a packed and important agenda, it was Him. He knew He had three years. He knew He had a job to do, and yet we see Him quite often in the Scriptures taking time to hang out with little children, heal the sick, have dinner with some "sinners," and have a conversation with a woman who had a pretty bad reputation (see John 4).

We've GOT to listen to the Holy Spirit on this one. We've GOT to allow HIM to shape our agenda. And, if our agenda NEVER includes the people we are called to serve, then there is a good possibility that we are pursuing our agenda, not His.

How to Do Justice and Not Undermine Evangelism

D. A. Carson

1. By doing evangelism.

I know numerous groups that claim to be engaging in "holistic" ministry because they are helping the poor in Chicago or because they are digging wells in the Sahel, even though few, if any, of the workers have taken the time to explain to anyone who Jesus is and what he has done to reconcile us to God. Their ministry isn't holistic; it's halfistic or quarteristic.

2. By being careful not to malign believers of an earlier generation.

The popular buzz is that evangelicals before this generation focused all their energies on proclamation and little or nothing on deeds of mercy. Doubtless one can find sad examples of such reductionism, but the sweeping condescension toward our evangelical forbears is neither true nor kind. To take but one example: The mission SIM has emphasized evangelism, church planting, and building indigenous churches for a century—yet without talking volubly of holistic ministry, it built, and still operates, many of the best hospitals in sub-Saharan Africa.

3. By learning, with careful study of Scripture, just what the gospel is, becoming passionately excited about this gospel, and then distinguishing between the gospel and its entailments.

The gospel is the good news of what God has done, especially in Christ Jesus, especially in his cross and resurrection; it is not what we do. Because it is news, it is to be proclaimed. But because it is powerful, it not only reconciles us to God, but also transforms us, and that necessarily shapes our behavior, priorities, values, relationships with people, and much more. These are not optional extras for the extremely sanctified, but entailments of the gospel. To preach moral duty without the underlying power of the gospel is moralism that is both pathetic and powerless; to preach a watered-down gospel as that which tips us into the kingdom, to be followed by discipleship and deeds of mercy, is an anemic shadow of the robust gospel of the Bible; to preach the gospel and social justice as equivalent demands is to misunderstand how the Bible hangs together.

4. By truly loving people in Jesus' name—our neighbors as ourselves, doing good to all people, especially those of the household of faith.

That necessarily includes the alleviation of suffering, both temporal and eternal. Christians interested in alleviating only eternal suffering implicitly deny the place of love here and now; Christians who by their failure to proclaim the Christ of the gospel of the kingdom while they treat AIDS victims in their suffering here and now show themselves not really to believe all that the Bible says about fleeing the wrath to come. In the end, it is a practical atheism and a failure in love.

This article originally appeared on TheGospelCoalition.org.

Do You Lead with a "What If" Faith?

Steven Furtick

I was swimming with Elijah this past summer, and he started getting really brave and jumping off the ledge of the pool. To make it safe, I would stand in the pool and catch him.

But then he got really cocky and started jumping before I was looking. There was no danger. I was right there to pick him up, which is why he was doing it in the first place. But still, it was the principle.

So I warned him, "Elijah, you've got to stop that. What if you fall in the water and daddy didn't tell you to jump yet?" He looked straight at me and said, "Well, what if?"

He had me. The truth is I wasn't going to let him drown, and he knew it. His faith in my love and my ability to save him compelled him to be bold and take a risk. He wasn't testing my willingness or power to save him. He was jumping because he knew they were already there.

This is the essence of childlike faith. It sets you free to risk, to say *well, what if*. Even to the point of coming off as cocky in your faith. You're not testing God or trying to prove His power or love towards you. You're taking bold steps because His power and love have already been proven.

Peter had *well, what if* faith.

What if you sink into the water when you try to walk on it? *Well, what if? Jesus is there.*

Peter's faith wasn't that he could walk on water. It was that Jesus could catch him if he fell. And so he became one of two men in history to walk on water. The other was God in the flesh.

Not bad company.

Paul had *well, what if* faith.

What if you're beaten and tortured for your faith? *Well, what if? I consider that my present sufferings aren't worth comparing to the glory that will be revealed in me.*

What if they kill you? *Well, what if? To die is gain.*

What if they let you live and put you in prison? *Well, what if? To live is Christ. I'll convert the guards.*

See why he turned the world upside down?

There is always going to be a *what if* standing in the way of your dream or your desire to radically obey God. Resolve yourself to respond with a *well, what if* of your own.

What if you're wrong and you're not supposed to take that risk for Christ? *Well, what if? I think God would rather me take a sincere risk for Him and be wrong than sit safely in the comfort of my own complacency.*

What if you fail? *Well, what if? As others have said before, I'm much more afraid of succeeding at something that really doesn't matter.*

What if you ruin your life? *Well, what if I waste it?*

What if...*Well, what if?*

The local church is the hope of the world, and its future rests primarily in the hands of its leaders.

—*Bill Hybels*

AUTHORS

Kent Anderson is the Dean of Northwest Baptist Seminary and an Associate Professor of Homiletics at ACTS Seminaries of Trinity Western University. Learn more from Kent at Preaching.org.

Matt Appling is a school teacher and pastor of a house church, Levi's House, in Kansas City, Missouri. Read more from Matt at his blog, TheChurchofNoPeople.com.

Ben Arment helps people launch great things. He's the founder of Dream Year, The Whiteboard Sessions, and STORY in Chicago, and he also wrote a book called *Church in the Making*. He blogs often at BenArment.com.

Greg Atkinson has been writing, speaking, and training church leaders since 2000. Greg produced an online church planter training program for the Association of Related Churches at ChurchPlanter. tv and now travels the country as a secret shopper/mystery worshiper for churches of all sizes. Find out more about Greg's ministry at WorshipImpressions.com.

Greg Baird is a children's ministry veteran with over 20 years ministry experience. Greg has had the privilege of serving in four San Diego-area churches, including under the leadership of both John Maxwell and David Jeremiah. He continues to fulfill his life calling through the ministry of Kidmin360, offering an experienced voice in equipping and connecting Children's Ministry leaders around the country and around the world. Learn more from Greg at Kidmin360.com.

Mark Batterson is the lead pastor of National Community Church in Washington, D.C.,

a multi-site church and a leading fellowship in the nation's capital. Meeting in movie theaters and Metro stops throughout the D.C. area, NCC is attended by more than 70 percent single twentysomethings. Mark's weekly podcast is one of the fastest growing in America. His book, *In A Pit With a Lion on a Snowy Day: How to Survive and Thrive When Opportunity Roars* peaked at #44 on Amazon.com's best-seller list. He also wrote *Wild Goose Chase: Reclaiming the Adventure of Pursuing God* and *Soulprint: Discovering Your Divine Destiny.* Read more from Mark at Evotional.com.

Brady Boyd is the lead pastor of New Life Church in Colorado Springs, Colorado. Before coming to New Life in August 2007, Pastor Brady served as the Associate Senior Pastor of Gateway Church in the DFW Metroplex. While there, Gateway grew from 100 to over 12,000 active members in just six years. Author of *Fear No Evil*, he's really serious about caring for the people of Colorado Springs by opening numerous Dream Centers. Learn more from Brady at NewLifeBlogs.com/BradyBoyd.

Brenton Brown has written some of the best-loved worship songs in the world today, including "Everlasting God," "Lord Reign in Me," "All Who Are Thirsty," and "Hallelujah (Your Love is Amazing)." He currently has five songs in CCLI's Top 100. Originally from South Africa, Brenton came to the U.K. in 1996 and joined Vineyard Church as a worship leader. He would eventually lead the development of the Vineyard worship movement, which has grown to impact the Church

worldwide. Explore Brenton's music and learn more about him at BrentonBrown.com.

D. A. Carson is a research professor of the New Testament at Trinity Evangelical Divinity School in Deerfield, IL and co-founder (with Tim Keller) of The Gospel Coalition. Read more from Don at TheGospelCoalition.org/blogs/LoveofGod.

Francis Chan is an author and church leader, formerly the pastor of Cornerstorne Church in Simi Valley, California. Chan has authored three books, *Crazy Love, Forgotten God,* and *Erasing Hell: What God Said About Eternity and the Things We Made Up.* He has also written several books for children. He is the founder of Eternity Bible College and sits on the board of directors of Children's Hunger Fund and World Impact. Read more from Francis at FrancisChan.com.

Tom Cheyney is the co-author of *Spin-Off Churches* (B&H Publishers), a conference speaker, and a frequent writer on church planting, new church health, and church revitalization. You can contact him at Tom@Revitalization101.com or visit www.BoomerangChurches.com. You can connect with Dr. Tom Cheyney and the Church Revitalization Coaching Network additionally via Facebook at the Church Revitalization Network.

Joel Comiskey (Ph.D. Fuller Seminary) is an internationally recognized cell church coach and consultant. He has served as a missionary with the C&MA in Quito, Ecuador and is now founding pastor of a cell-based church in Southern California. Joel has written best selling books on the worldwide cell group movement. He teaches as an adjunct professor at several theological seminaries. Joel Comiskey Group is a tax exempt, non-profit organization dedicated to helping complete the Great Commission in this century by providing resources and coaching to plant new cell churches and transition existing churches to cell-based ministry. For further reading on this topic, see Joel's books *Making Cell Groups Work Navigation Guide* and *Home Cell Group Explosion.* You can also read more from Joel at JoelComiskey.com.

Phil Cooke, Ph.D. is a speaker, media consultant, and filmmaker who blogs at PhilCooke.com. His latest book is *Jolt! Get the Jump on a World That's Constantly Changing* by Thomas Nelson Publishers.

Terrace Crawford, a popular speaker and writer, is the youth channel editor at ChurchLeaders. com. Terrace has been a mentor to students and youth workers for more than 15 years and connects with people everyday through his blog, www.TerraceCrawford. com, and through Twitter (@ terracecrawford).

Sarah Cunningham is the author of *Dear Church: Letters from a Disillusioned Generation* and *Picking Dandelions.* Read more from Sarah at SarahCunningham.org.

Alan Danielson is the senior pastor of New Life Bible Church in Norman, Oklahoma and the Small Groups Channel Editor for ChurchLeaders.com. Previously he served as Central Team Leader for LifeGroups at LifeChurch. tv in Edmond, where he led over a thousand small groups on LifeChurch's thirteen campuses in six different states. He then founded

3Threat.net to help leaders master three essential leadership skills: vision-casting, creating strategy, and fostering relationships. Alan is a popular conference speaker and consults regularly with ministries and leaders on topics relating to small groups and leadership. Learn more from Alan at 3Threat.net.

Artie Davis serves as lead pastor of Cornerstone Community Church, a multi-ethnic church in Orangeburg, South Carolina. Read more from Artie about church planting and leadership at his blog, ArtieDavis.com.

Kevin DeYoung is the senior pastor at University Reformed Church (RCA) in East Lansing, Michigan, and a popular church leadership conference speaker. A graduate of Hope College and Gordon-Conwell Theological Seminary, he is the co-author of *Why We're Not Emergent* and author of *Freedom and Boundaries.* Learn more from Kevin at TheGospelCoalition.org/ blogs/KevinDeYoung.

Ron Edmondson is a pastor and church leader passionate about planting churches, helping established churches thrive, and assisting pastors and those in ministry think through leadership, strategy and life. Ron has over 20 years' business experience, mostly as a self-employed business owner, and he's been in full-time ministry for over 8 years. Learn more insights from Ron at RonEdmondson.com.

Dave Ferguson is lead pastor at Community Christian Church, a multi-site church in central Illinois. He is responsible for providing the visionary leadership for both the church and NewThing, a network of reproducing churches. He loves working with the remarkable group of leaders and artists that make up his staff.

He has co-authored several books, including *Exponential, On the Verge,* and *The Big Idea.* Dave blogs often at DaveFerguson.org.

Chris Folmsbee is the chief ministries officer at YouthFront, a ministry designed to bring youth into a growing relationship with Jesus. He's the author of *A New Kind of Youth Ministry* and the upcoming books *Clear: Bringing Your Faith into Focus* and *Story Signs and Sacred Rhythms: A Narrative Approach to Youth Ministry.* Chris also has a regular column in the *The Journal of Student Ministries* and speaks to and trains youth workers and students throughout North America. He's been involved in youth work for more than 13 years as a youth pastor, coach, and high school teacher. Learn more from Chris at YouthFront.com.

Mike Foster leads an organization called People of the Second Chance, which provides innovative strategies on failure and crisis. Mike also serves as the Creative Principal at PlainJoe Studios in southern California. He blogs daily at POTSC.com and is @ MikeFoster on Twitter.

Bob Franquiz is the founding and senior pastor of Calvary Fellowship in Miami, Florida. Bob is also the founder of Church-Strategies.com, an organization that provides training and resources to pastors and church leaders. Bob is also the author of *Elements: Starting a Revolution in your World, Watermark: An Explanation of Baptism* and *Zero to Sixty: 60 Principles and Practices for Leading a Growing Church.*

Steven Furtick is the lead pastor of Elevation Church, an incredible move of God in Charlotte, North Carolina with more than 6,000 in attendance each week among three locations. He is the author of the book, *Sun Stand Still*, and blogs about pastoral leadership at StevenFurtick.com.

Josh Griffin is the high school pastor at Saddleback Church in Lake Forest, California and the author of *99 Thoughts for Youth Workers*. He has served in youth ministry for 15 years. Read more from Josh at his blog, MoreThanDodgeball.com.

Craig Groeschel is the founding and senior pastor of LifeChurch.tv. Meeting in multiple locations around the United States and globally at Church Online, LifeChurch.tv is known for the innovative use of technology to spread the Gospel. Craig speaks at conferences worldwide and has written several books, including *The Christian Atheist: Believing in God but Living As If He Doesn't Exist, It: How Churches and Leaders Can Get It and Keep It, Chazown: A Different Way to See Your Life, Confessions of a Pastor*, and *Weird: Because Normal Isn't Working.*

Tina Houser is the publications director for KidzMatter; she oversees the content of *K!* Magazine and develops the totally downloadable year-round elementary kids' church curriculum called The Kitchen. She absolutely loves being able to train volunteers and professionals who have a heart for seeing kids become disciples of Jesus, whether that is through writing curriculum, writing her eight idea books, or being able to speak at conferences. She has 32 incredible years in children's ministry within the local church. Get to know Tina and her ministry to kids at TinaHouser.net.

Rick Howerton has one passion: to see "a biblical small group within walking distance of

every person on the planet." He is presently the Global Small Group Environmentalist at NavPress Publishing. Rick has authored or co-authored multiple books, studies, and leader training resources, including *The Gospel and the Truth: Living the Message of Jesus, Small Group Life Ministry Manual: A New Approach to Small Groups, Redeeming the Tears: a Journey Through Grief and Loss, Small Group Kickoff Retreat: Experiential Training for Small Group Leaders*, and *Great Beginnings: Your First Small Group Study*. Rick has varied ministry experiences as a collegiate pastor, small group pastor, teaching pastor, full-time trainer, and church consultant, as well as having been a successful church planter. Rick is a highly sought-after communicator and trainer speaking at or leading training in forty settings annually.

Dale Hudson has been on the children's ministry journey for 21 years. He was recently named as one of the top 20 influencers in children's ministry by *Children's Ministry* magazine. He is the director of children's ministries at Christ Fellowship Church in Palm Beach, Florida, where he oversees the children's ministry at the church's five campuses. He is the co-author of *Children's Ministry in the 21st Century, Turbo Charged Children's Ministry*, and *Turbo Charged Preschool Ministry*. In addition, he also writes for children's ministry leadership magazines on a regular basis and speaks at children's ministry conferences across the country. Learn more from Dale at RelevantChildrensMinistry. blogspot.com.

Bob Kauflin currently has the privilege of serving as the Director of Worship Development for Sovereign Grace Ministries.

He equips pastors and musicians in the theology and practice of congregational worship, oversees Sovereign Grace Music, and leads worship in his own church. Learn more from Bob at his blog, WorshipMatters.com.

Brian Kaufman is the founder of Tipping Media, a web strategy and social media agency based in Phoenix, Arizona. He also co-authors the *STc* online magazine. Follow Brian at twitter.com/briankaufman.

Dan Kimball serves on the staff of Vintage Faith Church in Santa Cruz, California, where his current role is overseeing the Sunday gatherings and teaching as well as the missional aspects of the church. He also serves on the Vintage Faith Church Leadership Council. Dan's role also includes extending the mission of the church through writing and speaking. Learn more from Dan in his regular column in *Outreach* magazine.

Charles Lee is the CEO of Ideation, a consultancy that specializes in helping organizations and businesses take ideas to implementation via innovative strategy, branding, design, marketing, web, social media, and creative event development. He is also a founding member of JustOne, a NPO committed to addressing issues of poverty, orphans, and slavery. In addition, Charles is the creator of grassroots efforts including the Idea Camp, Ideation Conference, and the Freeze Project. Charles regularly speaks around the country on topics such as creativity, innovation, leadership, new media, and compassionate justice. Read more from Charles at CharlesTLee.com.

Sam Luce has been the children's pastor at Redeemer Church for over 13 years. A prolific blogger and popular children's conference speaker, Sam has worked in children's ministry for over 23 years and is also a contributing editor to *K!* magazine.

Gabe Lyons is the founder of Q, which serves to educate Christians on their historic responsibility to renew culture, and author of *The Next Christians: The Good News About the End of Christian America* (Doubleday, 2010). His first book, *unChristian*, was co-authored with Dave Kinnaman and revealed exclusive research on pop-culture's negative perception of Christians. His work represents a fresh perspective on Christianity's role in culture and has been featured by CNN, Fox News, *The New York Times* and *Newsweek*. Learn more from Gabe at QIdeas.org.

Mike Mack is the Connect Minister at Northeast Christian Church in Louisville, Kentucky. His most recent book is *The Pocket Guide to Burnout-Free Small Group Leadership* (Touch Publications). Mike is a small groups coach, consultant, writer, speaker, and cheerleader. In 1995, Mike founded SmallGroups. com, now owned and operated by Christianity Today; he continues to serve on the ministry's advisory panel. He also regularly blogs at SmallGroupLeadership.blogspot. com.

Will Mancini emerged from the trenches of local church leadership to found Auxano, a first-of-kind consulting ministry that focuses on vision clarity. As a "clarity evangelist," Will has served as vision architect for hundreds of churches across the country, including such notable pastors as Chuck Swindoll and Max Lucado. Will holds a Th.M. in Pastoral Leadership from Dallas Theological Seminary and has authored *Church Unique: How Missional Leaders Cast Vision, Capture Culture and Create Movement*; he

also co-authored *Building Leaders* with Aubrey Malphurs. Gain more insights from Will at WillMancini. com.

Brian Mavis leads Community Transformation at LifeBridge Christian Church, and he helps other churches in their missional efforts in his role as the executive director of the Externally Focused Network (ExternallyFocusedNetwork.com). Brian also leads a new website designed to challenge young Christian risk-takers (MoreAtStake. com). Brian was the first G.M. of SermonCentral.com from 2000–2005. He has written curriculum for campaigns including Bono's "One Sabbath Campaign", Mel Gibson's *Passion of the Christ,* World Vision's "Faith in Action" and "The Hole in Our Gospel." God's specific call on his life is to strengthen other Christian leaders.

Joe McKeever is a pastor-to-pastors who served for five years as Director of Missions for the 100 Southern Baptist churches of metro New Orleans. These days, he has an office at the First Baptist Church of Kenner where he's working on three books, and he's trying to accept every speaking/preaching invitation that.comes his way. He loves to do revivals, prayer conferences, deacon training, leadership banquets, and such. Usually, he's working on some cartooning project for the denomination or some agency. Learn more from Joe's more than 50 years in ministry at JoeMcKeever.com

Kem Meyer is the Communications Director at Granger Community Church. Kem leads worskshops, speaks at conferences, and blogs about finding ways to remove the barriers that keep people from connecting with Christ. Kem is also the author

of *Less Clutter. Less Noise.* Learn more from Kem at KemMeyer.com.

Don Miller is the author of multiple *New York Times* best-sellers, including *Blue Like Jazz* and *A Million Miles in a Thousand Years*. He has served on the Presidential Task Force on Fatherhood and Healthy Families and is a sought-after speaker regarding narrative structure as it relates to a person's life and their projects. Don recently launched the Storyline Conference that helps people structure their lives using a cohesive narrative. He is the founder of The Mentoring Project and blogs almost daily at DonMillerIs.com

Dr. R. Larry Moyer is a veteran evangelist and a frequent speaker in evangelistic outreaches, training seminars, churches, and universities around the world. Born with an inherited speech defect, Larry vowed to God as a teenager that if He would allow him to gain control of his speech he would always use his voice to declare the gospel. God has so worked that he is often referred to as "The clearest communicator I know." In 1973, Larry founded EvanTell, where he now serves as President and CEO. He has written several books on evangelism and frequently contributes articles to ministry publications. Learn more from Larry and his great team at EvanTell.org and Evangelism.net.

Randall Neighbour is president of TOUCH Outreach Ministries, Inc. (TouchUSA.org), a non-profit organization located in Houston, Texas. His threefold ministry focus is to consult, train, and resource churches as they fulfill the Great Commandment and Great Commission through a highly relational holistic small group-based model for church life. Randall is the author of six additional resources for small group members, leaders, coaches, and groups, including the book, *The Naked Truth About Small Group Ministry*.

Perry Noble is the founding and senior pastor of NewSpring Church in Anderson, Greenville and Florence, South Carolina. At just nine years old, the church averages over 10,000 people during weekend services and is launching another campus in Columbia, South Carolina. Perry is convicted about speaking the truth as plainly as possible. A prolific and outspoken blogger at PerryNoble.com, he's also the author of *Blueprints: How to Build Godly Relationships*.

Shannon O'Dell is lead pastor of Brand New Church. Through a God-given passion for healthy churches in rural America, Brand New Church is currently leading five campuses and three satellite house churches. Shannon is the author of *Transforming Church in Rural America* and blogs at BreakingAlltheRurals.com.

Brian Orme is the general editor of ChurchLeaders.com. He works with creative and innovative people to discover the best resources, trends and practices to equip the church to lead better every day.

Larry Osborne is the senior pastor at North Coast Church in Vista, California. With 20 weekly services on five campuses, North Coast is known for both its innovation and its small back door. Larry is the author of several books on church leadership, including *Sticky Church, 10 Dumb Things Smart Christians Believe, A Contrarian's Guide to Knowing God: Spirituality for the Rest of Us,* and *Sticky Teams*. Learn more about Larry's ministry to leaders at the North Coast Training Network, NorthCoastChurch.com/Pastors, or at LarryOsborneLive.com.

Glenn Packiam is an executive pastor at New Life Church in Colorado Springs, Colorado, where he oversees Spiritual Formation and serves as the teaching pastor for NewLifeSundayNight. He is one of the founding leaders and songwriters for the Desperation Band and the writer of the well-loved worship songs, "Your Name," "Everyone (Praises)" and "My Savior Lives." Glenn is also the author of *Butterfly in Brazil: How Your Life Can Make a World of Difference* and most recently, *Secondhand Jesus: Trading Rumors of God for a Firsthand Faith*. He recently released his first solo album, *Rumors and Revelations*. Visit Glenn at GlennPackiam.com.

David Padfield is the local evangelist for the Church of Christ in Zion, Illinois. He was born in Kokomo, Indiana and began preaching while he was still in high school. Read more from David at his blog, ExpositorySermonOutlines.com.

Marie Page is a founding partner of Musicademy.com, an independent music school specializing in DVD and online training resources for church musicians. As well as a MultiTrack backing track player for churches with no musicians or half a band, its acclaimed range of worship instructional DVDs covers guitar, bass, drums, keys, vocals, and orchestral instruments at levels from beginner to advanced player. Musicademy also hosts a comprehensive website crammed with free worship related resources.

Thom Rainer is the president and CEO of LifeWay Christian Resources (LifeWay.com). He was founding dean of the Billy Graham School of Missions, Evangelism, and Church Growth at The Southern Baptist Theological Seminary. His many books include

Surprising Insights from the Unchurched, The Unexpected Journey, and *Breakout Churches*.

Hal Seed founded and pastors New Song Community Church in Oceanside, California. Over the past 18 years, New Song has seen over 9,000 people come to Christ, planted four daughter churches, and helped launch four parachurch ministries, including Outreach, Inc., Dynamic Church Planting International, and Church Community Builder. Learn more from Hal at PastorMentor.com.

Dan Scott serves as the elementary director at Ada Bible Church, which is outside of Grand Rapids, Michigan. He establishes the vision for programming including curriculum, volunteer care, and environment. Dan enjoys sharing ideas and encouragement from his life and ministry. He has a busy speaking and writing schedule and was recently named one of *Children's Ministry* magazines' "20 Leaders to Watch."

Leon Sievers, with more than 20 years professional audio experience, founded Sound Advice, a message board on Experiencing Worship especially for audio technicians and leadership. Read more of Leon's insights at ExperiencingWorship.com/Sound.html.

Judah Smith is the lead pastor of The City Church in Seattle, Washington. He is a featured speaker at church conferences and other Christian church-related events in the U.S. and around the world. His video podcast (GCTV) is consistently ranked among the top 100 religious podcasts. He is the author of *Soul Seekers: Our Call to People and the 13 Challenges We Must Face to Reach Them*.

Andy Stanley is an acclaimed pastor, communicator, author and the founder of North Point

Ministries, Inc. Since its inception in 1995, North Point Ministries has grown from one campus to three in the Atlanta area; each Sunday, over 20,000 adults attend worship services at one of them. Andy has written several books on Christian leadership principles, including *It Came From Within, Communicating for a Change, Making Vision Stick,* and *The Principle of the Path.* Explore the breadth of leadership resources available at NorthPoint.org.

Ed Stetzer is president of LifeWay Research and LifeWay's Missiologist in Residence. He has trained pastors and church planters on five continents, holds two masters degrees and two doctorates, and has written dozens of articles and books. Ed is a contributing editor for Christianity Today, a columnist for *Outreach* magazine and *Catalyst Monthly,* serves on the advisory council of SermonCentral.com and Christianity Today's Building Church Leaders, and is frequently cited or interviewed in news outlets such as *USAToday* and CNN. Read more from Ed at his blog, EdStetzer. com, or at LifeWayResearch.com.

Paul Steinbrueck is co-founder and CEO of OurChurch. com, which has been providing web hosting, design, search marketing, and advertising services to Christian organizations since 1996. You can read OurChurch. com's Christian Web Trends blog at Blog.OurChurch.com and follow on Twitter at @OurChurchDotCom.

Greg Stier founded Dare 2 Share Ministries, committed to mobilizing teenagers to relationally and relentlessly reach their generation for Christ. Dare 2 Share's youth evangelism training conferences, curriculum and books motivate and equip teenagers to share the gospel with their friends. Learn more from

Greg at his blog, GregStier.com, or at Dare2Share.org.

Brian Taylor serves as worship leader at Church of the Redeemer—a growing, multi-campus congregation based in Gaithersburg, Maryland under the leadership of Pastor Dale O'Shields. His passion is seeing God advance His kingdom through the work and support of the local church. Read more about worship leadership at Brian's blog, LeadingSkillfully.com.

Carlos Whittaker is an artist, pastor, thinker, experience architect, and Web 2.0 junkie. Carlos currently serves as Director of Service Programming at Buckhead Church in Atlanta, GA, one of the three campuses of North Point Community Church. Previously, Carlos worked for 10 years as the Pastor of Worship and Creative Arts at Sandals Church in Riverside, CA. Recently he signed with Integrity Music to pursue a recording career and, as he says, "disturb and disrupt the church as a whole." He blogs prolifically at RagamuffinSoul.com.

Jim Wideman is an internationally recognized voice in children's and family ministry. He is a much sought after speaker, teacher, author, personal leadership coach, and ministry consultant who has over 30 years experience in helping churches thrive. Jim created the Children's Ministers Leadership Club in 1995 that is known today as "theClub" which has touched thousands of ministry leaders each month. Jim believes his marching orders are to spend the rest of his life taking what he has learn about leadership and ministry and pour it into the next generation of children's, youth, and family ministry leaders. Learn more from Jim at JimWideman.com.

Scott Williams is the Outreach channel editor for ChurchLeaders. com and served as a key leader and Campus Pastor for LifeChurch. tv. He is the Chief Solutions Officer for Nxt Level Solutions, a consulting company he founded to help businesses, non-profits, and individuals go farther faster. Scott is gifted speaker, strategist, and a natural developer. Scott is passionate about leadership development and diversity in the church. He is the author of *Church Diversity—Sunday: The Most Segregated Day of the Week.* He is an avid blogger at BigIsTheNewSmall.com and leverages Social Media to make a Kingdom impact. You can give him a #FistBump and follow his tweets @scottwilliams

Jeremy Zach has been a youth pastor for nine years and serves with Orange in the student ministry XP3 department. He places a high value on connecting with and learning from student pastors, deliberatively researching, reading, and blogging about student ministry and family ministry, dabbling with online technology, and experimenting in ministry lifestyle design and productivity in the church. Learn more from Jeremy at his blog, REYouthPastor. com.

Heather Zempel finally landed as the pastor of discipleship at National Community Church in Washington, D.C. after working as an environmental engineer for a few years and a policy advisor on Capitol Hill for a few years. She is a sought-after conference speaker on the subjects of discipleship and small group dynamics. Read more from Heather at her blog, HeatherZempel.com.